MONEY BY INTERNET

HOW TO GET STARTED MAKING MO

VOLUME 1 OF 2

By Burt Anderson

Amazon Paperback
ISBN: 978-1-893257-53-5   First Edition
Copyright 2012   Lions Pride Publishing Co., LLC

Every effort has been made to make this book as complete and accurate as possible. However, there may be mistakes in typography or content. Also, this book contains information on earning internet income only up to the publishing date. Therefore this document should be used as a guide only – not as a definitive source of internet income information.

This book is for information purposes only and does not impart legal, accounting, financial or any other form of business advice to readers who must consult their own professional advisors before taking action of any kind related to any internet business. The author and publisher do not warrant that the information contained in this book is fully complete and shall not be responsible for any errors or omissions. The author and publisher shall have neither

To my beautiful wife Melanie, whose patience and understanding allows me endless hours writing on the computer while she works a demanding 9 to 5 job and still keeps our household from falling apart!

To Napoleon Hill for writing *Think and Grow Rich,* the book that can change lives.

And to the late internet commerce genius and visionary Cory Rudl who paved the way in the '90s for the countless internet millionaires that followed. Without his wisdom and personal inspiration I would never have embarked on my successful personal cyber- journey.

FORWARD TO VOLUME 1 OF 2

You are about to embark on the adventure of a lifetime!

For the past month I worked on this book about eighteen hours a day, every day. When I began to write I had no idea how long the book might end up being. As it turned out, it became a far too long to fit into a single Volume. I decided to split it into two Volumes, each designed to stand alone, each designed to contain key information of equal value to newbie and experienced internet marketer alike.

Each Volume is in itself a rather long book, 90,000 words give or take a few. To someone new to internet commerce, this must seem pretty overwhelming. I was torn between two Volumes or splitting this book up even further into a number of smaller books, a "series" if you will. From a commercial standpoint I could surely have made more money had I done so. (Believe it or not writers have to eat too!) But I decided to make it a two-volume compendium of everything I have learned over the past decade and a half, and to allow the reader to pick and choose to decide which path to internet wealth to follow. Either Volume can stand alone.

This necessitated putting some information into each Volume that exactly duplicates that same information in the companion Volume. Chapters 1 through 3, and my Conclusions, along with the obligatory "About the Author", and a useful Glossary, needed to appear in each Volume. In this manner it is less important for anyone, especially a newbie, to purchase both Volumes to quickly establish an internet business. Either volume will suffice.

Over the years I have purchased countless internet courses for anywhere from $197.00 to $2,500.00. I still have all of them in my library. **I am certain that either Volume of this book, which you have purchased at a very tiny fraction of the value of the information they contain, will prove to be the best purchase you have**

ever made! Please do not judge their **value** by their low price.

My associates believe I have lost my mind to sell these books so inexpensively. I disagree. It is my genuine intention to expose as many unemployed and under-employed individuals as possible to the incredible opportunity to earn a living offered to everyone by the internet. I'm 75, very comfortable, and well past the time when I need to earn a few extra bucks. I want this book to be my legacy. If I can help **one** individual to reach the American Dream that will be great. If I can help hundreds, or even thousands, I will consider my life to have found its true purpose.

With all that said, I believe I should list below the Chapters in this Volume 1 that are best suited for persons at various levels of internet experience. That is not to say that the best approach would not be for you to at least read through the entire book once, and then return to the Chapters that I suggest or you find most appealing. This can, however, be your guide.

FOR EVERYONE: Chapters 1, 2, 3, Conclusion. *READ THESE FIRST!!!*

FOR A NEWBIE WANTING TO EARN MONEY QUICKLY:

Chapters 10, 11, 12, 14.

IF YOU, AS SOMEONE UNFAMILIAR WITH THE INTERNET AND NEEDING TO EARN MONEY AS QUICKLY AS POSSIBLE, FOCUS 100% OF YOUR EFFORTS ON THE ABOVE EIGHT CHAPTERS, YOU SHOULD BE ABLE TO BEGIN EARNING INTERNET CASH QUICKLY WITH AN ABSOLUTE MINIMUM OF INVESTMENT.

FOR A NEWBIE WANTING TO WORK A TINY BIT HARDER AND MAKE A LOT MORE MONEY:

Chapters 4, 5, 6, 7, 8, 9.

FOR A NEWBIE, NEXT LEVEL: Chapters 15, 16, 17, 18

THESE FOUR CHAPTERS ARE THE "CLASSIC" INTERNET BUSINESS MODEL THAT HAS CREATED MORE INTERNET MILLIONAIRES OVER THE YEARS THAN ANY OTHER OF THE POSSIBLE MULTIPLE STREAMS OF INTERNET INCOME.

FOR THE NOT-SO-NEWBIE: Chapter 21.

FOR THE MORE ADVANCED READERS:

Chapters 13, 19, 20.

Do not lose site of the fact that most internet entrepreneurs (infopreneurs) engage in most or all of the above pursuits at the same time. It is the **combined** multiple streams of internet income that merge to become a mighty river of internet wealth.

It is my most sincere hope that you will take up the challenge of reading and learning this material. If you truly want the freedom of earning a very good, perhaps spectacular, income from the comfort of your home, you have before you the blueprint for that success.

God speed.

WHAT IS NEW IN VOLUME 2 OF 2 [CHAPTER 22 – 50]:

MODULE FIVE – ADVERTISE FOR HOT TRAFFIC
CHAPTER 22: KNOWING INSIDER ADVERTISING KEYS
CHAPTER 23: WRITING KILLER ADS FOR BIG BUCKS
CHAPTER 24: PAY PER CLICK ADVERTISING SOLUTIONS

CHAPTER 46: THE SUCCESS TOOLS

MODULE ONE – INTRODUCTION

CHAPTER 1: YOUR SUCCESS BLUEPRINT

CHAPTER 2: HOW TO MAKE A WONDERFUL LIVING FROM HOME

CHAPTER 3: GET WEALTHY WHILE STAYING OUT OF TROUBLE

CHAPTER 1

YOUR SUCCESS BLUEPRINT

I wrote this Chapter in an effort to create a mind-set through which perhaps you can extract real life-changing value from the many pages of this "how-to" internet instruction manual.

In 1934 a brilliant author named Napoleon Hill published a book titled: "*Think and Grow Rich*". Every salesperson and marketer should own a copy, and should read it and re-read it frequently. It is as valid today as it was seventy-five years ago. If you do not already own a copy, get one. You can download it for free at Amazon last time I checked. If you do own a copy, even if you read it recently, reading this short Chapter will help reinforce Mr. Hill's life-changing philosophy.

I live an extremely comfortable life. My wife and I want for little. Almost everything we have achieved over the years we attribute largely to the words of wisdom penned by Mr. Hill. I first read his book in 1955. It changed my life, and it can change yours. **So can internet commerce.**

What I am writing in this Chapter is a brief summary of the ideas and concepts contained in Hill's book that I personally have found to be the most useful. Reflect deeply on each gem of wisdom. There's very little fluff offered here. They may not be exact quotes, and I have added a few ideas from other great minds, but I have lived by and applied this wisdom for decades with great success.

Mr. Hill had profound insight on higher education. He states that formal schooling does very little more than to put one in the mind set to learn how to **acquire** practical knowledge. Pleasantly drifting through an unspecified academic curriculum without purpose or without a definite future course of action (true of the vast majority of college students, especially the "BA" crowd) is a total waste of time and money. He states: "You do not get any **practical** knowledge in college….NONE."

Personally possessing a Bachelor of Science (BS), a Master of Business Administration (MBA), and a useless PhD, I could not agree more than I do with Mr. Hill's analysis. I truly never learned anything in college that could be directly applied to any real-world job. I wasted countless hours in night-school and more money than I care to calculate.

Hill points out that college professors specialize in teaching knowledge, but do not specialize in teaching the **USE** of knowledge. Knowledge itself is not power, it is **POTENTIAL** power. It becomes power only if and when it is organized into definite plans of action and directed to a definite worthy end. Knowledge has no value except that which can be gained from its application towards that end.

Any man is educated once he knows where to get knowledge when he needs it (for example this book) and how to organize that knowledge into definite plans of action. As knowledge is acquired it must be organized and put into use for some definite purpose.

A young Abraham Lincoln, arguably our greatest President, lived by one rule: "I will study and get ready and someday my chance will come". He recognized the need for practical knowledge. He studied, learned, and became a great President.

It pays to know how to <u>purchase</u> knowledge. There is no fixed price for sound ideas. Behind all sound ideas is **specialized** knowledge. This is why so many internet entrepreneurs have become wealthy. <u>This is why I wrote this book of specialized knowledge.</u>

Hill lists the six great fears of every human being. Understanding human fears can guide your internet marketing efforts, because addressing and in some way ameliorating these fears with your product offerings is your key to marketing success:

The Fear Of Poverty (The need to make money);

The Fear Of Criticism (The need for praise and envy by others);

The Fear Of Ill Health (The need for better health);

The Fear Of Loss Of Love (The need to find love);

The Fear Of Old Age (The need to extend one's life);

The Fear Of Death (The desire to live forever).

Some studies have suggested that The Fear Of Public Speaking is stronger than any of these, but Mr. Hill failed to mention that!

The fear of poverty manifests itself through indifference, indecision, doubt, worry, over-caution, and procrastination. Procrastination, the opposite of decision, is a common enemy that everyone must conquer. **Both** poverty and riches are the offspring of thought.

Hill states that ALL fears are nothing more than states of mind, and as such are subject to control and direction. The author Henley penned famously: "I am the master of my fate, I am the captain of my soul". Hill adds: "...because we all have the power to **control** our thoughts. Every human being has the ability to completely control his own mind".

Hill points out that even more powerful than the six human fears listed above is one's own **SUSCEPTABILITY TO NEGATIVE INFLUENCES.** Without a doubt the most common weakness of all human beings is the destructive habit of leaving their minds open to the negative influence of other people.

Strip such "low tone" (a Scientology expression) people from your life and you derive immense benefits. (Apparently Mr. Hill was a Scientologist before L. Ron Hubbard stole his ideas!).

Never forget: **SUCCESSFUL PEOPLE DO WHAT THEIR CRITICS SAY CAN'T BE DONE..........EVERY DAY**! Your critics greatest fear is that you, God forbid, might actually succeed.

Hill outlines six steps to personal riches. He credits Dale Carnegie for teaching these steps to him, and points out that the amazing inventor Thomas Edison adhered religiously to this formula:

Fix in your mind the exact amount of riches you desire;

Determine what sacrifices you are willing to give in return for them;

Establish a definite date to possess them;

Create a definite plan and begin immediately (ready or not) to put this plan into action;

Write out the above steps **in longhand.**

That's the easy part!

Hill then insists that twice a day you read aloud your written statement. Do this once before bedtime, and again once on rising in the morning. As you read, <u>see and feel and believe yourself **already** in possession of the riches.</u>

The key is to create in your mind a burning desire for a definite form of riches. Riches can be financial, spiritual, mental or material. Success comes to those who become **SUCCESS CONSCIOUS**. Failure comes to those who indifferently allow themselves to become **FAILURE CONSCIOUS**.

You must cultivate a persistence that does not even **recognize** failure as a possibility. The three most important roads to riches are **persistence, persistence and persistence!**

Every failure brings with it the seed of an equivalent success. Every adversity, every failure, and every heartache carries with it the seed of an equivalent or greater benefit. <u>**No one is ever defeated until defeat is accepted as a reality. There are no limitations to the human mind except those we acknowledge.**</u>

Forty years ago I attended an excellent motivational seminar run by a gentleman named Joel Weldon. He handed out to his audience a great marketing gimmick to get his point across. It was a tin can with a label that read: <u>**"Success Comes In Cans And Not In Cannots".**</u> I still have the can on my desk. I have never forgotten that profound wisdom. Neither should you. Truer words were never spoken.

Weldon added: "Forget the excuses. Accept responsibility. And take ACTION! **Whether you think you can or you can't, you're right!"**.

Basketball great Michael Jordan is credited with saying: "Most people fail because they make up imaginary excuses (the "cannots") The only person that can stop you is yourself." Don't make up excuses. Don't focus on CANNOTS. You CAN do anything you make up your mind to do.

Will every plan you start succeed? Probably not. Mine certainly did not. Thomas Edison tried hundreds of filament materials for his light bulb before achieving success and changing the world! If the first plan you adopt does not work replace it with a new plan. If the new plan fails to work replace it with another. Lack of persistence is why most fail. **No man is ever whipped until he quits in his own mind.**

A quitter never wins and a winner never quits. The only "good break" anyone can afford to rely upon are those self-made breaks brought about through persistence. Riches do not respond to wishes. They respond only to definite plans backed by definite desires through constant persistence.

Definiteness of purpose is the starting point from which one MUST begin. Ideas can be transmuted into riches through the power of definite purpose plus definite plans.

And remember, the starting point of all achievement is **desire**. Anyone can wish for riches, and most people do, but only a few recognize that a definite plan plus a burning desire for riches are the only dependable means of accumulating wealth.

It is often said that "good things come to those who wait". In my experience **BETTER** things come to those who

REFUSE to wait. Wait not for someone else to decide to make something happen. You can make it happen by yourself, **NOW**.

Desperation can be a very positive influence. Leaving oneself with no possible way of retreat you either win or perish. Hill points out historic examples of how this philosophy won military battles in the past. Winston Churchill is credited with saying: "The only sure way to accomplish something positive is to create a situation that is so untenable that you must solve it or perish".

Napoleon Hill stated one overriding truism: "**WHATEVER THE MIND OF MAN CAN CONCEIVE AND BELIEVE IT CAN ACHIEVE. Thoughts are things! And powerful things at that, when mixed with definiteness of purpose, and burning desire, can be translated into riches.**"

Earle Nightengale, a great motivational speaker, used the phrase: "You are what you think about". It was the keynote phrase of his "The Strangest Secret" seminar.

All achievement, all earned riches, have their beginning in an idea. More gold has been mined from the thoughts of man than has ever been taken from the earth. One sound idea is all you need to achieve success. One book, such as the one you are reading, can make all the difference in the world.

Hill is convinced that once riches begin to come they come so quickly, in such great abundance, that one wonders where they had been hiding during all those lean years. When one is truly ready for riches they magically put in their appearance. I know this was true in my life. It can be true in yours, through internet commerce, through this book.

Do not ever envy those who have become great. Success is to be envied, not reviled. Hill states that "Experience has taught me that the next best thing to being truly great is to emulate the great, by feeling and action, as nearly as possible". The great always have persistence and a determination to repel failure. They make definite plans and execute them <u>without hesitation.</u> Emulate, not envy, nor hate, these individuals. Don't fall into the trap of today's "class warfare" rhetoric as is being waged constantly by various political figures.

Remember: Life is like a checkerboard. The player opposite the board from you is TIME. You are playing against an opponent who will not tolerate indecision. If you hesitate to move, or fail to move quickly, your pieces will be wiped off the board by time. Take action NOW!

<u>Get involved in internet commerce today. Read this book, choose your path, and ACT ON IT.</u>

Good luck and GOD speed!

CHAPTER 2

HOW TO MAKE A WONDERFUL LIVING FROM HOME

UNEMPLOYED? UNDER EMPLOYED?
YOU HAVE NO EXCUSES WHATSOEVER!

I've often said: "I'd gladly participate in any experiment that would test the effects on me of sudden great wealth". Can money buy happiness? All I ask is the chance to prove it can't! **If you share these feelings, this book is for you.**

What is the information in this book worth? Let me give you an idea of what it would cost you for at least one of the academic internet marketing college credentials you can actually earn on-line while sitting at home.

For a mere **$21,000.00** (!!!!!) one fully accredited on-line University will issue you seven different "Certificates of Achievement" for completion of online "eight-week or less" internet commerce courses they offer. I assume these are really super-great courses. They'd better be for that kind of money. **At that rate this 300+ page book would be a major bargain at $1,997.00!**

The irony is that all of the many internet millionaires I know invested at the most a few hundred dollars to get started. Others, the so-called "Bum Marketers", didn't even invest a dime! Some of these earned their first million dollars within two years. Their "Certificates of Achievement" are their bank statements!

At first glance this book might look overwhelming. I grant you that there is a lot of information you can eventually absorb, but taken in little bites (and bytes!) it really is not at all difficult. Warren Buffett is credited with saying: "There seems to be some perverse human characteristic that likes to make easy things difficult".   Just take it slow and **let it be easy**.

Making serious money marketing on the internet is NOT difficult, unless you decide to make it so. Don't. Many newbies starting with zero knowledge and few if any liquid assets have become very successful internet entrepreneurs. It just takes a bit of time and patience.

The more people you listen to, the more products you buy, the more confused you are likely to become! Many newbies buy lots of stuff from dozens of different "gurus", seeking the magic silver bullet to internet riches. What they end up with is lots of excellent information and not a clue what to do with it. It is called the "Paralysis of Analysis".

Are you perhaps gainfully employed but sick of the nine to five rat race? Or perhaps working two jobs to make ends meet? I recall seeing a cartoon years ago, probably in the *New Yorker*. There's a bum sitting on a bench in a large city watching masses of business-clad people racing to and fro. He asks the simple hypothetical question to no one in particular: "Who's Winning?" Profound. These days the answer apparently is: "No One". No one, that is, except internet entrepreneurs! They are today's winners in a very difficult employment market.

Being an internet entrepreneur is not just about making money. Working from home, far from the nine-to-five rat race, is all about **you** being able to do what **you** want, whenever **you** want, wherever **you** want, with whomever **you** want, for as long as **you** want. Internet commerce is, in my opinion, about making the most money you can with the greatest possible freedom. Nothing could be more American!

It is reported that unemployment in the United States, if one includes those who have simply "given up looking", today may top twenty percent. The "official" government figure is stated as being well under half of that, but still terribly high. The "safety net" created by various government stipends and food stamps has led some to simply adjust their lifestyles accordingly and survive as long as possible without working at all or even looking for a job.

I am absolutely dumbfounded by certain behavior I see all around me. There are countless unemployed people receiving decent monthly checks, and receiving food stamp cards, and making ends meet quite well. In theory I have absolutely no problem at all with a social safety net for the **truly** needy due to unforeseen negative circumstances not of their own doing.

What I do have a BIG problem with is that many, if not most of these on-the-dole people see themselves as sort of "temporarily-retired". They figure that if their benefits ever do give out they will eventually need to find work. Until then they choose to make zero effort to find employment. That is especially true if the employment they might find pays them even less than their "free" income.

They sit around and watch TV and smoke and drink beer and get fat, and love every minute of it. I know quite a few that have greatly lowered their golf handicap! What has happened to American initiative? What are we becoming? "To each according to his needs; from each according to his ability to pay." Isn't that Marxist? Very sad.

Many of these "poor and/or unemployed" folks of whom I speak have cell phones and iPads and iPods, and Kindles, and cable TV, and decent cars. They spend untold thousands on cigarettes and beer. They live as well as **aristocrats**, the very top few percent do, in most of the 200+ under-developed countries in the world. Yet they are counted as "poor" here in the USA. **They are not poor**. The truly poor starve to death. No one in America dies of starvation unless they choose to do so. Few if any make that choice.

I've tried to share with many of these folks the information in this book. The most common response I hear is: "I can't afford to do that". This is followed closely by: "I don't know anything about computers". But when probed, the clear reason is: "I'm comfortable, leave me the hell alone". Remarkable.

I am certain that there are some unemployed individuals really trying as best they can to support their families. They wish they had a real full-time job. Many work multiple menial jobs to make ends meet. It has reportedly caused a large increase in the number of persons diagnosed as clinically depressed. **It is these people who are really trying to get out from under by working hard with whom I wish the most that I could share this how-to book of internet commerce knowledge.**

FACTS:

Computer knowledge? You need virtually none.

Up front money? You need virtually none.

Must one have money to start an internet business and earn a decent living income? NO. It <u>can</u> be done with virtually <u>zero dollars</u>, no money at all up front . Sure, it's harder and slower that way, but quite doable. And I share how this can be accomplished in the pages of this book.

For the annual cost of a daily pack of cigarettes or a few less brewskies one can buy everything ever needed to succeed on-line <u>big time</u>. A $500 investment spread out over a year, much of it one-time investments, can provide everything needed to quickly create and run a prosperous internet business that can provide income for the rest of your life.

The time the average person spends watching mindless TV programs and sending Tweets and interacting with "friends" on Facebook and watching moronic videos on YouTube and pinning nonsense on Pinterest is reported to be thousands of hours a year. Applying a portion of this time to developing an internet business would open up the opportunity to achieve the American Dream that most complain is unattainable because of our "bad economy". I say: "Hogwash".

Some will say they just don't have very good luck. To those I say that luck is where opportunity and creativity meet. You make your own luck, not wait for it to drop out of the heavens. Thomas Jefferson said: " I'm a great believer in luck, and I find the harder I work the more I have of it." **The American Dream is attainable, without luck, and I can show you how.**

I can say unequivocally that **THERE IS NO EXCUSE FOR ANY MENTALLY-CAPABLE REASONABLY-LITERATE PERSON EVER BEING UNEMPLOYED.** The reality of internet commerce has created the opportunity for almost anyone to earn a very good living working from home in front of a computer screen.

Being unable to read English at a high school level, being unable to understand and follow simple English-language instructions, and being unwilling to work hard are the only disqualifiers I can think of. **No one else *need* ever be unemployed or under-employed.**

It is absolutely true that in the present economy, and for the foreseeable future, conventional jobs in both the private and public sectors will continue to be difficult to find or keep. This is especially true for those with limited formal education or a lack of specific skill sets. **But EVERYONE has absolutely unlimited employment opportunities working from home using a computer.** I am certain that after you read this book you will believe this to be true.

I once saw a cartoon where two guys are sitting at a bar and one says to the other: "Not only am I not on line, I don't even know what 'on line' means"! And to be sure there are many who know nothing about computers, or the power of the internet, or the unlimited opportunities offered by internet commerce.

Fortunately, very basic beginner's training (as in the "For Idiots" book series) is available for FREE from any public library. Any large bookstore has many books for sale that are written for individuals who are totally clueless about computers. If you fall into that "clueless" category, your first step is to learn how to use a computer. It is not rocket science. The average kid in kindergarten does it. So can you.

The good news is that the actual amount of computer knowledge needed to be successful making money from home is <u>very small</u>. Basically all you need to know is how to turn the computer on and learn how to access and "surf" (look around) the internet, **and** follow the basic information found in an internet commerce "how-to" book such as this one.

Once one reaches that small level of competence all that is needed is a set of step-by-step instructions on the many ways one can make money sitting in front of a computer screen. **<u>I share these many ways in this how-to internet commerce book.</u>**

If you are reading this Chapter and already possess basic computer skills so much the better. You are well on your way to making as much money as the effort you are willing to expend will allow. If you already have advanced computer skills you may find some of the material in this book a bit elementary, but you can easily skim through the basics.

If you are one of many who have tried in the past to earn money using your computer and failed to do so to the full extent you hoped, there are many reasons why this might be true. **Do not be discouraged.** Just pretend you know nothing at all, start from scratch applying the techniques shared in this book, and you just might be amazed!

As pointed out earlier, success with internet commerce requires three things**: PERSISTANCE, PERSISTANCE, and PERSISTANCE!** Most persons fail at almost anything new because they give up too easily.

There is no "free lunch", **_EVER_**. It is not at all difficult to make money from home sitting at your kitchen table in front of a computer screen if you have a willingness to learn, a willingness to work hard, and have **persistence.** What I most like about internet marketing is that it is like pulling cash out of your head simply by knowing the right steps to take.

This how-to internet commerce book is the distillation of knowledge gained over the past sixteen years. I also bring a certain amount of additional background knowledge into the mix. Aside from an academic engineering and marketing background, I have been a real estate broker for over thirty years, securities principal for twenty, and licensed for ten years or more in insurance and mortgages. And I've been a prolific published author since 1970. All of this background helps me break down seemingly difficult and complicated material into easily handled step-by-step bites.

Every individual has a different set of life-skills. Some have almost none. Because of this, every individual will have a different experience learning how to make money with a computer working from home. Sadly, many will fail because they are simply not sufficiently motivated to even give it a try or to stick with it when initial progress may seem painfully slow.

Do not be misled by ads you might see on TV or hear on the radio or read in the media that would lead you to believe that riches await you for simply investing a few hours a week in some computer internet marketing program or other. **Nothing could be farther from the truth**. If there is a magic bullet to internet success I've yet to find it, and I have tried!

It **is** true that after some period of time, once you have learned many of the basics and set everything up so that it all virtually runs itself you can spend far less time than you must spend initially. Eventually you will be able to take many days or even weeks off at any time you want and it will have virtually no effect on your residual internet commerce income. You can sit on a beach in paradise somewhere with a laptop and watch the money coming in to your accounts and do little else. It took me years to reach that point. Was it worth it? Damn skippy!

There is no limit to the amount of money one can make in internet commerce of one kind or the other using a computer from the comfort of one's home. Thousands of individuals are reported to have proven that fact beyond a doubt. The purpose of this book is to share with you what my wife and I have learned over the past sixteen years. I hope to provide you with an awareness of the many creative ways that anyone, regardless of formal education, background, or prior computer knowledge, can make a wonderful living with a personal computer from the comfort of their home.

Many millionaires have been created in the past decade applying one or more of the techniques shared in this book. I personally <u>know</u> (not know OF) a number of them. I know <u>of</u> a great many more. Some are quite famous in internet commerce circles. Many more go about their profitable internet business entirely "under the radar". Personally I prefer the latter approach, which I why I publish under a number of different pen-names.

Aside from those who have made millions, many others have simply supplemented their incomes, or made their lives much easier. Some have paid off their bills. Others have bought the luxuries they only previously dreamed about. A few I know have been able to start charitable foundations to help those less fortunate than themselves. This latter pursuit is presently my personal goal, though for years non-altruistic "survival" topped the list!

Keep this in mind: **THIS BOOK IS ABSOLUTELY NOT INTENDED TO OFFER A "GET RICH QUICK" SCHEME.** If such a thing exists I have never found it, and believe me I have looked! Hard. It is, however, a very real potential vocation, the income from which can exceed anything you have ever earned in the past from a typical 9 to 5.

The reason this book isn't many thousands of pages long….and well it could be…is that I expect you, no matter how new to internet commerce, to be able to self-navigate the various websites I suggest that you visit. Remember to enter "http://www." before all of the website addresses that I suggest you visit (although most browsers today will enter the " http://www." for you). As you progress you will find a vast amount of valuable information on line. I especially find that periodically accessing *Website Magazine* at websitemagazine.com keeps me up to date on the rapidly changing world of internet commerce.

I did not feel the need to include computer "screen shots" in this book. These can fill up ten pages instead of ten lines of descriptive text. Any website worth visiting has excellent tutorials, often videos, and extensive FAQs (Frequently Asked Questions), and discussion forums. I do not need to add illustrations from these sites to make this book ten times longer than it already is or needs to be. I assume you can browse to a website and read it for yourself. (Please don't prove me wrong!)

I could spend thousands of extra pages describing to you everything that I can simply point you to online. There is no reason for you to pay me for including that information. I have seen 5,000+ page internet courses that contain far less real usable information than I am sharing with you in this much shorter book.

You will find, however, that certain information is repeated, often even within the same Chapter. This was not done to lengthen the book! If I believe it is particularly important information it will be repeated as often as I feel it is necessary for emphasis.

If you want an at-home internet business to be a full-time great paying job it will take your full-time commitment. Don't forget, a conventional nine-to-five job, including commute time, is a ten to twelve hour a day commitment, five days a week. Your internet commerce job will also require a serious time commitment for you to make comparable money. Can lots of money be made in your spare time? Yes. It will just take a lot longer to make it happen without a full-time effort.

At least at the beginning of your quest for internet riches you could well need to devote twelve or more hours a day seven days a week for a couple of months. The good news is that it gets MUCH easier as you gain some experience.

After six months to a year many successful internet commerce entrepreneurs find themselves earning far more money than they ever have or ever dreamed possible. They often find that they are devoting less time than the normal nine-to-five demands. **It is those first months of commitment that can make the difference.**

Remember: Every day millions of innocent people are forced from their homes by a disaster called "work". You need not be one of them. You are on the edge of a cliff standing on the brink of something called "the rest of your life". Don't ask: "Should I proceed?". And don't jump off! Just back off the cliff, get off your duff, and simply get in gear!

I'm a si-fi fan big time. I love Star Wars. The single most profound dialog occurs when Yoda explains to Luke that: "There is no try. There is either do or not do." This may have been inspired by Winston Churchill's WWII assertion that to get anything serious accomplished you need to set up a scenario wherein you have no choice but to succeed.

Unemployed? Underemployed? Hate your job? Need more money? Yoda's and Churchill's profound statements relate directly to you.

You do not even need to <u>own</u> a computer. Almost any library has computers connected to high-speed networks that can be used at no cost. They will even instruct you on how to use it! If you do not own a computer and want to do so, most computer stores sell excellent used computers at very reasonable prices, often well under a hundred dollars.

For a hundred dollars or less you should be able to find "last year's model", which is more than adequate for your purposes. In fact, most five-year-old computers will do just fine, at least until you have a thriving on-line business, at which time dropping a few hundred bucks on a hot current model with various bells and whistles will seem to be a non-event.

The fact of the matter is that at Walmarts today you can buy a top-quality laptop computer for under four-hundred dollars that has capabilities that,
if they were even available ten years ago, would have cost four-hundred-**thousand** dollars!   Incredible computing power has become ridiculously inexpensive, and will continue to drop in the coming years.

Though the library high-speed internet connection is free, you should get a "high-speed" internet connection at your home if you can afford to do so. It is possible to connect to the internet over a standard telephone line at no added cost, but it is painfully slow. Time is money. High speed connectivity is least expensive where either your telephone company or electricity provider can directly connect you, often at very low additional cost, if any. Cable TV connectivity is another excellent option where available.

If you are unfortunate (from an internet connectivity-speed perspective, like me) enough to live in a **very** rural area where high-speed internet connectivity is not possible, there are satellite services (such as Hughes Net) that are available as long as a receiver placed on your roof has an unobstructed shot at the satellite. Unfortunately, this is the most expensive way to get high-speed service, but as a last resort it is a viable, and perhaps only, alternative.

I would not care to try to have an on-line business using a slow-speed telephone modem, but it is not impossible. There are many people doing it. I just do not personally have that much patience!

Many of the money-making techniques I will share with you in this how-to internet commerce book require zero money to implement once you have a computer and internet connection. This is known in the trade as "bum marketing", and it can be very profitable. In fact, at least one technique requires no computer at all! Other techniques require varying amounts of money to accomplish. None require a huge up-front investment as is the case with starting almost any other business or "brick and mortar" store or franchise.

On the internet the old adage: "it takes money to make money", is not strictly true. Making money with virtually no investment of money is an internet- reality that can be learned. I hope to teach you how in this book.

Please read the following statement more than once, because it expresses the reason why marketing on the internet is easier than one might imagine: **"MAKING MONEY FROM HOME ON THE INTERNET IS A PURE _NUMBERS GAME!_"**

The number of individuals using computers to find information, gain knowledge, and buy things is in the multiple-**billions**. The number who purchase everything from $0.99 reports to $100,000+ cars is in the many hundreds of millions.

The key fact to grasp is: **A VERY SMALL PERCENTAGE OF A LARGE POPULATION CAN STILL BE A HECK OF A LOT OF PEOPLE!** You don't even need a small slice of the internet commerce pie. **All you need to do is lick the knife!**

Your internet commerce job is actually very simple. **You will be finding whatever a focused group (your "niche") of people want to buy and then selling it to them.** That's the whole enchilada!   I will share with you how to do both. There need be no cost involved to develop this information, and then provide it.

Let's discuss just what it is you will be "selling". It is important to understand that there is no "face-to-face" selling involved, and no "telephone selling". Everything is done on your computer. But what exactly will you be "selling"?

You have two basic choices: physical products (such as cameras, TV sets, books, clothing, etc.) and "virtual" products (items that can be delivered electronically). Most of the successful internet entrepreneurs I know have chosen NOT to sell physical products for a number of reasons.

It is true that one can find internet-based warehouses in the United States that will sell you virtually any product you can imagine at below-retail prices for you to re-sell on the internet for a profit. They will even ship directly to your customer without you ever touching the product. These programs **abound** in late-night TV commercials.

"You can charge your customer whatever you want and keep the difference between your cost and your selling price." Sounds easy, and the TV and radio commercials for companies that "teach" you how to do this would have you believe it is easy. It isn't, and here is why:

For starters, you find yourself in competition with the Walmarts and Costcos of the world who can buy almost anything in huge quantities at discounts that simply are not available to us regular folk.

But more important, you are competing directly with hundreds, if not thousands, who, just like you, responding to the **same** TV ad, and are trying to sell the same stuff. Consequently each marketer has to cut prices to the bone, ever and ever lower, to beat out everyone else.

What this leads to is you ending up with so little profit on each item that it becomes almost impossible to make a lot of money. I've heard of people selling $900.00 TVs for $5.00 net profit. That's just nuts.

I imagine that there are a few individuals who have found a way to actually make selling physical products profitable. Perhaps some specialize in a tiny market segment that is unattractive to the big retailers. But the percentage who fail at this sort of internet marketing is reportedly vastly higher. Very few succeed.

There are a few exceptions to the "no physical products" rule. Beyond a doubt many individuals make money selling physical items on eBay and Craigslist and similar sites.

Collectable items such as coins, stamps, antiques, old postcards and the like find a ready market there. So do CDs and DVDs that you can resell or create yourself. But the "warehouse drop-ship of expensive large items" business model is a very tough road to internet riches.

There is another "exception" involving physical products in a roundabout way. This involves you sending customers to the web addresses of companies of all sizes that sell their **own** physical products direct to consumers on their own websites. You can get paid just for sending them the customers! You personally offer no product, physical or virtual. This is called **"Affiliate Marketing"**, and it is one primary means of creating internet wealth that I share with you in this how-to book Volume..

Aside from the insanely profitable Affiliate Marketing, we will be focusing our attention on "virtual" products that you can create and sell. A virtual product is anything that can be sent to a customer electronically over the internet. It can be a book, a report, a "how-to" booklet, a course of instruction, or specialized information on almost anything imaginable.

It is important for you to understand that you do NOT have to actually write anything yourself. You can learn how to obtain all of the **free** written material you will ever need.

The following two lists are important summaries. The first represents the many ways to earn internet income that I will be sharing with you throughout this how-to book Volume 1. The second list summarizes the talents that you will acquire, over time, that will enable you to earn a very good income from the comfort of your home.

Both lists are alphabetical, not in order of importance. You will learn that many of the income streams can be achieved with little or no investment of your money up front. You will certainly not be learning it all at the same time!

Once you become aware of the possibilities open to you, and the specific talents you need to apply to each, you can choose your own internet marketing destiny.

Don't panic, but below is a long list of possible ways for you to profit from your new internet business. All will be discussed to the best of my ability within the pages of this Volume:

YOUR 10 KEY MULTIPLE STREAMS OF INTERNET INCOME

Affiliate Marketing (you should **start** here)
Amazon Direct Marketing
Benefiting From Your Own Affiliate Network
Earning With Blogs
EBay Sales
Google AdWords
Podcasting
Placing Classified Ads (free and paid)
Selling From Your Own Websites
Selling Virtual Products

THE 25 KEY INTERNET MARKETING TALENTS YOU WILL LEARN

Creating Blogs
Creating "Hard" Products (CDs, DVDs, Videos)
Creating Headlines & Sub-Headlines
Creating Landing Pages
Creating Sales Letters For Websites
Creating Squeeze Pages
Creating Virtual Products (ebooks, reports, articles, ezines)
Creating Your Own Affiliate Network
eBay Domination
Keyword Search
Mastering Affiliate Networks
Niche Selection
Placing eBay Classified Ads

Placing Free Classified Ads
Private Label Rights
Public Domain Search
RSS Feeds
Search Engine Optimization
Tools Of The Trade
Virtual Product Creation
Website Creation
Web Surfing and Mining Of Information
Writing Descriptions
Writing Headlines
Writing Sales Letters

Please do not be overwhelmed by the above. Your learning will be step-wise. Any one of these can be learned in a week or less, some in a day. You can focus on one limited means of creating internet income, become proficient at it, and then move on to another, and another, and another. You can even decide to focus on **just one**, such as Affiliate Marketing, and make a very fine income.

The key to your success in internet marketing is that many potential customers are just plain lazy. They want instant gratification with minimum effort. The main fact to understand here is: **PEOPLE WILL PAY FOR GOOD INFORMATION THAT THEY CANNOT FIND EASILY OR FIND COMPILED IN ONE PLACE.** Fortunes are being made on that one single principal by clever internet entrepreneurs (known as "**Infopreneurs**") all over the world.

JUST LEARN HOW, AND DO IT!

CHAPTER 3

GET WEALTHY WHILE STAYING OUT OF TROUBLE (LEGAL AND ETHICAL CONSIDERATIONS)

Let's get this "legal Chapter" out of the way early. Before I share with you the various techniques learned over a decade of trial and error, failures and successes, **you should read this Chapter**. After you have completed this book, read this chapter again. It will mean more to you then, after you have a fuller context within which to consider the legal implications of your new internet business.

I am not a lawyer, nor an accountant, and nothing I write in this book should be construed as legal or tax or investment advice. You should **ALWAYS** seek the advice of professionals, lawyers and accountants and financial pros, whenever you decide to start a business, or if you have any legal, tax, financial or estate issues once you begin to score internet profits.

Having a successful internet business is fun and profitable. It offers a freedom that few vocations offer. (Aside from being a golf pro I can't imagine a better money-making pursuit!) It offers the opportunity for considerable wealth. But it takes time and focus, care and persistence. The absolute last thing you need is any sort of legal or ethical problem. An awareness of possible pitfalls is a good start towards achieving a clean business profile. Consider the public's perceived value of a top Better Business Bureau rating. Point made?

Let's first look at Federal laws that regulate internet practices at this writing. Surely there will be more laws coming along down the road.

A big part of your marketing will of necessity be email based. Done correctly email is perhaps your best marketing tool available. <u>Done incorrectly it can land you in jail!</u>

The "Can-SPAM Act" was passed by both houses of Congress in 2003 and became law in January 2004. It is an acronym for: "**C**ontrolling the **A**ssault of **N**on-**S**olicited **P**ornography **A**nd **M**arketing Act". From that date on all unsolicited email has been referred to as **SPAM**.

Back in the '70s there was a famous Monty Python skit about SPAM, the meat product. The final punch-line was: "I HATE SPAM". I suspect some government genius reverse-engineered the acronym to create the name of the Act to fit the universal hatred of unsolicited email.

Whether this notoriety has helped or hurt the marketing of Hormel and their ever-popular SPAM meat product (reportedly an acronym for **S**pecially **P**rocessed **A**nonymous **M**eat) remains to be seen! (Obscure irrelevant fact: the SPAM meat product is **incredibly** popular in Hawaii and is even found there at McDonald's! Having lived in Hawaii for five years I developed a passion for eating SPAM to this day!)

For the ten or so years prior to enactment of the act, sending out unsolicited marketing emails was the primary source of income for most internet entrepreneurs! In fact, there were " How To SPAM " seminars galore, with names such as "Creative eMail Marketing", and "Email Your Way To Wealth". There were many serious written courses available for many hundreds of dollars. I still have many that I purchased in the '90s gathering dust in my library!

Back then you could even legally send pornography to a minor! There were simply no rules governing commercial emails. Obviously the government stepped in for the public's protection. It is your responsibility to study and abide by the Can-SPAM Act. Check out at the government

site: ftc.gov/bcp/conline/pubs/buspubs/canspam.shtm
This site has all of the relevant updates. Be **certain** to check this out. It is your sole responsibility to learn the letter of this law. Ignorance of the law is never an excuse.

The following list is far from complete, but it represents areas that are most easily and often violated, many times innocently and with no malice of forethought:

For starters, NEVER use a false or misleading header. "From", "To" and routing information must be accurate to allow the recipient to contact you.

Do not use deceptive subject lines. Make the subject line relevant to the content.

You should clearly identify your email as an advertising message.

You must include your current physical address.

Primary to this law is the requirement that if a recipient of one of your emails asks to be removed from your list you **MUST** do so. Neither you nor anyone affiliated with you may ever send another email to that recipient. To facilitate this you MUST have an opt-out link in your email (tied to your autoresponder), and you have ten days after a removal request in which to comply.

You are required to keep a list of everyone who has ever unsubscribed. This is known as your "Suppression List". And you may not sell, rent or give out this list to anyone.

Penalties for violation of the act are rather strict. EACH violation can cost you $11,000.00.! The Federal Trade Commission (FTC) can actually seize your property. And should you involve minors, or do something particularly egregious, or are a repeat offender, you can do hard time in a Federal prison. You don't want to do that. Don't SPAM.

If and when you decide to join an Affiliate Program, be CERTAIN to take a long, hard look at their email-marketing policy. Perhaps the ugliest provision of the "Can SPAM Act" is that any company can be found in violation of the Act even if they themselves did not send the email message! Ouch!   Because of this, understandably nervous potential-affiliate merchants may stipulate:

No email marketing of any kind to market our products;

Prior approval of your email messages;

Prior approval of your entire list of email addresses;

The merchant may require you to "scrub" your email list against   suppression lists that they themselves keep. There are services you can hire yourself to do this. Check out unsubcentral.com, or do a Google search for "list scrubbing services".

Some merchants may even require you to add, in addition to your own signature, address and opt-out link, THEIR email signature and opt out link.

All of this might seem like a giant pain in the ass. It is not only for the better good of society as a whole but it is definitely in your best interest as well. "Trust" is a very critical issue in internet marketing, and showing clearly that you take the laws seriously goes a long way to instilling that trust in your visitors and customers.

Incidentally, these laws are in effect in the United States only. Massive amounts of SPAM still originates "legally" from foreign-based companies.

Now let's look at another important Federal Law, the "Unfair or Deceptive Acts or Practices Act". <u>Internet advertising is strictly governed by this act.</u>

As with Can-SPAM, you should access and print out the FTC publication at: ftc.gov/bcp/edu/pubs/business/ecommerce/bus41.pdf.

Some highlights of this law are:

You will find that the laws governing internet advertising are essentially the same as for off-line advertising. This is to the delight of every **legitimate** internet marketer who now can compete on a level playing field with the internet slime-balls that abound.

Ads should be clearly identified as such and should not be misleading in any way.

Disclaimers, disclosures and warnings must be conspicuous and clear. They must not be in "fine print", but must follow the general style of the website regarding size and color.

If your visitor will be receiving email from you they must be clearly told to expect your advertising email messages.

There can be no inflated claims about the value of your product.

You must disclose any dangers or limitations of your product.

If your website sales letter is very long, repeat your disclosures relative to your claims about your product.

Know the law. As I mentioned before, and it needs repeating, ignorance of the law is absolutely no defense whatsoever should you ever get caught in a violation.

There are many other activities that are closely regulated. The government has placed very strict restrictions on the installation of software on your visitor's computers. Prior to these regulations affiliates and advertisers were able to easily and remotely install software without visitors' consent. These are known as "black hat" techniques. Some are still practiced.

The three types of software (also collectively called "malware") in question are "Spyware", "Adware", and "Parasiteware".

Spyware transmits information about the internet activities of anyone using a computer on which this software is installed. Quality virus protection software can generally remove these programs.

Adware software is used to display advertising on a computer based upon their on-line behavior.

Parasiteware is your worst nightmare as an affiliate marketer. It allows a thief to steal your affiliate commissions by changing and redirecting your unique affiliate identification links.

If you have reason to believe that you are the victim of parasiteware (because your once-steady commissions have dropped off suddenly or dramatically) you should immediately contact your affiliate network's manager. They can often determine the origin of the problem. Unfortunately it is very unlikely that it would be economically feasible to attempt to sue the offending parasite-marketer once identified.

One reason to only use large and reputable pay-per-click advertisers such as Google is the documented fact that some of the smaller PPC networks (beware the penny-a-click crowd) are known to install Spyware and Adware on your computer.

There are also specific Federal regulations governing adult-content websites, and on-line gambling sites. As with all of our Federal laws, foreign-based companies are not obligated to adhere to them. This is why there is still a huge amount of spyware, adware, and parasiteware, as well as pornography, and gambling sites, found throughout the internet.

Until recently the U. S. Department of Justice held that online gambling in all forms was illegal under the Wire Act of 1961. This act bars bets via telecommunications across state lines or international borders. A new interpretation by the Office of Legal Counsel states that the Wire Act only applies to wagers on a "sporting event or contest". This opens up a considerable window of opportunity for such endeavors as online card games.

The matter of tracking cookies is coming under increasing scrutiny. The European union recently passed a set of privacy directives known affectionately as "The Cookie Law". It is well worth noting. You should look carefully at your own websites to avoid problems in the future regarding your use of tracking visitors. Your Privacy Policy should list the cookies on your site by name and purpose. For other-party cookies be certain to identify their source. You should also disclose any social-sharing buttons that might link to outside sites that gather data.

It is not only necessary to follow all of the Federal laws. You must also comply with Local, County and State laws as well.

Local Home Owner Association or zoning codes can be found at most City Halls. There may be rules that could apply to your affiliate marketing business-from- home. Your County may have its own business regulations, usually available at the County Courthouse offices. Permits are a wonderful way for all government entities to scrape up additional revenues.

Equally important to you are your State laws regarding businesses. These relate to incorporation, taxes, unemployment insurance, workers compensation, minimum wage, and business licenses. These can usually be checked out on-line at your State government websites.

Aside from strict adherence to all Federal and local laws, there is also the area of ethical behavior that all serious internet marketers must address. To run a truly ethical web business you must:

Keep your visitors private information private;

Not spread false rumors about your competitors;

Comply with your merchant's advertising rules;

Not make false or misleading claims about your products;

Not make any promises that you or your affiliated merchant cannot keep;

Deal with visitor's complaints promptly and fairly;

Not lie about your internet income.

One of the "gray" areas of internet commerce law is in regard to collecting sales taxes from every buyer and remitting them to each buyer's state. This would be a daunting if not almost-impossible task for any internet marketer, but with States all looking for new revenue sources it is an obvious potential pain.

My tax accountant shrugs his shoulders on this one. It is also unclear whether sales to buyers even in my home state should includeaState sales tax. One problem is often my not even knowing the physical location of buyers of my virtual products. Be certain to check this matter thoroughly with your tax advisor.

Of course you have to pay Federal personal or Corporate income taxes on all of your net internet profits. Up until 2011 there was apparently no way for the IRS to accurately monitor your internet income. You were obligated by law to report this income, but it is said that many did not voluntarily comply. Enter the shiny new IRS 1099K form.

As I understand it, effective for 2011 payment-collection middlemen such as PayPal are required by law to send you and the IRS 1099Ks documenting your internet income. Not reporting all of your internet income will now open you up to a tax fraud audit. You do not want that. It is a very compelling reason for you to keep very detailed records of your expenses spent in generating your 1099K income.

One almost inevitable change that is coming is a universal internet sales tax designed by Uncle Sam as one route to reducing the Federal deficit (or more likely providing them with more money to find some creative way to waste). What impact this might have on overall internet sales is impossible to assess, but no-one in the industry is looking forward to its implementation. It is quite likely to happen in 2013.

Laws change, and as internet marketers it is our duty to keep up with the changes. For example, recent court rulings have redefined the gambling laws and actually made certain formerly-illegal practices absolutely legitimate. The new interpretation is that the law only applies to "sporting events or contests". (Theory: permit and regulate everything else to raise tax revenues.) This has opened up a whole new area of internet marketing opportunities.

One very important thing to remember is to NEVER exaggerate the merits of a product. The Federal Trade Commission (FTC) actually monitors this sort of fraud rather closely. It is also a VERY bad idea to "fake" endorsements and testimonials. The FTC has hit one website owner with a $250,000 fine for doing just that. Not exactly a cost-effective website.

It is a fact that sex and gambling are extremely profitable ventures on-line. Legal involvement in certain of these areas of commerce are more governed by one's personal moral code than by law. There is so much money to be made in other areas of internet commerce it just isn't necessary to participate in these "adult" endeavors. Then again, perhaps, I'm just an old prude. If that shoe fits you, wear it.

Knowing the various laws and ethical expectations governing internet commerce is essential to your marketing success. Once you get in the habit of doing things correctly, staying out of trouble becomes second-nature. Always err on the side of caution.

In the long run nothing is more important to you than your reputation as an ethical and law-abiding internet businessperson. **Do everything you can to establish and maintain that reputation.**

MODULE TWO – NICHE MARKETING

CHAPTER 4: FINDING YOUR BIG-MONEY NICHE
CHAPTER 5: KEYWORD SEARCH FOR TOP MARKETING DOLLARS
CHAPTER 6: CREATING FAST-SELLING VIRTUAL PRODUCTS
CHAPTER 7: PRIVATE LABLE RIGHTS (PLR) EXPOSED
CHAPTER 8: FREE WRITTEN RICHES FROM THE PUBLIC DOMAIN
CHAPTER 9: THE MILLION DOLLAR TOOLS OF THE TRADE

CHAPTER 4

FINDING YOUR BIG-MONEY NICHE

"If you want to get rich, target a niche; if you want to be broke, target **all** the folk!" **This is the founding principal behind all internet marketing.**

A market "niche" is an area of interest held by some definable group of individuals. We will be considering "niches" first as "general areas of interest", for example, "dogs". Then we'll split this down further into sub-niches.

As a "sub-niche" we could search, "dog training". Refine the sub-niche further down to: "How To Train A Doberman". Further? "How To Train An Older Doberman". Get the idea?

If possible you will want to share your personal passion with other people, whatever it may be. There is a market for virtually any information product. Are you a golfer? Then "golf" could be your general niche, and "Learn To Hit Straight Drives" could be a sub-niche.

Health nut? Survivor of some illness? Poker player? Fanatsy sports nut? Dog or cat lover? Biker? Swimmer? History buff? Sci-fi lover? Great at picking up dates at bars? The best swordsman in town? Great cook? Grow great petunias? There are limitless possibilities. Anything about which you are passionate, or have some knowledge fits the bill. Working within a familiar niche can be more fun. It may make your creation of a product easier for you. Of course you can work in any niche imaginable, passion notwithstanding. Do not ever choose a niche only because it is your passion.

Marketing principals are exactly the same regardless of the niche you choose. Some just find it easier to write about topics they care about. Personally I care about making money, so "niche passion" is not a big consideration in my internet marketing!

The general idea is to find a starving crowd, and sell them whatever it is they are starving for. What do you think you could sell a desperately hungry, starving crowd when it comes to food? Just about anything at any price. Get it?

Think about your last trip to a ball park or airport. The food sucks, it's poorly prepared, it's vastly overpriced, and served by nasty people with questionable hygiene. There you are, standing on a long line, praying to God they don't run out of what you want before you can overpay for it! Get the point?

But you cannot sell everything to everybody. Only Sam Walton figured out how to do that and you ain't Sam! You have to focus on specific narrowly-defined niches. You want to find the marketplace of individuals starving for something.

These hungry folk just simply **must** have that information that is tucked away in your report or book. They don't know how they can live without it! You want THOSE people, irrationally, insanely, passionately craving your information.

Some factors to consider before you even look for a niche is whether you will be:

Selling your own product;

Creating an affiliate website;

Creating a Google AdSense ad website;

Planning to do a pay-per-click campaign for any one or all of the above three;

Planning to market on social media only.

Of course, since this is your first exposure to the wonderful world of internet commerce, you have absolutely no idea what I'm talking about! Just read on and hopefully it will all fall into place.

Your "keywords" need to be really specific so that when buyers search for your particular keywords they know that your product is the one they must have. There is a word of caution here which you must heed if you are going to be a successful niche marketer. When you study the marketplace (by searching Google and Yahoo! and Amazon) you will find many areas where there are very active areas of focus by a large universe of internet professional marketers. Wow, that definitely looks like a winner since everyone else seems to be selling that certain "whatever"! **Don't fall into this trap.** I did years ago, before I awoke to reality!

First of all, you don't need to go up against massive competition. That is counter-productive. You don't want to try to compete in broad niches such as "mortgages" or "how to make money on the internet" because you will be going head to head with large companies with virtually unlimited marketing and advertising funds, and individuals with decades of marketing experience, both of which you very probably lack.

<u>Your task is to find many **tiny niches** where there are few or no competitors.</u> You could write mediocre material addressing specific needs in these niches and still make a lot of money. That is the ultimate secret to internet riches.

A few thousand monthly searches from one tightly-focused niche keyword can bring in good money. You can target other minimally searched keywords on other pages of your website or on additional websites. Never lose site of the fact that this entire internet marketing business is a pure numbers game.

The other side of the coin is that a competitor can sometimes be your best friend. Finding one that is successfully selling a product similar to yours is powerful market intelligence if you can acquire it. It proves that buyers (not just visitors) actually exist for products in that niche.

Does every niche product sell? Not at all. For example, there are a zillion searches for "Jokes". Would a well-advertised joke website get visitors? Absolutely. Everyone likes to be entertained! But with all the free jokes available on line would anyone be likely to pay for more yucks? Probably not.

Just how much will these niche-focused buyers actually pay for **your** special information? The answer is**: As much as you can convince them it is worth!** Take someone who is passionate about growing orchids. They own everything they could ever find ever written about orchids.   If you can do some in-depth internet research on orchids, find some gems of knowledge they might not know about, they'll likely pay $19.97 or $29.97 or whatever you ask for a report containing some tidbits of knowledge they do not possess on a subject they are so passionate about.

One way to find "who is passionate about what" is to visit any store that stocks a selection of different magazines. In my area the local Walgreens pharmacy and the local Safeway supermarket have a serious variety of magazine titles. Look for areas of interest addressed by more than one magazine. Realize how much it must cost to produce and distribute these magazines. If people weren't buying them they wouldn't exist. Bingo, a hot general niche!

You should also check out magazines.com for ideas.

Believe it or not there is a goldmine in your email spam box! The more emails you see about a particular market niche the more likely it is that this is a hot current topic on which you could consider focusing. Your task is to do a better job of reaching interested buyers than the idiot spammers are doing.

Check out Google Zeitgeist for general niche ideas. To access this free program go to: google.com/press/zeitgeist.com Here you can choose between "Trends", "Trends for Websites", "Hot Trends" and "Insights for Search". Good stuff.

Another great FREE tool for finding general niches is a monthly .pdf (free download) from eBay at: pages.ebay.com/sellercentral/hotitems.pdf.

Google "Trends" at: google.com/trends is another great research tool. You can mess around with geographical regional data and time frames. You can even see if a particular search, for some obscure reason known only to God, spikes on a particular day of the week! You can even compare two or more different search terms by entering them in the general Google "Search Terms" box separated by a comma ",". Google does a lot of work for you, and it's all free!

To see what digital products are being sold in your target niche go to:
marketplace.clickbank.com. Again, this is FREE. You can easily spend a full day at that site!

When I look for a target niche market the first thing I do is determine as best I can what people want to learn about, what training they seek, what special tips they need, and most important, what they are actually looking to buy.

There are four keywords for you to search are: **training, learn, buy and tip.**

If you type in "training" or "learn" or "buy" or "tip" in any of the keyword suggestion tools we will discuss later you will find lists such as "learn to play piano", "piano training", "buy a piano" and "piano tips". This preliminary search will give you an excellent general list of possible niches on which to focus.

Another approach is to take the words: "How to…." and "How do I…" followed by: learn; quit; get; stop; fix; get rid of; prevent; or cure, or any similar words. Then follow with anything imaginable: "How to fix a faucet"; "How do I quit snoring". Get the idea?

Up at 2:00AM? Can't sleep? This could just be your most valuable niche/product finding time! The TV infomercial volume at that hour is almost beyond belief! You can bet that if a vendor is paying out big bucks to create and run 30-minute TV infomercials these are great niches on which you should focus. One or more might even offer an affiliate program wherein you can piggy-back on their expensive TV ad marketing.

To get free information on internet search trends, check out:

Yahoo! Buzz at: buzzlog.yahoo.com/overall/;

Amazon Best Sellers at: amazon.com/gp/bestsellers/;

Technorati Top 100 at: technorati.com;

eBay Pulse at: pulse.ebay.com;

Google Hot Trends USA at: google.com/trends/hottrends;

SearchSpy at: dogpile.com;

Lycos Top 50 at: lycos.com;

Top Searches at: shopping.com;

Digg best stories at: digg.com;

America On Line Top Searches at: aol.com;

Alexa Top 100 Sites at: alexa.com/whatshot;

Frequently Asked Questions at: wiki.answers.com;

Top Searches at: ask.com (the IQ section);

Frequent questions at: answerbag.com;

The 100 Top "Lenses" at: squidoo.com;

Browse topics at: about.com.

Another free tool for finding niches is a .pdf download from eBay:
pages.ebay.com/sellercentral/hotitems.pdf.

To find a niche AFFILIATE program do a Google search: "(YOUR KEYWORD[S])" + "AFFILIATE PROGRAM".

If you can find a narrow niche with decent traffic within some of the general hot-topic areas you have a great start towards affiliate marketing success. The key is finding merchant offers of value to people within that narrow niche. If you cannot find relevant products, those products that people searching your keywords simply MUST have, find a different niche.

After you search through the above sixteen sites you should come away with a list of at least fifty topics that look like good candidates for a focused niche keyword search. Cut this down to the twenty or so with which you can imagine enjoying working.

You should also access the learning centers at Yahoo! and MSN:
searchmarketing.yahoo.com and adcenter.microsoft.com.

Another good tool for determining trends is found at: pulse.ebay.com. Yahoo Buzz is also useful for this purpose.

Take a long, hard look, at Quantcast.   Quantcast.com is a site dedicated to internet demographics. Study this site in detail, because it can be of great value to you in all of you internet marketing. For example, do a search on a product niche to find related sites. Here you can check out the sites where your product niche would get great exposure. Taking the time to learn Quantcast will be time very well spent.

There are many other free tools to check out: kwbrowse.com; adlab.msn.com;   spacky.com; traffictravis.com;   wordpot.com.

Wordstream.com is a paid service that will allow you to perform a **limited** number of niche searches for FREE.

Next we need to see how many on-line searches there are for keywords in these niches. I do all of my keyword research using an internet keyword generator sold by Brad Callen called "KeyWord Elite". It is well worth the cost. There is also a useful tool available called "PPC WebSpy".

There is a free trial of a keyword niche finder located at wordstream.com. You should check out this resource, and also take a look at some of their other useful products.

Two very useful niche-finding tools you can purchase are:

NicheBot, at: nichebot.com. There are three versions with daily pricing of $0.60, $1.12 and $3.62. There is a 14-day trial for a buck.
MicroNicheFinder, at: micronichefinder.com, is a valuable tool for deciding in which niches you want to market products or affiliates. Download for a hundred dollars, or try for 30 days for eight dollars.

Perhaps the most profitable approach to finding hot niches that I have found is going through lists of keyword searches made by potential buyers. I then search for information products that utilize those keywords.

Amazingly I often find NO relevant products! Even if there are only one or two, this becomes an absolute no-brainer. <u>Just create a product utilizing those keywords, and you have a sure winner.</u>

A summary overview of your niche search process suggests:

Collect ideas. Take notes as you watch infomercials. Look at magazine racks;

Search the four general key words shown above for more ideas;

Find the correct "category" for your niche. Google search: "article directories", and learn in which categories articles in your niche appear;

Click on your niche category and look at the most recent articles in your niche;

Look at fifteen of these, and rate them from one to fifteen based the number of views each received;

Rate the same articles based on your opinion of the content;

Make a list of those that have the highest combined rating;

Look for "product review" articles with high traffic to see whether such reviews exist in your niche. Add these to your list.

For all of the best articles you determined from the above searches, click through to their landing pages and study how they are built and what affiliate products they promote.

To see articles that have been actually published in a potential niche go to: ezinearticles.com. Check the number of views. This can be a real eye-opener, and a great indicator of interest. Plug in any term and see a list of articles related to that term. Click on an article and you will find the date published and the traffic available to you.

At some point all of your niche study will boil down to your own subjective assessment of niche profitability. For each of your choices ask:

How well do current related products sell?

What is the price of these related products?
How easy would it be for me to create a better product?

How many different products might I create?

How much potential is there for "backend" sales? (Offering an upgrade-version of the product.)

Once you choose your niche your job is to either find appropriate affiliate products, or decide to create your own offering. You will obtain a domain name and a hosting company. Then you will create appropriate articles. You will create dynamite headlines, and user-friendly landing pages, followed by whatever type report it is that the successful competitors in your niche are offering. There is no need to re-invent the wheel. Copying success is the way most wealthy internet marketers, myself included, got that way! All of the above "create" references will be covered thoroughly in this book.

If you find that your chosen niche brings in little or no traffic DON'T GIVE UP. Just pick another niche and try again. The only possible way to fail in the internet commerce business is if you give up and stop trying. Once you give up there is nothing the world's most expensive training can do for you.

Take advantage of our catastrophic economy. Thousands are searching for information related to bankruptcy, foreclosures, mortgages, loans, credit check, credit cards, cash advances, debt reduction and jobs. Don't be shy. Sell it to them!

OK, so now you have a list of possible niches, what now? This is where you must decide just how profitable a niche or product might actually be. This is the world of "Keyword Research", which is an entirely new topic that will be covered in detail in the next Chapter 5.

Just to get started, let's look at Google's FREE "Keyword Tool". This appears within the Google Adwords pay- per-click site, so you will first need to open an AdWords account. This costs nothing but a few minutes of your time. Google keeps detailed records of all of the millions of searches on their platform!

It is reported that the search statistics they publish are some fraction, probably far less than half, of the actual searches for a given keyword. (No sense in letting their competition know how well they are doing!) Keep this in mind when you are looking for profitable niches. Once you type in a keyword or keyword phrase you will see a list of many related terms, with the traffic to each. This is where your detailed keyword search work begins.

Focused niche marketing is the key to success in selling information products. Find your niche and you **CAN** become rich! Take this task seriously, enjoy the task, and you are well on your way to internet commerce success.

HAPPY NICHEING!

CHAPTER 5

KEYWORD SEARCH FOR TOP MARKETING DOLLARS

One of the great things about the internet commerce business is the availability on-line of an incredible amount of helpful relevant information. Some of this can be accessed at a modest cost, but almost anything you will ever need can be accessed for **FREE**. Keyword Research is your "key" to low up-front-investment riches.

The reason keywords are so important is to insure that search engines "Query Software", such as Google and all other search engines employ, sends searchers to **YOUR** website rather than to your competitors' site. Query software matches search terms with relevant keywords on websites. **All success in search engine marketing begins with keywords.**

Your main objective in all of your internet commerce work, in website development and affiliate marketing, is to develop lists of relevant key words and keyword phrases (known as "long-tail" keywords). These words and terms are related to whatever niche and product you are trying to market. Searching for, and finding, useful keywords and phrases that others haven't found or used can give you a big leg up over the competition.

People buy from those who can solve their most pressing problem, and solve it **NOW**. Instant gratification. Many are looking to learn something. It is very simple to use any ""keyword tool" (an item of specialized software) to search the four simple words mentioned earlier: **"learn", "training", "buy" and "tip"**.

Search the word "learn" and you will get a long list of results pertaining to exactly what people want to learn. Do the same with "training" and find out what training they seek. Then click on each keyword phrase (e.g., "learn piano" or "guitar training") to uncover dozens of additional tightly focused keywords.

The same technique is used to find people who are specifically looking to buy something. Just type in "buy". Not exactly rocket science! This will provide you with a list of the exact things people are looking to buy.

Want an idea for an ezine or article? Search the word "tip". This will give you a wealth of ideas. What tips, bits of information, are people actively seeking?

Just those four short words, **learn, training, buy and tip**, are your keys to opening up the Pandora's box of internet commerce.

GOOGLE IS KING

Google gives you a mind numbing number of ways to do your keyword research. Three important ways to do general research in your niche are Google "Alerts", Google "News", and Google "Reader".

You can use "Google Alerts" to gather information based on specific search terms you choose. You fill in your search term, then choose from dropdown boxes: TYPE > HOW OFTEN > VOLUME, & give your email address. I suggest setting up a free Google Gmail email account just for receiving these alerts.

Get blog-post ideas for really fresh news based on the term you select by using "Google News" advanced news search. You can set this up for fresh news in the past hour, day, week, or month. You can also study archived material published in the past. An amazing statistic, reported by Google, is that 25% of all daily searches are for a keyword phrase or term that has never been used before!

"Google Reader" is a free tool that helps you stay up to date with what is going on in an industry. Great aid in coming up with fresh content ideas

Let's first look at what else Google has to offer you:

Go to any Google page with a Google search function, and enter your keyword. When the search list appears, go to the long list on the left side and click on "Related Searches". At the top of the search results will appear a list of very useful related terms. Clicking on one of these will show you the sites that are rich in those particular keywords.

Google has an excellent keyword search tool. It also has a valuable contextual (words within the body of your text) targeting tool for you to use to analyze your competition. Both tools are within the Google AdWords program.

For starters, open up a FREE AdWords account, which you must have to access this useful tool. Go to AdWords.Google.com. (You will need a website address [URL/domain name only; a developed site itself is unnecessary] to complete this initial sign-up form.) Get any cheap domain name, such as your own given name .com, at godaddy.com (inexpensive and fast). If your own given name or nickname is not available, try "ask(yourname).com"; "follow(yourname).com" until you find one that is available.

Next you go to "Create Google Account" where you will give your name and email address and make up a password. (If you do not have an email account set up a free one at Yahoo! mail or Google gmail.) Next step will be choosing a time zone and currency in which you want to be paid. You will then be sent an email.

The email contains an account number (copy and keep it, though I've never actually needed it for anything!) and a special link. Click on the link, and you have confirmed your new account. You then go back to the home page and sign in with your email address and the password you created.

Incidentally, if you have any other Google account, such as gmail, you can sign in to AdWords with your sign-in info for that other account.

This site has an immense amount of helpful information on it. You would be well advised to spend an entire day clicking on every tab and watching every training video.

Probably the best known and most useful Google tool can be found at: adwords.google.com/select/KeywordToolExternal. By typing in keywords in "Keyword Tool External" you can see how many people searched using that term in the past month. It is generally believed that the ACTUAL number is as much as four times what is stated. The reasoning is that Google does not want its competitors to know their statistics exactly.

To access the keyword tool click on the "Reporting & Tools" tab, and on the drop-down menu click on "Keyword Tool". Then by entering your keywords and phrases, and choosing the general category from a menu, you will get a huge list showing the searches made for many terms in your niche. By checking a small box you can narrow the list down to searches more closely focused to your term. It is a good idea to do both.

To access the contextual targeting tool, click on the "Opportunities" tab, enter a few words that describe your offer, and the tool will create a series of "Adgroups". When you click on the "Expand" button you see updated lists of relevant keywords.

Google AdWords has a particularly valuable tool called "Traffic Estimator". This tool shows how much you would have to pay to get the number one position for given keywords. You can access this tool without actually setting up a real campaign that you really do plan to run and pay per click.

Set up a dummy campaign with an obscure term. Log in and "create a new campaign". Create ad group "TEST" with Headline TEST, descriptions TEST. Enter your keyword(s) & "save".

Google will now tell you the dollars it will take for high position when you click "Calculate Estimate". (To be sure the dummy ad never runs click "Pause Ad".) Incidentally, because Google frequently changes their various tools, adding new ones and deleting old ones, this may no longer be available when you are reading this.

Google's "Mass Keyword Search" allows you to find out how your website ranks for up to ten keywords at once. You can also study the top hundred sites for your specific keyword. Access this at: googlerankings.com/mkindex.php.

It is a good idea to spy on your competition. You can be certain they are spying on you! Conduct a search at Google for certain keywords for a week or two. See if any affiliates are running the same ad all the time. You can also determine whether he or she is tracking that keyword. Click on their link, go to the extreme bottom of their vendor's order page (you don't have to BUY anything) and you will find a code. If it is obviously your competitor's ClickBank (an affiliate/vendor facilitator) name alone, that keyword is not being tracked.

If the name is followed by a period and a series of letters and/or numbers that keyword **is** being tracked. So if you find a keyword associated with an ad for a week or so and that keyword is being tracked you have found keyword gold! Go back and copy your competitor's ad, and run a similar campaign. You should have a sure winner.

For under a hundred bucks you can purchase a great spying program at:
dayjobkiller.com. Many top gurus use it, and you should surely consider doing so.

Here is a useful technique for expanding your keyword list. Do a Google search on some profitable keyword. Copy the URLs for the first four websites that show up. Then go to a FREE tool in your AdWords account:
adwords.google.com/select/keywordtoolexternal. Click on "Site Related Keywords", and enter these four URLs. Google will show you a great list of keywords that may not have shown up using your other keywords tools.

When you do any Google search, do these searches three ways. Start with quotation marks, " " (known as phrase match), and without quotation marks (known as broad match). Then also search with [ ] brackets to get an "exact match". You will get somewhat different results from each search.

BUT IT'S NOT ONLY GOOGLE

Keyword popularity is your basic starting point. You should be aware, however, that the numbers you see will differ from one keyword source to another. This is because they are based on the figures from different search engines. Also, different search engines may publish different percentages of their actual total traffic for reasons mentioned above.

Some programs (such as WordTracker) provide figures for only a small segment of searches. Google's figures are generally reported to be one-half or so of the true number of Google searches for a particular key word or phrase. (Multiply Google's figures by two (or even three) to get a number closer to the actual number of monthly searches for a given keyword or keyword phrase.) The point here is that you must treat all keyword search numbers as rough estimates and not as absolutes.

If you want to buy a keyword search tool that gives you many different keyword choices along with other valuable tools start with Word Tracker at: wordtracker.com. They have a free trial so you can see whether it is worth its price of a bit over a dollar a day to actually own it. It is not a bad idea to save up a large number of searches that you can perform these all within the free trial period.

Another trial worth pursuing in the same manner is Key Word Spy at: keywordspy.com. And you might find Micro Niche Finder's Keyword Tool at: micronichefinder.com to be worth a long hard look at.

Another fine product can be found at: goodkeywords.com. Their "Keyword Strategy Studio" has a free trial. It sells for under fifty bucks, and is well worth it. An excellent **FREE** keyword suggestion tool can be found at wordstream.com. They also have a very useful negative keyword tool that indicates wasteful keywords to avoid.

Between Google and these five sites you can get a massive amount of keyword information with proper planning at zero cost during free trials.

For years I have used a tool by Brad Callen called Keyword Elite available at: keywordelite.com. It goes for around a hundred bucks. It is well worth it.

On "eBay Pulse" you can find the keywords and phrases most frequently used to search their massive site. At ClickBank (clickbank.com) you can find their best sellers by clicking on "Marketplace". You can find the keywords used by these sites by doing a Google search and then looking at the keywords used by those sites.

A rather useful site which provides a somewhat different set of website results than Google when you search with your keywords is: quintura.com. (Ignore the occasional result in Russian!) Enter your search term in the box provided and click on the almost-invisible little arrow on the right side of the box. You will find the URL results to be quite specific to your search terms.

The search engine Bing has very useful "webmaster tools". Using its keyword tool "Phoenix" you can search multiple keywords simultaneously, same as with Google. Bing also has an organic keyword search tool that displays organic search volume across different languages and countries.

ALEXA

Now check out alexa,com.   According to their website: "Find And Evaluate Businesses Worldwide With Alexa's Free Web Analytics". This may well be the most useful web site out there. It is widely reported that it is the only site that has a truly unbiased website ranking system. It is owned by Amazon.   Alexa ranks websites purely on traffic volume. I strongly suggest you study what the site has to offer.   They only provide statistics for popular websites, but if you want every imaginable analytic about one of their listed sites you can find it. Studying details of successful sites can offer you guidance in creating your own marketing campaigns.

You can also learn up to the minute "hot topics", "hot products" and "hot web pages" all at no cost. Once you get deeply established in internet commerce Alexa can also provide a number of sophisticated website audits for you, but these services are quite costly.

It is absolutely essential that you spend as much time as you can studying these keyword search sites and what they have to offer. In fact, from a time-spent perspective, you will find that keyword search together with selection of vendors to represent as an affiliate (see Module Four) will occupy at least half of your working day. I find both of these tasks to be fun, because I know they are the key to much of the money I make on line.

HOW SEARCH ENGINES WORK

A discussion of keywords is incomplete without a thorough understanding of search engines and how they find websites to provide the searching public with the best possible viewing experience. A search engine basically consists of three distinct software programs:

Spider Software requests pages from websites. It "sees" text and links and the URL. It does not see images, logos or videos, unless you include a text "alt tag" associated with these elements. It especially loves links.

Index Software contains an algorithm that takes all of the spider software information and analyzes and stores it.

Query Software checks through everything in the index software and responds to searches by matching search terms with relevant websites.

The reason keywords are so important is to insure that the query software sends searchers to your website in deference to your competitors' websites.

UNDERSTANDING KEYWORDS

The are two general types of keywords that you MUST always have in your campaign. These are the keywords that are the most targeted and qualified and most likely to make you lots of money. These are **ACTION-BASED** and **PRODUCT-BASED**.

Action based keywords are those that indicate the person searching is actually looking to buy something and not just looking for information. Searches beginning with (or having it within the search term) "buy…..", "purchase……", "order……" "cheapest……" and similar action terms are best. "How To….." is fine only if you are selling a relevant "How To" product. Otherwise it qualifies as a negative keyword and must be listed as such.

Using a **product-name based keyword** is great except for one unfortunate fact. Google will only allow one advertiser's ad to use that product's exact keyword connected to the product "Display URL" in AdWords. However, if you use as the "Display URL" a different extension (e.g., .net) or tack a number on the end of the product name before the .com this seems to pass muster.

One can look at keywords in three ways:

Keywords that bring in great traffic but poor sales. These are words people use when they are researching, "just looking".

Keywords that bring in good traffic and decent sales. These are words people use when they are in a buying mood.
Keywords that bring in low traffic but huge sales. This is the buying behavior you will find in a tightly-focused niche market.

Using the any of the keyword statistics analyzers you will be finding:

The number of times our EXACT keyword or keyword phrase (also called a "long-tail keyword") was searched over the past month.

The number of website pages that contain that exact keyword, which is a measure of your competition.

A "**K**eyword **E**ffectiveness **I**ndex" (**KEI**), found in WordTracker) which is a very useful numerical representation of how effective the keyword may prove to be.

Once you have a list of the best prospective keywords, create some headlines using those keywords. There is a very interesting free tool for evaluating the "emotional" value of your headlines from 0 to 100%. It rates your headline on three bases:

Intellectual. Ads effectiveness where your product requires reasoning or careful evaluation.

Empathetic. Ads crafted to bring out positive emotional reactions in your visitors.

Spiritual. Ads designed to have the deepest emotional appeal.

The program is found at: aminstitute.com/headline/index.htm. Apparently they employ a scientifically researched algorithm to create an EMV rating (**E**motional **M**arketing **V**alue). I certainly do not use it to entirely guide my headline creation or the keywords used to create them, but it offers some very interesting insights into the emotions induced by certain words that may trump the actual dictionary meaning of a word.

It is reported that a 50% EMV is minimum for a good headline, and that "headline pros" achieve between 75% and 100%. It is worth taking a look at. You can't beat the price!

A list of your keywords having both a high KEI (preferably greater than 50) together with a high EMV (minimum 50%) should be a great starting point in your quest for the optimum conversion of visitors to buyers.

A word of advice: I have seen keyword training that suggests that you should find and make a list of hundreds, even thousands, of keyword phrases for each product. I find this to be a total waste of time and effort.

Most experts agree that you should try to determine what are in your judgment to be the ten best keywords for each campaign and focus exclusively on their proper use in your headlines, sales letters and advertising. Don't over-complicate the process. Time is money.

You can go to websitemagazine.com for a list of "Keyword Research Tools". The following list summarizes the tools I use most often:

Micro-niche Finder at: micronichefinder.com (my personal favorite);

KeywordElite by Brad Callen, at: keywordelite.com;

Word Tracker at: wordtracker.com (KEI);

AM Institute at: aminstitute.com/headline/index.htm (EMV);

Keyword Strategy Studio Tool at: goodkeywords.com;

NicheBot, at: nichebot.com;

KeyWord Suggestion Tool, FREE, at: google.com/adwords;

Micro-Niche Finder at: micronichefinder.com;

WordStream at: wordstream.com;

Keyword Spy at: keywordspy.com;

Keyword Discovery at: keyworddiscovery.com;

KeywordCountry at: keywordcountry.com;

TrafficTravis at: traffictravis.com;

SpyFu at: spyfu.com;

MisspelledKeywords at: misspelledkeywords.com;

Good Keywords at: goodkeywords.com (searches out MetaTags from competitor's websites.

You will find **many** free trials available. It is a good idea to save up a number of different campaigns so that you can take advantage of free trials during the time before they expire.

To find long-tail keywords with these tools start by doing a general search using three short keywords that are most relevant to your book's content. Next re-order the "Global Monthly Searches" with the lowest number on top and work your way down the list to locate relevant long-tail keywords with some reasonable volume.

It is important to recognize the need for "long tail" keywords. They appeal to visitors searching for specific tightly-defined products. Most important, there is less competition for them and therefore they cast less. Lower cost plus focused searches equals better profits! The emphasis here is quality over quantity.

Never underestimate the power of being found on the first page of search results using the right keyword. If you can identify your keyword "findability" you will connect with searchers who are ready to take action, not just window shopping.

Keyword search in and of itself is not the absolute last word. You need to base your research on "supply and demand" factors, not just on keyword searches (demand) alone. You need to research the number of sites responding to those keywords with good relevant information (supply).

Do a keyword search and copy the URLs of the top five sites that appear. In the Google keywords tool click on "Site Related Keywords" and you will see a list that may not have shown up in your other searches.

What you are seeking is a keyword phrase you hope to use that turns up little or no good information when you key it into your browser. That is the niche on which you should focus, high demand with low supply. A program (such as "Keyword Strategy Studio) at goodkeywords.com can be purchased to facilitate your search for this winning combination.

As a vendor- affiliate one approach is to focus on finding any **new** products that are hot and cash in on them before they become saturated. Even better, you can even promote products pre-launch! This is made simple by joining a FREE site that specializes in new product announcements. Go to: jvnotifypro.com and sign up.

Many affiliate marketers make it a point to register unique domain names as close as possible to the name of their affiliate product. In connection with this technique there are two very valuable sites for you to use in your keyword research. They are alexa.com and quantcast.com. Once you have decided on a general niche theme, go to Quantcast and individually enter the URLs of the top sites in a Google search related to that theme.

As discussed earlier, Quantcast will deliver to you a wealth of information about the site you entered. You will learn the monthly traffic and demographics related to that traffic. But most important to you are three data columns: "Audience Also Likes", "Audience Also Visits", and "Audience Also Searches For".

Take some of the top URLs shown and enter them back into Quantcast. If they get a lot of traffic add them to your keyword list of domain names to bid on. Next go to Alexa and go through a similar process. You want "Traffic Rankins">"Get Traffic Details". You will find information appears similar to what you got from Quantcast.

Now click on the "Related Links" button. Here is the mother-lode of information on other sites to which visitors go. Voila'! You now have many possible new domain choices within your general theme.

Then by making logical variations, misspellings (typos) of each URL you can create a massive new keyword list as well! An aid to this is: visualthesaurus.com. Many of the keywords you found might be searched for with a synonym. Add as many as possible to your keywords.

You can even use a search engine such as ask.com to find additional keywords. Type in any keyword and it immediately gives you a list of related keywords that people have searched.

Here is a very simple formula for getting started:

You choose a product or service that you would be comfortable selling as your own product or representing it as an affiliate.

Think of the most common words related to that product that you can imagine someone searching for the product would enter into a search engine. Answer: "What would I enter"?

Do searches in at least five different search engines entering those words. Visit each of the top ranked sites. View the "source" of each homepage and record their "meta name = keywords".

Repeat the above but visit each of the "sponsored links" and "paid ad sites". Again do the "source" search for even more and different keywords from the meta tags.

Take a thesaurus (if you do not own one go to thesaurus.com) and copy synonyms for every keyword, greatly expanding your list.

Now you have a great starter list to feed into all of the keyword search tools to determine possible high traffic keywords to use in your AdWords campaign.

REFINEMMENTS OF THE PROS

There are many "tricks of the trade" that are seldom taught. These are used quite effectively by the top affiliate marketers, known in the trade as "super-affiliates".

After you have acquired your keyword list using all of the tools and techniques outlined above, consider expanding your list in the following ways:

Consider adding "cities" to some keywords, for example: "grow better roses in New York City".

Glom some keywords words together. Some people might search for "gardeningtips" rather than "gardening tips". Some might even enter "gardening-tips". Incidentally, capitalizing any letters has no effect on searches. You can add plurals to some keywords, though some search engines ignore the plurals as if they were singular.

Misspelled keywords can be a gold mine! "Weeding" for "wedding" is a common example.

Another gold mine is typographical error entries. Say you are marketing "hybrid roses". How about "h6brid roses" or "h7brid roses"? The 6 and 7 keys are directly above the y key. Check out the number of searches for the typo version and compare it to the number without the typo.

If there happens to be the name of some famous person associated directly with the product be sure to associate it with phrases in your keywords list.

When you right-click to "view source" of competitor's websites you may find some good suggestions within their Meta Tags.

There might be thousands of searches for the accurate search-term version, equating to massive competition, but only a handful for the typo where you might well be the **ONLY** landing site!

Be certain to EXCLUDE "negative key words". If you are trying to sell something you certainly do not want "free" to appear in the visitors search entry! Many other words such as: "hate", "sucks", etc. can eliminate lots of clicks. This is particularly important when you are paying for every click!

You might well end up with a list of thousands of relevant keywords. There is a free tool at: seochat.com/seo-tools/keyword-optimizer that will "clean" your entire list. It will eliminate any duplicates, and alphabetize the entire list!

Once you have a website in place and a keywords campaign going, a freebie called hittail.com will track the amount of organic "natural" traffic your site receives (visitor typed in your URL directly).

Look at keyword search as a fun game, not a chore. I actually enjoy it as much as any other aspect of this wonderful internet business. There is nothing on which your time can be better spent.

JUST DO IT!

CHAPTER 6
CREATING FAST-SELLING VIRTUAL PRODUCTS

Your day to day "job" as an internet entrepreneur is not what you might imagine. Your job is to answer three questions, and the much of your time will be spent answering them:

Who is my target audience?

What do they want?

How can I motivate them to act now?

Notice I didn't say: "What can I <u>sell</u> them?" Remember, you are marketing, not selling. You must spend the majority of your time, perhaps sixty percent, answering those three key questions. Creating your actual "product", a report or ebook, or choosing a vendor to represent, accounts for the other forty percent.

In writing your reports and ebooks you must anoint yourself as the expert on whatever it is you have discovered your target visitors want. Then you must create an ever deepening relationship with those visitors that could last a lifetime.

Jeff Bezos, the genius who conceived of Amazon back in the mid '90s did so by focusing on being consumer-centric. He recognized that he did not want to be a "book company". He stated that he wanted to create a "customer company". He did, and most successfully. <u>You must also be customer oriented.</u>

Back in the days of mail order marketing (basically the 50s to 80s) a successful guru preached the need to create what he called a **USP**, a **U**nique **S**elling **P**roposition to use in his promotional material. Just what exactly is it that sets your product apart from what your competition is offering? That is your "USP".

You can think of your USP as articulating your **U**ltimate advantage over your competitor's offering; creating a **S**ensational Offer; and making a very **P**owerful Promise. That is your **USP** formula. You have to sit down and think of every possible benefit you can that will set your offering apart from the competition. Then and only then create that product.

Look at your competition and differentiate your product in some significant way. You are faster, more complete, or better researched You offer better service, a better guarantee, a better whatever you can think of. This is your **"U".**

Your goal is to reward your customer for taking action. For example, offer a free ebook, a free report, a free newsletter, a free anything. This is your **"S".**

Your **"P"** is to consider making some outrageous promise, then see if you can reverse-engineer it to figure out a way to deliver on the promise. Here is where your "guarantee" comes in to play.

CREATE SPECIAL REPORTS

Let's talk about "Special Reports". I know of three companies that have founded extremely successful businesses based upon this concept. One such company is Scoopified. I have personally bought many of their reports, which sell for a few dollars each. Their catalog lists hundreds.

What amazes me is that some of the "reports" contain one single piece of information, the name and address of the location where you can access the **actual** obscure report or study itself. They don't sell the product itself, just the source of the product! The copy in their catalog creates the perception that this one hard-to-find bit of information is worth a few bucks. **And it is!**

Dr. Jeffrey Lant is a very prolific writer/entrepreneur who has written a number of extremely useful books on writing for profit and marketing written material (easy to access him through a Google search.) But for years he has also successfully sold short reports on 8 1/2 x 11 sheets stapled in one corner. I've bought many of them from him. I've met Dr. Lant. He is a unique and very wealthy genius. **Information reports sell.**

A third company from whom I have bought many fine reports is Adventures Unlimited (adventuresunlimitedpress.com). They sell an eclectic mix of new age and weird science and conspiracy theory stuff, but it all falls into the "information product" category.   In fact their website is one that anyone with a large selection of their own information products to offer could very well copy. NOTE IN PARTICULAR THE VERY ATTRACTIVE COVERS ON THEIR REPORTS.

The absolute fact is that **PEOPLE BUY INFORMATION**. Just accept the fact. There are many fortunes being made based upon an understanding of this one reality.

What sort of information must you create? Two general types: New, fresh, hot information always sells. But well-researched, timeless information aggregated by you and **available only through you in one place** always sells well too.

Short on ideas? Let's get some product ideas that others have thought to offer. Go to amazon.com, and look up the Kindle genre. Study what people are selling. Look at the "best sellers". Study how they title their books. Study how they design their covers?

We are not going to try to reinvent the wheel here. It is perfectly ethical to learn from

the successes of others and copy their successes. This is fundamental to your success. Check out "short reads" at: amazon store/kindle/ebooks/singles

GO BEYOND THE VIRTUAL

It is a great idea to convert ALL of your reports and ebooks into audio format. It is easy, and it gives you a whole new world of profit opportunities. The idea is to create an "mp3" audio file. Your customers can access these and burn them to a CD or add them to their mp3 players. They can add them to their iPhones and iPads, iPods and Blackberries too.

You can accomplish this by downloading FREE "Audacity" software at: audacity.sourceforge.net. All you need is an inexpensive microphone from Radio Shack or Walmart or wherever and you are ready to record. Instant new profit maker!

Carrying this concept to the next logical level, consider making video recordings. Here again, there is FREE software you can download at: techsmith,com/download/cantasia. You may want to edit the results you obtain using this program. If your computer came with video editing software (such as "Windows Movie Maker) that is all you need. If not, you can purchase "Camtasia Studio", which has a FREE trial.

To summarize, any written report or ebook can be **enhanced** in value by creating audio and video files (though some may not lend themselves to a video format).

Buyers will always pay more for audio and especially video than for an e book not containing these elements. They also make great "upsells" and "one-time-offers", or can even be offered as a freebie on a squeeze page to build your email list.

Do not overlook creating "hard copies" of your own virtual material. Having your local print-shop run off Xerox copies and spiral bind them is one path taken by internet infopreneures. One commonly used marketing approach is to have a buyer purchase some virtual info product, and after securing their mailing address send them a spiral-bound "something".

That "something" can be a copy of the virtual product they just bought, or better, a new report on-topic, for FREE. When your buyer receives that report you will have included in the package all manner of upsells! Lots of special offers and directions to different websites, possibly even to an affiliate offer. This is the ultimate combination of "dinosaur" snail-mail-order and modern internet marketing. Brilliant!

You can even consider sending an inexpensive 1gb thumb "flash" drive (they cost around $10 at Walmart) containing not only the product they bought but any number of creative offerings. Of course this will include direct links to anywhere you want them to land to take some action that adds to your bank account!

Yet another nice "extra" product is your own audio CDs. These can be sold as an upsell, one-time-offer, or as a stand-alone product. They always command a lot more dollars than a digital download. The beauty of this business model is that you do not have to create the CDs yourself. Just create an audio file. Then enlist the help of a company called Kunaki at kunaki.com. They do a great job of creating beautifully packaged CDs at a <u>very</u>

affordable price. They create the CDs from your recorded .wav file which you send them electronically. They will do this one at a time on demand (no inventory to carry) and ship direct to your customer, beautifully packaged.

Of course you can simply record on CD blanks yourself and make duplicates on your PC, but this takes time, and the product you send out will probably look amateurish. There are specially-coated CD blanks that allow you to print titles on your CDs directly from your personal computer, but they still look cheesy.

A few very creative infopreneurs have focused on a special genre of CD product that sells very well. These are especially easy to produce if you happen to have a friend or relative who is an expert at something, for example an attorney, accountant, mortgage pro, real estate pro, or whatever. If you do not know someone, simply find willing local experts in the yellow pages. A recorded interview, the special product to which I am referring, can be done face to face or even over the phone. The local individual, in exchange for the interview, gets free publicity. Win-win!

You will need to prepare a list of questions to give the expert in advance. In exchange for the interview, you can offer to promote their website, email, business name, address, etc., in effect trading free advertising for the interview. These can be really hot products in the right niche.

Once created, your virtual products or hard copies of them, can provide an income stream for life. They can be offered in myriad ways, packaged together to create a new product, set up sequentially as a study course, and used as freebies on squeeze pages. If there is time-sensitive information, be certain to periodically update your reports.

The wealthiest internet infopreneurs have made millions of dollars doing nothing more than creating simple, short, virtual information products. The fact that the internet and devices with which to access it are in themselves so dynamic, changing almost daily, creates in itself the opportunity for new and different "how to" information products.

DO I HAVE TO BE A GOOD WRITER?

Most people are not particularly good writers, so creating an original written report or ebook seems like a daunting task. It need not be. There are a number of options available to you:

Write it yourself. It does not have to be Pulitzer Prize material. Believe it or not, simple and mediocre sells. It sells because many of the buyers frankly would not know top quality writing from lesser quality. If it answers their questions and provides the information they were seeking they will be quite satisfied with writings that your 8th grade teacher might grade C-.

Pay someone else to write it. Check out elance.com and rentacoder.com. Check out the amazing fiverr.com. From these sites you can access the talents of literally hundreds of thousands of freelance writers. You put the details of what you want out for bids, sit back, and wait for results. You will get many responses, and your task becomes simply deciding who to hire to write your virtual report or ebook material. You will be surprised at how inexpensively you can have good reports written for you.

You can use PLR (Private Label Rights) material;

You can use Public Domain material.

There are many places to market your ebooks and reports. If you want to give away articles in the hope of them going viral and spreading around your signature links or contextual links, check out : brandable-ebooks.com.

When you decide to sell your content, there are many choices. Using eBay and Craigslist and all manner of classified advertising to drive traffic to your website is critical. Selling books and reports from your own website is Basic Marketing 101.

You can sell your books directly on Amazon.com, Barnes and Noble, Borders, Amazon Kindle, Nook, or CreateSpace. There are also a host of other virtual bookstores from which you can sell: Booklocker.com; Ebooksonthe.net; Mypublish.com; Ebookmall.com; Ebooksnbytes.com; Ebooksubmit.com; Download.com; Ebooktags.com; Jogena.com; Ebookcrossroads.com/ebook-sellers.html; Ecourseweb.com; Blish.com; Ideamarketers.com; Ebookpalace.com; Published.com; Bowindex.com; Ebookjungle.com; Cyberread.com; Ebookbroadcast.com.

A Google search for "virtual book sellers" or "where to sell my ebook" will turn up more than you will ever need. As pointed out above, **PEOPLE BUY INFORMATION**. It is a fact proven over and over by successful infopreneurs. Millions of dollars have been earned by authors of virtual material. It isn't difficult.

JUST DO IT!!!

CHAPTER 7

FREE WRITTEN RICHES FROM THE PUBLIC DOMAIN

The biggest problem that most internet marketers have is creating their own original written information. They either cannot write, or do not like to write, or find the thought of writing an entire original work of any length absolutely beyond all reason! Write a book or have a root canal? Root canal wins every time!

Having a freelance writer from elance.com, rentacoder.com, or fiverr.com create your reports, or obtaining Public Label Rights material, are two common ways infopreneurs create products. There is yet a third way to create your saleable virtual information products. It is one on which many infopreneurs focus almost entirely. The concept is that of using material in the Public Domain.

Creating highly saleable virtual products can be no more difficult than copying exactly something that someone else has previously created. The catch here is the absolute need to abide by the strict Federal Copyright Laws. These laws give all authors, including you, protection from anyone copying their material for a very long period of time. The rules differ from country to country, and even by the type of creative media (e.g., books, films, etc.).

Copyrights do eventually expire, and/or are never renewed, or many works are never copyrighted at all. The final result is that you can pick and choose from literally millions of items, turn these into your own fully-copyrighted products, and sell as many as you can at whatever price you set. Sweet!

Marketing of information products where your product costs you virtually nothing and you keep 100% of the profits has to be the very best business model ever created! And as you will learn elsewhere in this report there are many free or very inexpensive ways to attract buyers. Sure, it takes work, but the return on investment (ROI) can be off the charts.

Nothing in this report should be construed as legal advice. That's why God created intellectual-property lawyers. When you do find something you believe you can use legally it is your responsibility to determine whether it is, in fact, actually in the Public Domain. "Public Domain" refers to items that have no definite owner, belong to no one, and are available to copy, change, sell and distribute in any legal and ethical manner.

The following parameters are accepted by most everyone in internet commerce who are using Public Domain material to create their profitable products. Public Domain material is recognized as:

"A work that was first published before January 1st, 1923, or 95 years before January 1st of the current year, whichever is later, OR a work where the last surviving author died 70 years or more before January 1st of the current year, OR a work was first published in the USA between 1923 and 1963 and the copyright was not renewed within the 28th year after first publication (IF renewed, it then gives it an additional 75 years protection), OR a work that was published in the USA between 1923 and 1978 without a legal copyright notice posted in the work itself."

United States Government works are not copyright protected unless written by non-government authors under federal funding which then may be copyrighted.

The above list is modified in that:

Any work published before 01/01/64 has 75 years added protection from the time of renewal if a renewal was filed. If no renewal was filed the expiration is 28 years from date of publication.

Any work published INITIALLY after 01/01/64 and up to 01/01/78 expires 75 years after publication without any renewal needing to be filed.

Any work initially published after 01/01/78 is protected for the life of the author plus seventy years.

Obviously it takes some research to be absolutely certain you are working with Public Domain material unless you stick with pre-1923 material, which I prefer to do.

There are a few country-specific copyright-law exceptions, the most notable being Mexico. You can do some further checking at:
onlinebooks.library.upenn.edu/okbooks.html, or at Wikipedia.org.

Rather than copying a Public Domain item exactly, it is beneficial for you to make some major changes to it for a number of reasons. First of all, it allows you to copyright your "new and unique" work yourself! No changes, no copyright.

Once altered it is now yours alone until your death and 70 years thereafter, which is the current USA copyright law. (Exception: reports you derive from United States government material cannot be copyrighted.)

But more important, the more changes you make the more it sets "your version" apart from what could be the versions of thousands of other internet marketers working with the same Public Domain item. This has become increasingly important because giants Google and Amazon look for highly-original copy.

In fact, if you plan to publish at Amazon Kindle, CreateSpace or Smashwords the works you submit for publication will need to be as "original" as you can make them or they will be rejected. Of course you can sell anything you want, within legal and ethical constraints, on your own websites.

It is the best idea to think of any Public Domain material you find as "for research purposes only". The best scenario is finding a number of related items, reading them, putting them aside, and creating your own original material using the high-points of each.

A good way to get ideas for your own public-domain-derived-products is to look at ezinearticles.com and goarticles.com. Look for the most frequently viewed articles by niche category. Choose ten or so of these. Then derive something from the public domain that covers the full range of these.

For example, if you find popular articles on "Getting Married in the Caribbean", "Wedding Dresses", and "Special Hair Styles", you could produce "Wedding Dresses and Special Hair Styles for Caribbean Weddings"! The possibilities are infinite.

If you go to firstgov.org you will find a mind-numbing amount of government reports available to you at no cost. Click on "Explore Topics" and a list of twenty or so general areas pops up. Click on one of these, say, "Health and Fitness", and up comes a list that might show many hundreds of government-created articles.

Most government reports have titles that are not, shall we kindly say, "marketing oriented". Many reports are very short. Some really stink. But you can easily obtain a few that are focused on the same topic, create a decent combination report with each smaller report being a separate chapter, and market it as you would any other information product.

Some government sources to access for information you can use in your information products are:

The Library of Congress at: catalog.loc.gov;

The IRS at: irs.gov;

US Government Printing Office at: gpoaccess.gov/cgp/index.html;

Government Information Connection at: library.unt.edu/govinfo/subject/catsindx.html;

US State Department at: state.gov/;

US Government at: usa.gov;

National Security Agency at: nsa.gov/public/;

Citizens Information Center at: pueblo.gsa.gov;

The Federal Bureau of Investigation at: fbi.gov;

The Center for Disease Control and Prevention at: cdc.gov.

If you do a Google search for: ["public domain" site: .gov] it will provide an overwhelming number of places to look for information product ideas.

If you have any doubt about the copyright status of anything go to the US Government copyrights website and see "Circular 22": "How to investigate the copyright status of a work" and "How can I tell whether a copyright was renewed". Very useful free resource.

Again, one point to remember is that you cannot by law copyright any material you derive from US Government publications. That's a no-no. But you could sell it un-copyrighted with any changes you wish to make.

Although not cost-free as with government publications, you can find countless pre-1923 books at antique dealers and used book stores. You can buy them at abebooks.com. You can buy them on eBay. Major Public Libraries may have them available to copy. And a Google search I just did for "Public Domain Sources" turned up a mere 3+ million results!

In eBay look under Books>Antiquarian & Collectible>(date range) and you will see many choices, by category, of items you can buy inexpensively.

Project Gutenberg (gutenberg.org) is home to hundreds of public domain works. They have an excellent search box and download choices. And it's **FREE**.

Browsing the websites alibris.com, abebooks.com, and addall.com will allow you to purchase all manner of wonderful copyright-expired material. They all have excellent search features. And aside from books, look for old magazines from the late 1800s and early 1900s. These are rich in content you can use to create excellent products.

As you acquire old books you will find many that have beautiful illustrations, and many have old maps. These items can be copied, mounted, and sold on eBay as works of art. If you happen to be creative or know someone who is artistic these illustrations can be hand-colored and will achieve even higher profits. And as any eBay search will show, these items do sell very well.

There is even a company called "Café Press" that will take your images and reproduce them on mugs, pillows, table mats, greeting cards, coasters, clothing...you name it. These can be great products to sell on eBay as well.

In my experience the three best-selling products derived from out-of-copyright old books are children's stories, recipe books, and dog books. They are my favorites because they have a huge market and are easy to create.

I suggest you seek out old:

Children's stories;

Books on mind reading and anything occult;

Books on herbal remedies and natural healing;

Cookbooks;

Stock, bond and commodity trading techniques;

Cat and dog stories;

Golf books.

Any one of these can be pure gold! If no one else has done so, publishing these works, or chapters from them, can be very profitable. All of the above niches have proven to be big sellers. Uncovering something obscure that no one else has found can be your own gold mine!

If you can find an obscure old item that has exercise-tips or self-improvement- tips or golfing- tips you could easily create an entire new course of study. There are many credible stories of individual infopreneurs who have made tens of thousands of dollars doing exactly this in some sports niche or other.

Remember, if a particular item is easy for you to find it is just as easy for your competitors to find. The harder you have to work at finding something, the more obscure it is, the better. If you find an book in an antique store, and look for it on line (abebooks.com et al) and cannot find it anywhere you could have found a real winner!

Just because the material from which you are creating products can cost you nothing, do not be tempted to sell it cheap. Buyers actually do equate high price with quality.

Never lose sight of this fact. If something costs your buyer buck or two it is perceived to be almost worthless. "You get what you pay for." Psyc 101.

Charge $19.97 for the same item that you might be tempted to sell for $3.97and you are very likely to sell a lot more of them! And the buyers will be satisfied because they bought something they perceive, because of the higher price, to be of higher value.

On the other hand, because Public Domain information can cost you nothing it makes the perfect products to use as give-away incentives in your marketing efforts.

Incidentally, to create the copyright symbol on your computer hold down the "ctrl" and "alt" keys (left side keyboard bottom) and type "c". I once almost went nuts trying to figure out how to do this when I first started out! But when publishing ebooks on Kindle or Smashwords write out "copyright". The " c in a circle" symbol does not reproduce well electronically.

If you have trouble rewriting articles you might wish to try using some "rewrite" software. Check out:

Magic Article Rewriter at magicarticlerewriter.com;

SENUKE at senuke.com;

Unique Article Wizard at uniquearticlewizard.com;

Article Marketing Automation at article marketingautomation.com.

Personally I find that the rewrites these programs produce is far from perfect English usage and sometimes is almost unusable. Many marketers do use these programs, and publish the results without further reworking. That is a mistake, but it works for many infopreneurs. It is better to do some re-writing to create "clean" copy.

I keep focusing in this Chapter on written **reports**, but there are endless films, cartoons, broadcasts, commercials, music, photographs and sound bites available to you in the public domain. You can easily convert these to CDs or DVDs and sell these for serious profits. For starters, check out archive.org. Also take a look at the excellent UCLA Film and TV Archive at: cinema.library.ucla.edu/.

Study what is available at Kunaki (kunaki.com). They are the company mentioned earlier that will create, package and ship CDs and DVDs for you at incredibly low prices. This is a wonderful resource from which you can create extremely profitable items.

So if writing original material is something you cannot conceive of doing, take heart! The Public Domain is your road to internet wealth as an author of unique copyrighted material for minimal cost and minimal work. What business model can you mention that is the equal of this one? Don't even try!

HOW DO I PRICE MY PRODUCTS?

Pricing your virtual products is not hard if you follow some guidelines. In practice you should actually NEVER "sell" anything for an "even-number" amount, as in $10.00 or $15.00 or $17.00. This is "Pricing 101". Your pricing would be $9.97 or $14.97 or $16.97.

No matter what your price point, always end with "7". Why? The "end in 7s" paradigm apparently had its origin in *Life Magazine's* initial offer decades ago of a $7.77 subscription. But it is common knowledge today that *Life* had the right idea.

Because it has been tested by marketers for years $9.97 will outsell $9.99 or $9.98 or even $9.96 or $9.95. I'll leave it to the psychologists to explain just why this is true. I have split-tested it myself and it always proves to be true.

In general, $4.97, $9.97, $19.97, $29.97, $49.97, $99.97, $199.97, $499.97 and $999.97 are price points that seem to lower sales resistance. If your product justifies prices in these general ranges, stick with these price points.

An exception occurs when you are packaging a whole bunch of items together. It is always best to say they are collectively "worth $567.42" or whatever strange sum you want because it implies that a detailed calculation was done (as opposed to "$500" which would likely evoke the response: "Yeah, right".)

And always remember that large "looking" numbers are far more effective than rounded-off numbers. Remember, Ivory Soap is 99.44% pure! "517.7% more" is far better "looking" than "5X more" or "five-times more" although it means the virtually same thing.
You had a windfall of "$6,287.47 in less than 27 hours", not a windfall of "six-thousand dollars in a bit over a day"! That last ".47" actually makes the figure more believable!

There are ways that you can increase the average size of every order. Consider increasing your price. Every item has a price point called "the point of diminishing returns". Say you sell a product for $9.97 and find you sell twenty every day. You've made $200. You raise your price to $14.97, and find you sell fifteen a day. Wow, great idea, you've made $225! So you figure you'll try to squeeze a few more dollars and raise your price to $16.97. Ooops......your sales just dropped to ten a day, $170 out of the till! You just PAST your "point of diminishing returns". Economics 101.

There are two companies that are good resources for producing your reports in three useful formats, .pdf, ePub, and hard-copy. You will always be creating your ebooks and reports in a word-processor program such as Microsoft Word.

FORMATTING ISSUES

For products to be downloaded by a visitor from your website you will be converting to a ".pdf" format (portable document format). This can be done directly in later editions of MS Word, or by using any number of .pdf converters available on the internet. (Google search "pdf converters".) In pdf format you should number the pages at the bottom to correspond to your Table of Contents.

But hand-held reading devices, such as Kindle and Nook, require a special streaming, non-page-numbered/ table-of-contents-clickable format. This is necessary because each such device sees a different amount of text on its face at a given time. Unless your copy "streams" it will break up all over the place and not provide a pleasant reading experience. Visit kdp.amazon.com and smashwords.com for ebook publishing in different formats.

If you want to produce non-virtual products look no further than Blurb at: blurb.com. The can produce a wide variety of "hard" formats. Their work is excellent. Unfortunately, producing small numbers of books equates to a high per-unit cost, for example $40.00 each for a 250 page book. A better choice is CreateSpace at createspace.com, an Amazon print-on-demand platform.

Writer or not, there is no reason whatsoever why you cannot join the ranks of successful internet gurus marketing virtual reports and ebooks, earning a great living, and realizing the American Dream from the comfort of your home. **JUST DO IT!**

CHAPTER 8

PRIVATE LABEL RIGHTS (PLR) EXPLAINED

Another alternative for creating your products is to take advantage of the fact that there are a lot of writers who have no idea what to do with their creations except to offer them to the general public for reprinting. They offer to sell you "**P**rivate **L**abel **R**ights".

PLR is a bit confusing, because there are so many different varieties. Someone writes a report or ebook. They can, and often do, choose to market it themselves. But they are also aware that there are many infopreneurs who for whatever reason cannot or do not wish to produce virtual products themselves. Enter PLR.

There are two basic reasons for someone to release their works to others: profit, and/or promotion of their other offerings.

PLR material comes in many different flavors. When you receive PLR material (sometimes you buy it, often it is free) you receive a written license that gives you certain rights. Be certain to **READ THE LICENSE CAREFULLY**. You do not need copyright infringement lawsuits. They tend to spoil your day!

You will see the terms "resale rights" and "resell rights" used interchangeably. They mean the same thing. When a product comes with Resale Rights you are ONLY allowed to sell it to your customers. These customers only have "Personal Use Rights". They cannot do anything else with it other than to read and enjoy.

You keep 100% of the profits, but cannot alter the material in ANY way because the author has links within the report that sell products for the author. One could call these **"Basic Resale Rights"**.

Basic Resale Rights can be restricted to the extent that the owner can even tell you how you may and may not market the item. They may require you to use only **their** marketing material. They may not allow broadcast emails, or eBay sales.

More valuable products for you to acquire come from authors who offer **"Master Resale Rights".** These are similar in scope to the Basic Resale Rights except you <u>also</u> have the right to sell the Resale Rights to other marketers! Your license may allow you to sell Master Resale Rights to others, or may restrict you to re-selling only Basic Resale Rights.

Better still, if possible, focus on buying products that carry **"Private Label Resale Rights",** often simply called "PLRR". These give you the right to modify the product in some way specified in the license.

You can change or modify the copy itself, though some licenses will limit the percentage of text that you can modify. You may or may not be permitted to pass along various rights to others (called non-transferrable rights).

You may or may not be allowed to change the form of the product, say to a CD or hard-copy book. You WILL be allowed to use your name or pen-name as the actual author. Read your license carefully and abide by it.

Best of all are products sold with **"Unrestricted Rights"** which allows you to do anything you want with the product. Even here, however, the license may well include some minor restrictions.

It is important, especially if you are engaged in affiliate marketing, to obtain **"Rebranding Rights"**. These allow you to change the links in the product to your own links, to your affiliate's sites or to your own website or wherever. The license may or may not give you any of the other rights discussed above.

"Freebie Rights" (**"Give Away Rights")** often modify other of the above rights. You may only be permitted to give the product away (with your links in it if you have Rebranding Rights), or you may actually be <u>required</u> to sell it (so as not to dilute its perceived value in the eyes of the public).

"Reprint Rights" allow you to re-publish, in unaltered form, something that was previously published elsewhere. You generally cannot sell this information, but can use it in blogs, newsletters and on your website.

"Royalty Rights" allow you to control the marketing of a product, BUT you must pay the author some specified royalty for every unit sold. You cannot modify these works in any way.

"Foreign Language Rights" are often overlooked. These give you the valuable right to translate a report or ebook into other languages. The license might be language-specific, or allow unlimited language choices.

No matter what "rights" you are granted <u>DO NOT EVER CLAIM TO BE THE AUTHOR</u> of PLR material. You are not, and saying you are is a lie. Instead of saying: "By (your name)" an untruth, say: "Brought To You By (your name)" or: "Presented By (your name).

If you have any doubts about what rights you have in the use of any licensed product **ALWAYS** contact and ask the product creator for clarification in writing. This will avoid the inevitable grief over misunderstandings and legal complications.

One problem with using rights-based material is that there are hundreds if not thousands of <u>other</u> infopreneurs using the same material. If you have the right to do so, the more you can change the copy from the original, the more it becomes your <u>own</u> original report or ebook.

Remember, because of the dynamic nature of the internet, virtually anything written before 2012 will contain outdated, harmful to follow, information.

Do not be misled by all of the wonderful "Private Label Rights" material available to you at very low cost. Some will come as a free bonus associated with a product you buy. Some you will pay for. Look at the copyright dates. Many, if not most, will have copyright notices around 2003-2004! Some I've seen are as early as the late '90s. Rarely will one be as recent as 2010, and even that is probably mostly outdated.

There are more rights-based PLR products out there in cyberspace than you could ever read in a lifetime, most of them outdated and worthless. (Google search "PLR" items and a couple of hundred thousand results pop up!). For a nice supply of freebies that you can use, at zero cost, go to plrwarehouse.com. Sites that sell top quality material are: theplrstore.com and master-plr-rights.com

Remember, however, that you do not have <u>exclusive</u> rights to PLR material. Someone else has probably also bought the same resale rights to sell on one of the virtual ebook publishing sites. This is where your creativity can win the day.

Resist the temptation to load up your publishing accounts with crappy PLR material, or stuff you copy with no changes. This is irrespective of having the right to publish as written. You want quality over quantity. This will make you more money in the long run and keep you in good stead with your publisher. They DO review your material before approving it for publication, and if someone else is publishing something very similar you will be "slapped". A slap can literally ban you for life from using that particular publishing platform, so avoid being slapped by doing massive re-writes when permitted by license..

You **must** rearrange the PLR copy, and change as much of the wording as you can. Create a new title. Create new chapter names. Create a new cover. Add a picture or two. Add an article or two. By the time you are done it should pass the publishing police with flying colors!

CHAPTER 9

THE MILLION-DOLLAR TOOLS OF THE TRADE

Throughout this book you will see that for emphasis I have capitalized "FREE". The fact of the matter is that everything you need to do to
make money on line can be done with no, or "almost" no, investment at all. It is called "bum marketing", and many wealthy internet entrepreneurs are very successful at spending very little, if any, money up front.

I qualify "FREE" with "almost" because you may need to buy a domain name ($10/year) and hire a web host ($5/month) if you decide to have your own website to sell your own products or to promote affiliate vendors' products from that website. Having your own website can also help you build a list of customer's email addresses for future marketing efforts. So for the price of one pack of cigarettes a month you can have your very own profit-making internet website presence!

You do NOT, however, even need a website at all ever, if you limit your marketing to the FREE "affiliate/vendor business model" and obtain FREE traffic by employing FREE article marketing, press releases, blogging, and social site interaction to market your wares.

Even if you do not own a computer, or do not have access to a high-speed internet connection, these can be accessed without cost at most libraries. If you do have a computer but only have a dial-up connection, most McDonalds, Burger Kings and Starbucks have free high-speed net connectivity.

I do NOT recommend that you buy a website creation program such as Microsoft's "FrontPage" or the ever-popular "Dreamweaver". There are just so many excellent free website creation tools out there, especially those associated with web hosts, plus some fine blogging platforms, that buying these programs and learning how to use them is a total waste of time and money. I doubt whether the purveyors of these programs would agree!

The same advice is true with regard to Merchant Accounts, Visa, etc. Because of PayPal you simply do not need one. Almost all of the successful internet entrepreneurs I know use the PayPal payment system, which also allows your visitors to pay with credit cards even if they themselves do not have a PayPal account. Merchant accounts, which may offer a few minor additional features, are complicated to install, very expensive, and usually require extensive credit checking. They are simply not needed.

Learning the very simple basics of HTML (Hyper Text Markup Language) web code is helpful, but is not at all essential. For those who care to learn HTML there are excellent free tutorial guides on line and in books that can be found at any library. What little "HTML tweaking" you might need to do can be done intuitively without any real working knowledge of HTML itself.

You can, however, without an overwhelming expenditure, purchase a few computer programs that will greatly speed up the development of your internet business. If you can possibly afford to buy some of these up front you will find the entire internet marketing experience far easier and more pleasurable than the more time consuming "bum marketing" FREE alternative:

I highly recommend the following programs, many of which I cannot live without! Purchase them ONLY after you have learned to live without them. They are not mandatory, just very useful time savers.

Incidentally, neither the author nor publisher of this book has any connection (other than as a paying-customer/user) with ANY website or product mentioned anywhere within this book. We are not

compensated in any way for including this information, which simply reflects our personal experiences or those of others whose recommendations we respect.

PROGRAMS YOU WILL FIND USEFUL

GOOGLE TOOLS

One thing I can say about Google is that they want you to do things right and give you lots of FREE help along the way. Here are over a dozen really useful FREE Google tools:

"Mass Keyword Search" allows you to find out how your website ranks for up to ten keywords at once. You can also study the top hundred sites for your specific keyword. Access this at: googlerankings.com/mkindex.php.

A great "Guide To Google-Friendly Design" can be found at:
googlerankings.com/googlefriendly.php.

"Google Trends" at google.com/trends will allow you to analyze trends over time.

"Google Insights" at: google.com/insights/search/ enables you to compare search volume patterns across various categories and time frames.

"AdSense Preview Tool" at:
googleadspreview.blogspot.com/ allows you to see what ads Google is most likely to place on your website.

The "Ultimate SEO Tool" when presented with your URL will give you a list of the most frequently used keywords and the number of times they appear, as well as the keyword density. Access this at:
googlerankings.com/ultimate_seo_tool.php.

The "Position Report" button on "5" will tell you how your website ranks for each search term.
The "Website Optimizer" tool at: google.com/websiteoptimizer can help you compare optimization strategies.

Probably the best known and most useful Google tool can be found at: adwords.google.com/select/KeywordToolExternal. By typing in keywords in "Keyword Tool External" you can see how many people searched using that term in the past month. It is generally believed that the ACTUAL number is as much as six times what is stated.

The general Google learning center can be found at:google.com/adwords/learningcenter/.

You can find website tutorials , compliments of Google, at: google.com/intl/en/websiteoptimizer/tutorials.html.

At google.com/reader you can learn all about RSS feeds and how to take advantage of them on your website.

To find the "Page Rank" (a 0 – 10 Google ranking of popularity) of any website install the toolbar found at toolbar.google.com.

Google recently added "Search Plus Your World" for your international search work.

NICHE FINDING TOOLS

NicheBot, at nichebot.com another useful keyword research tool. There are three versions with daily pricing of $0.60, $1.12 and $3.62. There is a 14-day trial for a buck.

MicroNicheFinder, at micronichefinder.com, is a valuable tool for deciding in whichniches you want to market products or affiliates. Download for a hundred dollars, or try for 30 days for eight dollars.

KEYWORD SEARCH TOOLS

WordTracker. An extremely useful tool for doing your preliminary keyword research. Learn your "KEI", **K**eyword **E**ffectiveness **I**ndex, which is a prediction of your keywords' value. Three different programs: "Keywords" at $379/year; Link Builder at $59/month; and "Strategizor" at $57/month. Go to wordtracker.com. There are FREE trials available and a FREE "lite" version you must have.

Keyword Elite, at keywordelite.com. Similar to Wordtracker, but with some different features. This is the program I frequently use. Regularly $297 but often on sale. One-time download.

KeywordCountry at keywordcountry.com. At $49/month or $299/year this is not exactly inexpensive, but they do offer a free trial.
XsitePto at excitepro.com, $197, allows you to create a fine website in just thirty minutes (or so they say!).

Keyword Strategy Studio Tool, $49, at goodkeywords.com, is useful for background research. There is a free trial.

AdSpyElite at undercoverprofits.com, $297. Expensive but extremely useful tool to find high-converting keywords.

GoodKeywords v3 is a download at goodkeywords.com. Also offered are "Keyword Pad" and "Keyword Explorer" programs.

KeyWord Suggestion Tool is accessed at google.com/adwords. You need to set up a Google AdWords account to use this program. It is a FREE program.

WEBSITE BUILDING

OptimizePress. Go to optimizepress.com, $97 download. This program is extremely useful for building squeeze pages, creating sales letters, creating membership sites, crafting "One Time Offers" (OTOs), and integrating your autoresponder. Again, you can do all of this by yourself for FREE, but if you can afford the program it will pay for itself time and again in hours and effort saved.

Metatags.info/wizard for generating Meta Tags. FREE.

Instant Video Website at instantvideowebsite.com . You can add your AdSense code, Amazon Affiliate Link, and ClickBank affiliate links. All of the relevant videos are provided automatically from YouTube. Each video becomes its own page, and can be surrounded by your ads. (Product may no longer be available). Do a Google search for alternatives.

Camtasia Studio at: techsmith.com/download/camtasia has screen-capture video editing software for $299. There is a 30-day FREE trial.

Audacity.sourceforge.net has an "mp3" audio-creation program;

Camstudio.org offers screen-capture video software;

Addme.com/meta.htm for generating your Meta Tags;

Joomla.com to build your websites easily;

Bluevoda.com to build your websites easily.

SEARCH ENGINE OPTIMIZATION (SEO)

SEO Elite. Another extremely useful tool to save hours of manual searching in you website Search Engine Optimization work. It is also very valuable for studying every parameter of your competitors' websites. $167 at seoelite.com.

DIYSEO. Find it at: andyhagans.com/tools/hubfinder. If you are _really_ lazy these guys will do all of your SEO for you, for $129/month.

AUTORESPONDERS

AWebber. You can organize and send out emails manually at zero cost, but the amount of time and level of organization offered by an autoresponder will keep you from losing your mind! Most gurus apparently use this brand. Priced by list size, from $19/month for 500 email addresses to $149/month for 25,000, in five steps.

ANALYTICS AND STATISTICS TOOLS

HyperTracker. Find it at hypertracker.com. This is an analytics tool for evaluating the effectiveness of your marketing. $20/month, $180/year.

CubeStat at cubestat.com is my favorite free site! It gives an algorithm-based value-approximation of any website, the traffic to that site, and the ad revenue the site could obtain from its current ads.

Spyfu.com allows you for FREE to enter search terms and learn twelve valuable analytics. Pay $79/month for nine deeper analytics.

Metatags.info/wizard for analyzing the quality of the meta tags already on your websites. FREE.

Piwik.org, an alternative to Google analytics.

Ranking.com rates websites.

Cubestat.com provides comprehensive info on websites.

At compete.com you can get great information on many websites that shows you their traffic, and also ranks their major competitors.

LINK CLOAKING TOOLS

Linkcloakingsoftware.com, to cloak affiliate links, $27.

Stealthaffiliate.com, alternate link cloaker, $47 (compare features).

Linktrackr.com. at $9/month to $69/month will cloak affiliate links and track affiliate programs.

CLICKBANK TOOLS

EasyClickMate at: easyclickmate.com, $67, can help you organize your ClickBank marketing and protect you against some forms of commission theft.

DayJobKiller at: dayjobkiller.com, $97, will enable you to spy on the most successful ClickBank affiliates and emulate their campaigns.

CREATE YOUR OWN AFFILIATE PROGRAM

OmniStar Affiliate Software at: osiaffiliate.com costs $27-$97/month for 200 to unlimited affiliates. There is a free trial, and a $100 Google AdWords credit.

DOMAIN TOOLS

Domainpunch.com has domain name search and management software for $129, with a 30-day no-credit-card FREE trial. You can also access Domain Name

Analyzer, Domain Name Filter & Domain Name Status Reporter for FREE..

ARTICLE WRITING TOOLS

Dragon Naturally Speaking. Access at nuance.com. Two versions: "Home", $100, "Premium", $200. This software allows you to create website copy and articles by speaking into a microphone. It is a great time-saver for anyone who has ever spoken dictation to a secretary in a business environment and is comfortable organizing thoughts without putting pen to paper. If you are comfortable with it you can save a lot of time. One can speak a lot faster than one can write, or even type.

EZine Article Creator Pro will aid you in writing articles without being a great writer or paying ghost writers. Do a Google search for this because it is sold by many different affiliates at around $20.

Neevia.com has an excellent PLR text format-conversion product for $19.

BOOK COVER TOOLS

Ecover-go.com creates book covers online for $20/month. There is a one-day trial. (Save up your needs!)

EBAY TOOLS

MyDigitalDispatch at: mydigitaldispatch.com. For $97 you can own software that will greatly streamline your eBay participation and save you a lot of valuable time.

HammerTap at: hammertap.com for $19.95/month (under half that if paid yearly) can save you a lot of time in doing all sorts of eBay research.

An eBay Store. This is an investment you almost cannot do without if you hope to optimize the business you can enjoy from eBay.

KINDLE TOOLS

MobiPocketCreator for easy Kindle uploading, under $10, at: sevenbuckaroos.com/kindleformatting/.

OTHER USEFUL TOOLS

PayPal, at paypal.com, owned by eBay, is a transaction-processing program. (They do charge a small percentage of your sale.)

Primopdf.com for converting your Word documents to .pdf format. (If you have Windows 7 you can do it directly from Word).

Openoffice.org has a full suite of products that can be used in place of the Microsoft equivalents, some of which may not have been included in your computer purchase.

Calibre is a software program that will convert any written material created in any program into ePub format. Winportal.com/calibre.

Any pricing shown above is current as of this writing, but may very well change over time.

Even your browser can provide a wealth of useful information. Many consider Firefox to be more reliable and faster than Internet Explorer. . Personally I kept IE and use both interchangeably. But Firefox has an EXTREMELY valuable plug-in called "SEO QUAKE". It's FREE, and it is a great time saver. Google "download Firefox" and download it. Using your shiny new Firefox browser Google "Install SEO Quake for Firefox", follow the instructions to download the program.

What SEO Quake gives you is a toolbar in Firefox that automatically provides a wealth of information on any website you enter in the browser. It enables you at a glance to see some very important facts about your competition. These include:

Google PageRank. On a scale of 0 – 10, even a rank of 1 shows *some* traffic. A 4 rank is very good and indicates very decent traffic. A page rank of 5 or more is great. The higher the number you see the worse for you as a direct competitor.

Google Index gives an idea of the size of your competitor's website in the number of pages it has kept in its index. This can be from one to many thousands of pages.

The MSN Index of the actual number of pages in the site today.

Yahoo's assessment of the number of links pointing to the competitor's home page. Your hope is to exceed this number.

The Alexa rank of the site, a measure of search engine traffic the site is receiving. Anything below 1,000,000 is very good.

The "age" of the website. Google does rank older sites better all else being equal.

You can click on any of the above items and get a wealth of additional information, including the "meta tags" and "meta description" your competitor is using, as well as all of his keywords and their density!

Go to all of the above websites. Check them all out. Get all of the freebies. Try out those pay-for programs with FREE trials. Buy those you feel will save you time and make you money. There are many similar products available in each category, and some may be better for your needs than those listed. A simple Google search for any category will produce the names of many others for you to compare as to features and price.

May you live long and prosper for life in the incredible internet marketing universe! Dare to go where relatively few have gone before. Internet Infopreneuring: warp speed ahead to internet income!

MODULE THREE – AFFILIATE INCOME FOR LIFE

CHAPTER 10

SECRETS TO MASTERING AFFILIATE NETWORKS

NEWBIES START HERE!   This Chapter outlines your easiest keys to internet riches!

Becoming an affiliate, and sending visitors to merchants' commercial websites, can involve minimal or no cost to you, and be very, very profitable. **It is the recommended starting point for any newbie.**

You also have the option of spending any amount of money you might want to buy visitor traffic through a huge variety of paid advertising methods. The key in that case is to spend less in advertising than you receive in affiliate commissions, a positive "return on investment", referred to as ROI.

In my experience it is not very difficult to obtain a return on advertising investment of four to one.....spend a dollar on ads, earn four. But I know some very experienced affiliate marketers who claim they can regularly make a ten-fold or better return on investment. Based upon my own experience, I believe this is quite possible for anyone to achieve.

There are a large number of "Affiliate Network Marketing Companies". You can locate these with a simple Google search for: "affiliate marketing companies". These companies aggregate thousands of vendors that sell a huge variety of products. They offer their affiliates (you and me) a commission for some positive action at their website. They provide a wide range of statistics on each affiliate offer, marketing tools, and details of the commissions offered.

To find <u>an affiliate program</u> in your niche do a Google search:
"(YOUR KEYWORD[S])" + "AFFILIATE PROGRAM" .

Affiliate program networks are mostly free to join, and eliminate entirely any need for you to create your own products. You never need to think about processing payments, product delivery, or customer service. **You do not even need to have a website!** All of the hard work is done for you.

At zero cost you benefit from hundreds of thousands of dollars of marketing research and marketing efforts the vendors themselves have made. Your job is to focus 100% of your efforts on advertising the unique affiliate link you are given, driving visitors to the vendor's website offer, and earning hard cash for doing so. <u>This is a fantastic business model!</u>

Probably your biggest challenge as an affiliate marketer will be keeping up with the huge numbers of offers and opportunities presented by the many affiliate networks. You simply cannot spend too much time studying and too little time doing.

THE AFFILIATE NETWORKS

There are "public" affiliate networks, and "private" affiliate networks. The private networks often have exclusive affiliate offers unavailable elsewhere, some with very high-paying commissions. As a beginner with no track record of sending visitors to vendors you will not be easily able to access the private networks. The good news is that there are so many thousands of affiliate offers available on the public networks that one can become wealthy without ever joining a private network.

Where do you find all of the available affiliate program networks? A Google search of "affiliate networks" will provide you with a lifetime of possibilities. My personal favorites are ClickBank (mostly virtual products), LinkShare and Commission Junction. Just "drill-down" through the relevant major categories until you reach sub-categories that are a good fit for your chosen niche keywords.

If you want to see lists of companies that offer affiliate programs directly to you (not through a network) check out: associateprograms.com. They list fifteen general categories, within which there are hundreds of affiliate offers available for your consideration. (But I strongly suggest that you use the networks.)

Certain networks specialize in certain types of offers. For example ClickBank, one of the most frequently used networks, specializes in virtual products, the "How To" material delivered electronically. You can earn lots of money here.

It is a fact that the vast majority of newer affiliate marketers use the ClickBank Network. They have many fine virtual products to represent, are easy to join, and pay directly to you and pay on time. Great operation. But do not overlook other networks because the number of affiliates (your competition) promoting some product not found on

ClickBank may be relatively quite small. Less competition can translate into much higher profits for you.

Very popular **Public** Networks, that are rather easy to join, are: (approximate ranking in overall visitor volume as published in *Website Magazine)*:

CJ.com (Commission Junction) (6)
ClickBank.com (accepts anyone any time) (7)
ShareASale.com (9)
LinkShare.com (12)
Plimus.com
MarketHealth.com
E-Junkie.com
ICommissionsNetwork.com
PayDotCom.com

Some of these may require at a minimum that you at least have a basic website. These nine networks will provide you with more vendor choices than you should ever need in a lifetime to make serious money in affiliate marketing.

There are a vast number of other networks that have excellent affiliate vendors, but who require some level of demonstrated affiliate experience to qualify for acceptance into their program. More specifically, most require that you show an existing affiliate website receiving at least 5,000 unique visitors monthly. Some really exclusive networks require 500,000 uniques per month!

Among the top **Private** Networks are:
ClickBooth.com (1)
OurFreeStuff.net (2)
Copeac.com (3)
XY7.com (4)
RevenueLoop.com (5)
FriendFinder.com (8)
Zanox.com (10)
FluxAds.com (11)

Axil.com (13)
TradeDoubler.com (14)
Network.HydrantNetwork.com (16)
AdsMarket.com (17)
AdValient.com (18)
WebGains.com (19)

Additional well respected Networks include:
NeverBlue.com; CXDigital.com; PepperJam.com;
Hydra.com; DirectLeads.com;
EpicDirect.com; AsSeenOnPC.com; Affiliate.com;
UniqueLeads.com; AffiliateWindow.com (United
Kingdom);
LinkConnector.com; ShareASale.com;
Instantdollarz.com;
Azoogleads.com; ClixGalore.com; Rextopia.com;
JoeBucks.com;
DigitalRiver.com; MaxBounty.com; NCSReporting.com
(credit cards);
RegNow.com; FastClick.com; DirectResponse.com;
AdReign.com;
BulletAds.com; IncentaClickMedia.com; LinkMo.com;
LeadHound.com; TotalAccessOnLine.com;
EADExchange.com;
CuttingEdgeOffers.com; Fourex-Affiliate.com;
ESecure.CPAEmpire.com/signup

If you enjoy blogging, look to valueclick.com and
tribalfusion.com for "blog friendly" affiliates. The problem
with TribalFusion is that they are looking for affiliates with
500,000 unique visitors a month! Talk about pickey!

That is a pretty overwhelming list, and it if far from
complete. The obvious point here is that affiliate marketing
is a **huge** internet market segment. **Many fortunes are
being made by entrepreneurs just like you by just
adhering to this one business model.**

If you get rejected by one of these (mostly CPA) private networks give them a call, and ask: "Why?". Tell them you are a professional PPC marketer and media buying pro with a few years' experience and you have worked with other CPA networks in the past. If you are polite and sound convincing you have a fair chance of being accepted even if you do not have hard statistics to prove it! Once you gain experience and can prove your results you should definitely try to be accepted by one or more of these networks, where you might find some very high-paying affiliate offers unique to a particular network.

Do not be upset when you are turned down by one of these affiliate networks. The reason many of the best affiliate networks are very particular about who they accept into their programs is the prevalence of credit card fraud. The affiliate business model makes it particularly easy for scammers to abuse the system. Fraudulent affiliates buy stolen credit card numbers and use them to make fake purchases and drive up their commissions. The vendor is stuck with chargeback fees and can even lose their merchant account entirely. There are computer programs available to scammers that make very rapid and lucrative conversions automatically.

These same scammers have ways to use proxy software to hide their identity. Before the network can shut the affiliate down they take their commissions and disappear, only to re-emerge with another fraudulent affiliate site.

Merchants do have a few resources to mitigate fraud. IPVelocity controls the number of buys from a particular IP address. IPGeoLocation monitors the physical distance between a billing address and the IP location. There are time-velocity filters that will kill transactions made too close together. And of course there are databases of "black-hat" (bad guys) P addresses and credit card numbers.

Probably your biggest challenge as an affiliate marketer is keeping up with the huge numbers of offers and opportunities presented by the many affiliate networks. As I said earlier, you simply cannot spend too much time studying and too little time doing.

One approach is to focus on finding any **new** products that are hot, and cash in on them before they become saturated. Even better, you can even promote products pre-launch! This is made simple by joining a FREE site that specializes in new product announcements. Go to: jvnotifypro.com and sign up.

Watch late-night TV and make a note of the many infomercials. If you search the affiliate networks and can find that the exact TV-ad product has an affiliate program, BINGO! Take advantage of THEIR TV ad budget. Very popular programs are acne treatment, Botox, skin care, anti-aging and wrinkle removal.

The highest competition today is in the areas of dating, weight loss, and internet commerce (including FOUREX). Credit card offers & mortgage offers are highest paying. Many Real Estate vendor offers hit $27/click! But the competition is intense!

One of the keys to successful affiliate marketing is offering bonuses to people who buy through your link. Point out that these bonuses are available nowhere else. Clearly state the benefits of these bonuses and how they tie in with the product you are offering. The idea is to "out-bonus" the competition! Bonuses can take the form of one or more special reports, or audio files, and even video clips or CDs. It is a fact that a great bonus package is often more important to the visitor to obtain than the product itself! You just need great bonuses and great copywriting describing the benefits in conjunction with the offered vendor product.

IF the amount of commission can justify it, there are some fabulous bonuses that you can create with artscafe.com. Offering a physical product as an incentive bonus is not often done. If you were offering a dog-related product, wouldn't a mug with your buyer's dog's photo on it be a great incentive? Or even a mouse pad with that image of Fido?

Place easy-to-follow instructions for claiming the bonus at the bottom of your order page, or send them along in the "thank you" email. They will need to send you a copy of their purchase receipt with the affiliate network's unique purchase code, their shipping address, and a .jpg photo of Fido or Fluffy.

HOW VENDORS PAY YOU FOR YOUR MARKETING EFFORTS

You will get paid by affiliates based on "conversions", a term that means different things in different affiliate network programs.

The three basic payment plans are:

Cost Per Action (CPA): This is the easiest way to get a conversion and receive a commission. The visitor to the affiliate site will be asked for certain personal information. At the least, they will be asked only for a zip code. For this simple conversion you would get the lowest commission. Your commissions increase as vendors mine ever more information. Some may ask for an email address in lieu of or in addition to the mail address. Others ask for a full name and address. Some add the phone number.

I would suggest that you affiliate, if possible, with the largest and best known companies that offer CPA programs. Big name companies providing various gift cards make great affiliates. Piggie-back on their national advertising and name recognition.

Typical of these would be Best Buy and Home Depot. Expect commissions in the $1.00 - $1.50 per conversion. Many lesser known companies may offer larger commissions, but in general you will get fewer click-throughs because of lower name recognition.

Cost Per Lead (CPL): This is similar to CPA except the conversion occurs when a visitor signs up for a "free" trial and has to produce a valid credit card for "shipping and handling". This is a win-win-win business model. You earn a commission, your affiliate gets a new customer, and the visitor gets something free. You can earn commissions of $5.00 to $15.00 in these programs. Examples would be "Proactive" (acne medicine, the longest running TV commercial), and Netflix.

Cost Per Sale (CPS): The visitor to your affiliate's website must actually purchase something. You get paid a commission that is either a flat fee per sale, or a percentage of the sale price. (ClickBank is almost 100% CPS because it focuses on virtual download products). Examples: BestBuy pays a 15% commission per sale. Target pays a flat $40.00.

Some affiliate networks call every program a "CPA" which in those cases stands for "Cost per Acquisition", and can include CPA, CPL and CPS affiliate offers.**You need to take a great deal of time looking at possible vendors to represent.** This is the key to your ultimate success. Go for high commission items over theirs that are similar but with lower net payout in your pocket. It is just as easy to sell a high priced product as it is to sell a low priced product. You will end up doing the same work for more money representing the higher payout vendors' products.

You can surf the internet, go to the websites of thousands of companies, and apply directly to them to join their affiliate programs. Most on-line vendors have one. The advantages I see to using networks over going direct to vendors is that they closely screen all affiliate offers for you so that you can have comfort in their legitimacy and efficacy, and be certain of getting paid.

The networks make sure you get paid (you get paid directly from the network itself not the affiliate). The tradeoff (Truism: there is **NEVER** a free lunch) is that the networks take a small percentage of what the vendor pays them which means a slightly-reduced commission for you. Personally I prefer to use the networks, but there is an exception to this rule.

My exception is where I am **very** familiar with the affiliate because I have done business with them in the past. I have bought and liked their products, and I trust them. For example, I have no problem whatsoever working directly with The Internet Marketing Center or Anthony Morrison's diverse operations, among others. I know these people personally and I trust them implicitly.

Once you are satisfied that you have found one you want to represent you need to get your unique "tracking link". This is the coded unique-to-you code that you upload to anywhere you hope to attract a visitor. You imbed it in your ads. It identifies you as the person to receive the commission. Some affiliates refer to this link as the "Tracking ID", some call it the "Unique Link". All such terms mean the same thing.

Before we look at choosing vendor's affiliate offers, I want you to be aware of some cold hard facts that relate to your website. Most internet websites get ZERO visits per day. This is because most internet marketers are not properly taught traffic techniques. The overall average is reported to be ten visits per day per website.

At this rate you would average only around six sales a month, which is unacceptable. It is conventional wisdom that the average conversion rate for all internet offers is 2.0%, though ANY conversion rate is good. I do know of offers that have achieved 6% and higher CRs (I've even heard 15%) but do not expect these.

My personal goal, often achieved, is to get one hundred clicks per day per offer, 3,000/month minimum. NOW, at 2% (which I consider low) you are making 60 sales per month per offer! Depending on the commission per offer, and the number of offers you have out there, well, you do the math. **Big bucks possible**

This is why the very successful affiliate marketers (referred to as "Super Affilates") make tens of thousands of dollars a month once they have lots of offers on line converting well. Keep this in mind: There is competition for your business, especially if you are a proven high-producing affiliate. All Networks have a built-in cushion in their payouts to be able to reward high performers. The quoted payouts are the lowest they feel they can post and still attract new affiliates. It is your job to convince the affiliate manager (who is generally paid commissions based on your success) assigned to you that you are a super-catch as an affiliate and well worth higher payouts than they are offering.

There is no harm whatsoever in trying. Before you do it is a good idea to establish a friendly rapport with your assigned affiliate manager. The better the like you personally the better chance you will have to negotiate. Many managers have "pocket offers", vendors that they expose only to their favorite affiliate buddies. Getting chosen for one of these offers can minimize your competition and possibly maximize payouts.

There are a number of approaches you can try in your negotiations. You could simply tell the manager that you are considering similar vendors with other networks and would like them to come back to you with a more competitive offer. If you already have a successful program going with one network, consider pulling it and placing it in a different network. (Many networks have a large number of vendors that list with multiple platforms.) Then contact the manager where you pulled you offer and tell him or her that you will be happy to reinstate it if the will up the ante. This usually works!

Let's say you have spent a lot of time setting up a website and a plan to attract lots of traffic, and are confident you can pull this off. Call different affiliate managers, tell them you expect to draw $75,000 or more in commissions in the next thirty days, but you need a better payout than they are offering. Tell them you have better offers from others, but like their network.

HOW TO CHOOSE VENDOR AFFILIATE PROGRAMS

All affiliate vendors are not created equal. There are a number of factors that you should evaluate, though it is the rare affiliate program that offers everything you might want in one particular offer.

First of all, it must cost zero dollars to join, and you must not be obliged to buy any of their vendors' products. It is a big plus if the program pays you a commission for life on future sales of their products to customers you referred, known as "residual" commissions. (It is a good idea to voluntarily buy the product offered so you can offer an honest testimonial. It also could help you write your ad.)

They should pay out commissions at least once a month, and they should have a reasonably low minimum accumulation of commissions (like $50 to $100) to cut and mail you a check, add funds to your PayPal account, or wire funds to your bank account.

How the vendor handle "cookies" is very important to you. A "cookie" is a bit of code that the affiliate places on your visitor's computer. If the individual you referred does not act on the first visit, but returns a day or a week or a month or even years later, you still can earn your commission because of the cookie. Ideally the tracking cookie should not expire.

You also need to take a hard look at the actual amount of commission they pay to affiliates. This can be either as a percentage of sales or flat dollar amount per sale, or an amount based on visitor information collected. But you have to also weigh the "average sale amount" statistic compared between different affiliate offers.

A few affiliates will pay you in "tiers". If someone you refer ends up becoming one of their affiliates you get a second-tier commission.

Even fewer will put a limit on the number of affiliates they allow, but when you do find one of these it is a definite plus because it limits your direct competition.

START WITH CLICKBANK

I suggest you start your affiliate marketing with ClickBank, and try other Affiliate Networks later. They are the biggest and I find the easiest. There are literally thousands of vendor programs from which to choose, in dozens of general niches.

Let's run through a general example:

Register at ClickBank.com. Use a very generic nickname;

Access the email that is sent to you, and note your password;

Search the site (ClickBank.com/marketplace.html) entering your niche keywords;

Compare all of the offers that are relevant to your keyword;

You need to sort the offers by "Popularity", the higher the better;

Next Sort by "Gravity". You want 30 or higher. Closest to 100 is best;

Then check the % Referred, and look for 50% or better.

If you find a product with good popularity but low gravity it indicates that relatively few affiliates are promoting this program. This could indicate either a new product, or one where a small universe of affiliates dominate the offer. If it is a new product it is worth considering.

If you find a product with good gravity and popularity but low % referred it could indicate a "tired" offer, but is also worth considering.

If you cannot find any product in your niche that has decent popularity, gravity and % referred it is time to look for a new niche!

There are certain things on which you should focus in choosing a ClickBank vendor's product to promote:

Click Bank has a statistic called "Gravity". It's not exactly what Isaac Newton had in mind! Here it is a measure of the popularity of a product and the rate of conversions (click-through + action on vendor's site = conversion) achieved by affiliate marketers offering that vendor's product. It is calculated over the past two months using a complex algorithm. A high Gravity equates to lots of affiliates making lots of conversions….and lots of competition. Click on "Sort Results By" then "Gravity". The results are listed in descending order.

All else being equal look for products that show recurring payments after a customer makes the initial purchase. These are expressed as: "Avg. Rebill Total" and "Avg. % Rebill". You will make higher commissions with these "Rebill" vendors.

Go to: cbsurge.com/ and download a plug-in called "ClickBank Surge". This program highlights products with a high profit potential and little competition. Products that are not considered marketable are highlighted in red.

Keep an eye on the "ClickBank Marketplace for tends. Go to: clickbank.com/marketplace.htm. Sign up for lots of newsletters. Look at the "Top 50" for a new program that cracks the top 10 overnight.

To track your ClickBank keywords add this bit of code to the affiliate code you are assigned: "/?tid=(enter here the keyword to be tracked)". Let's say your ClickBank nickname is "joe26". Your link would be the following: Joe26.(vendor program name).hop.clickbank.net/?tid=(keyword).

You will want to cloak this long ugly link for three reasons. One problem here is, it's ugly! Second, it tips a buyer off that you are an affiliate, and some will go out of their way to bypass you (God forbid you should earn a commission) and find the vendor directly! Most important, a clever thief can steal your commissions.

ALWAYS cloak your affiliate links. It has been proven over and over that people are far more likely to click on a shorter cloaked link than on a long clumsy-looking "amateur link". Check out: linkcloakingsoftware.com; linktracker.com; improvely.com; zazzle.com/sell/affiliates; amazingcloaker.com; cloaknrotate.com; and stealthaffiliate.com. You can check out Google "link cloaking software" for a huge list of software that is inexpensive and easy to use.

With virtual (downloadable) products look for a minimum commission of 60%, 75% is best. An exception to this is a very high sales price product, e.g., $160 offered at 50% commission. Also, for recurring-billing subscription-based products I'll go down to 40%, but never lower.
On physical products, represent only vendors paying you $40 or more per sale.

Look for a vendor's sales page that is: visually attractive; long (which always converts better than short); has no affiliate links; and has no order-by-phone number shown.

No restriction on how you promote the vendor's product, e.g., "email only" or "no email".

On CPA (cost per action) programs, "Zip Code Only" are by far the easiest to convert. Never represent such a program paying under $1.00 commission per conversion.

The highest paying programs are mortgages and credit cards.

A good idea is to register a URL with the exact vendor product name if it is available, such as "makebigbucksfromhome.com", where the title of the book is "Make Big Bucks From Home". If unavailable, you could try the .net or .org version, or you could make a minor change in the URL such as "makebigbuckfromhome.com" or "makebigbucksfromhome1.com".

There are two schools of thought regarding choosing to represent a brand new untested affiliate program. Some believe that being a guinea pig for a totally unproven program often wastes time better spent on proven vendors. Others believe that the most money is made in the first few weeks of any new program where your competition is

limited. These are "The early bird gets the worm"
marketers.

The approach is to focus on finding any new products that
are hot and cash in on them before they become
saturated. Even better, you can even promote products
pre-launch! This is made simple by joining a FREE site that
specializes in new product announcements. Go to:
jvnotifypro.com and sign up.

IMPORTANT: If you see a late-night TV ad go to the
merchant's website and see whether they have an affiliate
program. Many do. If so, sign up at once. Piggybacking
on the TV revenue of a merchant can be a big plus. Very
common programs are for acne treatment, skin care
products, wrinkle removal, Botox, and anti-aging miracles!

Many affiliate marketers make it a point to register unique
domain names as close as possible to the name of their
affiliate product. In connection with this technique there are
two very valuable sites for you to use in your keyword
research. They are alexa.com and quantcast.com.
Once you have decided on a general niche theme, go to
Quantcast and individually enter the URLs of the top sites
in a Google search related to that theme. Quantcast will
deliver to you a wealth of information about the site you
entered. You will learn the monthly traffic and
demographics related to that traffic. But most important to
you are three data columns: "Audience Also Likes",
"Audience Also Visits", and "Audience Also Searches For".

Take some of the top URLs shown and enter them back
into Quantcast. If they get a lot of traffic add them to your
keyword list of domain names to bid on. Next go to Alexa
and go through a similar process. You want "Traffic
Rankins">"Get Traffic Details". You will find information
appears similar to what you got from Quantcast.

Now click on the "Related Links" button. Here is the mother-lode of information on other sites to which visitors go. Voila'! You now have many possible new domain choices within your general theme.

Then by making logical variations, misspellings (typos) of each URL you can create a massive new keyword list as well! An aid to this is:
visualthesaurus.com. Many of the keywords you found might be searched for with a synonym. Add as many as possible to your keywords.

You can even use a search engine such as ask.com to find additional keywords. Type in any keyword and it immediately gives you a list of related keywords that people have searched.

Beyond these FREE keyword searches, there are tools for which you can pay that provide even more information. The most often mentioned of these are: Wordtracker; KeywordElite; and KeywordCountry. You can do extremely well without ever buying any one of these tools, but if you can afford them they will help you squeeze every bit of keyword-based profit you can out of your campaigns.

It is definitely worth looking at every new program closely. If you find a new one that pays a good commission and you like the sales letter on the vendor's site and they provide decent affiliate marketing material, go for it!

Your ClickBank link will look like the following:
(your unique affiliate ID name).(vendor's ID).hop.clickbank.net
If you add /?tid=(keyword) after this you can track for that keyword. You can do this for each individual keyword, or for your groups of keywords in Google's AdGroups. Always track keywords.

Your email address is important. You need to be: "webmaster@(your domain URL) .com". No Yahoo!, MSN or Google-gmail free email addresses, which make you look like a rank amateur newbie. In fact, some affiliate networks will not even talk with you unless you have a "professional" email address.

ClickBank is the perfect place for a newbie to start their affiliate marketing. You will find higher commissions there than at most networks. Very important is the fact that you get paid by ClickBank directly. ClickBank has a very excellent reputation regarding payments. In many networks the individual vendors pay your commissions. Much less certainty there.

The only drawback to ClickBank is that you are limited to virtual products as opposed to physical products. This is not exactly a limitation in terms of making money, but it does preclude making easy commissions with product-vendors "free trials" where a simple ZIP code entry can earn you commissions.

ADDITIONAL AFFILIATE PROGRAM CHOICE PARAMETERS

We need to look at some specific parameters relating to the affiliate programs you choose to promote. The products you choose should add relevant value to your website. They should relate to the text you have written for your site.

Use ClickBank's "Marketplace" drop-down categories and sub-categories to find some interesting topics. Select "Society and Culture". You will be presented with a rather large list of possible vendors to represent in each topic. Ah, decisions, decisions. How shall we decide which one vendor to choose? Fortunately, Click Bank makes this analysis as easy as possible.

You are concerned with a number of their analytics. I always look first at the amount of commission I can earn. It is no more difficult to promote a product with a high commission payout than a low one. It's a no brainer.

Never take on a product vendor where your net commission is not at least $15.00. The higher the better. The percentage commission is irrelevant.
It's simple arithmetic. An 80% commission on a $19.95 product is a lot less commission than a 65% payout on a $39.95 product. Regardless of the dollars involved, never represent a digital product that pays less than 65% commission.

Next focus on the "% referred" analytic. This tells you what percentage of business comes in to this vendor through the affiliate program. The higher this figure the better. I consider 75% to be the lowest acceptable figure.

The next very important figure is something called "Gravity". This is a measure of affiliate interest in the product. It is a rather complex algorithm. Suffice it to say the higher the better. Over 100 is very good, over 500 excellent.

Once you find a vendor with the right combination of commission %, referral% and gravity, take a long look at the website to which you will be sending visitors. Would you buy the product at the advertised price?

Next take a long look at the tools the vendor provides. Aside from the affiliate link, how much back-up marketing material do they provide? It is also extremely valuable if a vendor offers you a platform where you can submit keyword tracking software (see below) to be placed on their thank you page.

Many do not have this tracking feature. In those cases you will need to contact the manager in an effort to get them to allow this. Before spending a minute of your time developing a program for this vendor determine this matter beyond any question or doubt.

Less obvious negatives: Do they have an 800# for your visitor to use to order instead of ordering on line (bad). Do they offer the visitor an affiliate program? If so, any savvy visitor will simply join it, and be customer #1and receive a commission. You receive nothing. Affiliate program offer bad.

OK, so we've gotten through all of that. Next see if you can determine how many of the vendor's affiliates are buying ppc traffic. Enter some keywords in a Google search and see if you can find your program high in the results. This would mean that someone has found that they can make money paying for traffic.

Next you must check out the "content" networks, where relevant articles reside. Go to ezinearticles.com, put in some keywords, and see what articles come up. Are any of these written by affiliates promoting the vendor you chose? How many times have these articles been read in the past month? Fewer than fifty is not particularly good. That's less than one per day. Hundreds would be much better.

Assuming after all of this you still have a number of programs you want to represent, it is time to contact each vendor directly by email. Tell them of your interest in becoming their affiliate. Ask them directly how much money their top affiliate is making each month. Ask them whether their top affiliates make their commissions mostly through paid search. Ask them how much help they will provide.

This is also a good time to ask them whether they permit you to use a keyword-tracking-code on their "Thank You" page. (See below for an expansion of this thought).

Because keyword tracking is so important you might consider representing only those vendors who allow it.

Some may not respond. Forget representing these. You want to establish a good working relationship with your vendor's affiliate manager right from the start if possible.

Most affiliate networks provide you with a great deal more information than simply the dollar or percentage amount of commission you can earn.

First in importance to you is the "Conversion Rate" (CR). This is the rate at which people you send to their offer do something that makes you money. The higher the better.

It is reported that "zip code submit" offers get much better CTRs than "email submit" offers by almost two to one. Though email submit offers generally pay higher commissions, if you do the math you will find out that you are probably better off to focus exclusively on ZIP Code Submit offers.

Two critical parameters are called "Gravity" and "Click Through Rate (CTR)". These are listed in the affiliate offer information.

Gravity is calculated by the network through an algorithm. It is an expression of conversion rate. Choose ONLY offers with a gravity of 2.00 or higher. (Not even 1.99!). Do not deviate from this.

Click through rate MUST be above 0.04%. Do not deviate from this.

I generally avoid any program with no gravity and CTR figures, or "N/A" for "not applicable". You generally do not want to be a guinea pig for an untested new program. However, do consider my "early bird" comments above.

You also need to look at the price an affiliate is charging for a product. Go to the offer. Would you pay it? Would you expect that your referred visitor would?

Incidentally, where you see a statistical "average sale" price LOWER than the "item price" this is an indication of a good "downsell" which creates the lower average figure. (A downsell is an item the visitor purchases after saying "no" to the initial offer but before he leaves the website).

You may find some affiliate offers that look "too good to be true". This is often the case with gambling offers. Make certain that any offer you decide to market "feels good" in your gut. If you have the slightest twinge of doubt, do not do that particular program. Trouble you don't need! Protect your on-line reputation.

There are lots of lucrative "good feeling" affiliate offers out there from which to choose. You just have to spend many hours, perhaps many days, searching and comparing. Offers come and go and are frequently terminated when they outlive their usefulness to a vendor for one reason or another. (I just found one with a 5.53 gravity that pays $8.42/sale! This one is obviously well worth considering.)

ADULT AFFILIATE SITES

It is a rather morally-unfortunate fact that the most money made on the internet is reported to be from adult sexually oriented sites. I've never gone that route, but I know others who have and done quite well. There are many affiliate programs available.

A Google search for: "adult affiliate networks" will turn up a large number, within which are endless vendor affiliate programs. You can also click on: adult-affiliate-guide.com or adultaffiliateprograms.org for comprehensive categorized lists.

Most web hosts restrict adult-content activity. Here again a Google search for "adult website hosts" will provide you with a long list of hosts who are no so morally challenged. If you have no particular moral objection to sex toys and legal pornography there is certainly a lot of money to be made in this area. If you do get involved be certain to seek legal counsel and obey all Federal and State laws.

YOU NEED *NO* DOLLARS TO MAKE BIG DOLLARS!

Possibly most important is the fact that you are not limited to the number of affiliate products you can offer. You probably would never have the time to create very many products of your own products from scratch by yourself. You can have one affiliate or ten or a hundred or more! And a very big plus is that most vendors provide you with FREE training and FREE advertising materials. It is an absolute win-win for both the vendor and you as an affiliate.

Many infopreneurs use "Yahoo! Answers" as an aid in promoting affiliate offers. Go to answers.yahoo.com, sign up for a FREE account, and enter some keywords. Look for a CPA offer with a $20+ payout and a short form to be completed. Select the appropriate question categories to find related questions. Select "Open Questions" in the questions status field. Once you find a relevant question answer it by explaining how a product would benefit the questioner, and mention a FREE trial. Put your CPA link in the relevant resource box called "What's Your Source".

If you need to find answers a good place to start is Wikipedia. Also, a Google search for virtually any question will turn up a wealth of material you can use to create a unique answer to almost any question. Just try to match CPA affiliate offers with questions.

One of the keys to successful affiliate marketing is offering bonuses to people who buy through your link. Point out that these bonuses are available nowhere else. Clearly state the benefits of these bonuses and how they tie in with the product you are offering.

The idea is to "out-bonus" the competition! Bonuses can take the form of one or more special reports, or audio files, and even video clips. It is a fact that a great bonus package is often more important to the visitor to obtain than the product itself. You just need great bonuses and great copywriting describing the benefits in conjunction with the offered product.

IF the amount of commission can justify it, there are some fabulous bonuses that you can create with artscafe.com. Offering a physical product as an incentive bonus is not often done. If you were offering a dog-related product, wouldn't a mug with your buyer's dog's photo on it be a great incentive? Or even a mouse pad with that image of Fido?

Place easy-to-follow instructions for claiming the bonus at the bottom of your order page, or send them along in the "thank you" email. They will need to send you a copy of their purchase receipt with the affiliate network's unique purchase code, their shipping address, and a .jpg photo of Fido or Fluffy.

You do not even need to have a website to do affiliate marketing. You can direct-link to a vendor's website. But in doing so you preclude being able to pre-sell the visitor. You lose the ability to gain valuable email addresses. It's difficult to measure results because your visitor isn't exposed to your analytics software. And most important, the search engines will not allow you to link to a site you do not own, so PPC and CPM are out.

There are benefits to direct linking, aside from the fact that it can be FREE. Visitors are assured of seeing the vendor's offer which can lead to higher conversion percentages. (Reality check: let's face it, some visitors will actually leave your webpage without clicking on anything.) If you choose direct linking be certain you choose vendors whose site does a great job of selling their product.

You can direct-link in all of your social site marketing, be it Facebook, Twitter, Pinterest, Google+ or whatever. You can direct-link in forums. You can direct-link in article marketing, and ezines, on CraigsList and eBay. You can direct-link in all of your off-line advertising. **NO WEBSITE NEEDED!**

HOW TO LOSE YOUR AFFILIATE COMMISSIONS WITHOUT EVEN TRYING

Choosing a vendor to represent as an affiliate goes beyond the considerations of commission dollars and program statistics. It is EXTREMELY important to be fully aware of ways in which your affiliate commissions can be **stolen**. Some vendors' programs are more theft-proof than others.

Commission theft is often referred to in the trade as "leakage" of commissions. It is the single biggest problem in affiliate marketing. It happens all the time, and very few marketers are aware of the reality of theft let alone how to minimize it. They just chalk up low revenues to their own lousy marketing. That is often a fact, but seldom the problem!

Here are some very real theft issues:

If the page your affiliate is sent to by the link on your website contains
"Join Our Affiliate Program" or "Become An Affiliate" or "Make Money" type of links, savvy visitors will simply join

your vendor's affiliate program themselves and then buy the product and get a discount by way of their earned commission. Pretty sneaky. The vendor couldn't care less because the sale is made. You get screwed. **AVOID AFFILIATES WITH THESE TYPES OF LINKS.**

Many vendors' landing pages have an 800# for convenient customer ordering. <u>Many visitors use it instead of the website.</u> The vendor makes the sale so they're happy. You don't get a commission so you are not happy. A very few vendors do track such phone orders to your affiliate link so you earn your commission, but they are few and far between. **AVOID AFFILIATES WITH 800#s.**

If the merchant you are promoting is selling a software product they may offer your visitor a "trial period" version as opposed to an outright purchase. If it is bought after the trial period, are you screwed out of your commission? In many cases the answer is "Yes". This problem is avoided if the merchant lets you set up the trial on <u>your</u> website with the affiliate link embedded in it. Best advice: **AVOID MERCHANTS SELLING SOFTWARE PRODUCTS THAT CAN BE USED ON A TRIAL BASIS.**

Some vendors join other vendors affiliate programs themselves. If your referred visitor does not buy their product they can still profit from your referral and you get nothing for your marketing efforts. **AVOID MERCHANTS WHO HAVE AFFILIATE BANNERS ON THEIR WEBSITES.**

Probably the most insidious theft occurs when a clever thief substitutes their affiliate ID in a link on **your** page. Ouch! (See below.)

Unfortunately there are "profession refunders" who will buy your vendor's product and request a refund shortly thereafter. Not much you can do here.

In regard to affiliate-ID substitution, this is the problem of "Parasiteware", a form of remote computer coding. Parasiteware is your worst nightmare as an affiliate marketer. It allows a clever tech-savvy thief to steal your affiliate commissions by changing and redirecting your unique affiliate identification links.

If you have reason to believe that you are the victim of parasiteware (because your commissions have dropped off suddenly or dramatically) you should immediately contact your affiliate network's manager. They can often determine the origin of the problem and stop it. Unfortunately it is very unlikely that it would be economically feasible to attempt to sue the offending affiliate marketer once identified.

There is a way to protect yourself. There is software available from easyclickmate.com/ that is well worth using. Aside from the protection it offers there are many other desirable features. Be certain to check it out. It costs less than a hundred bucks, and it can save you thousands!

It is a good idea to spy on your competition. You can be certain they are spying on you! Search at Google on certain keywords for a week or two. See if any affiliates are running the same ad all the time. You can also determine whether he or she is tracking that keyword. Click on their link, go to the extreme bottom of their vendor's order page (you don't have to BUY anything) and you will find a code. If it is obviously your competitors ClickBank name alone, that keyword is not being tracked. If the name is followed by a period and a series of letters and/or numbers that keyword **is** being tracked.

So if you find a keyword associated with an ad for a week or so and that keyword is being tracked you have found keyword gold! Go back and copy your competitor's ad, and run a similar campaign. You should have a sure winner. For under a hundred bucks you can purchase a great

spying program at: dayjobkiller.com. Many top gurus use
it, and you should surely consider doing so.

ARTICLE MARKETING SECRETS FOR AFFILIATES

One KEY to earning commissions in affiliate marketing is
the "ARTICLE MARKETING" model. We will discuss article
marketing again in Chapter 37.

Each week submit one short article (250 -350 words is a
good range) on your niche topic. Do not write this as "sales
copy". Make it informative in some valuable way.

Now you must submit your articles to "article directories".
This has proven to be the best way to drive fast and furious
traffic to your website, your blog, or your social site
presence. When website owners and ezine (on-line
magazine) publishers want free useful information-rich
material to reprint they always turn to the article
directories.

In exchange for getting this free content these publishers
agree not to alter your article in any way. Most important,
they must leave your resource box, which you placed at the
end of your article, containing the link to your website or
your affiliate offer exactly "as is". No changes whatsoever.

A Google search for "Article Directories That Allow Links"
turns up 242 million results! You do not need quite that
many! In fact listing in the top dozen or so will be more
than adequate. Be certain to list in: ezinearticles.com (by
far the most important); hubpages.com; technorati.com;
buzzle.com; articlecity.com; goarticles.com;
brighthub.com; thefreelibrary.com; articlesfactory.com;
squidoo.com; suite101.com; ideamarketers.com; and
articledashboard.com.

There is nothing to prevent you from publishing ten articles a day in each of the above twelve directories. That's 3650 different 250 – 300 page articles yearly for a total of 43,800 postings! Possible? Not very likely. My recommendation of one posting per week per directory, 624 total postings per year, is very easy to do. Some very wealthy affiliate marketers I know manage to do five times that number.

Keep in mind that many of these article directories get 50,000 visitors every day. When someone uses your article, others to whom they send it might also use it. This is known as "viral marketing", because your article with its link spreads like a virus across the internet! The word "viral" carries the negative "virus" connotation. No one wants to be sick. No one wants their computer to be sick. For these reasons I prefer to use the term: "Auto-Effective Marketing" whenever referring to "viral" marketing techniques.

There is more to article marketing than simply creating articles and submitting them to the many directories. It is called research. You need to check out what your competition in your niche is doing and do it better!

To locate articles written by others which are generating big-time traffic and thereby generating big-time profits go to ezinearticles.com. Click on your general topic under "Article Categories". Click on the top article that comes up. When it appears go to near the bottom of the page you will see a search box. Enter "Most Viewed Articles Last 120 days" and click search.

The articles that appear are not in any obvious order. Click on many of them and after you do scroll down to the bottom where in rather small type you will see the date the article was first submitted, and the number of views in the past 90 days. Print out the ones with the most views. Some will have under a hundred, some will have over a thousand!

Realize that this traffic has probably been comparable over the entire life of the article. Then note that many authors have hundreds of articles listed. Do the math. There are authors getting hundreds of hits a day from these short, 300 page articles. Can you produce similar stuff? No reason why not.

You can also use the link at the top of the article, "Ezine Publisher" to locate keywords used by the author.

One very effective "trick of the trade" is to publish a third or half of your article to the directories as a "teaser" and put the balance on a website. By including the resource box at the end of your partial article people who like the first part will usually visit your website to read the balance. Once there you can perhaps obtain their email address with a "squeeze", or offer a unique product, or display affiliate links or AdSense ads. Presto! Income.

Incidentally, in all of your internet marketing, but especially in affiliate marketing, you do NOT want a FREE email address. Yahoo!, Google gMail, scream "AMATEUR!" or "NEWBIE!". You need to be: affiliatemanager@(your website URL).com.

If you are a Twitter Tweeter there are a large number of Twitter accounts that are very well worth following. You can learn a great deal from: AM Navigator (@AMNavigator); Affbuzz.com (@affbuzz); Affilorama (@Affiloramo; RaveNews (@Ravenews); Int_Marketing (@intmarketingtip); AffiliatePaying (@AffiliatePaying); NoExpAffiliates (@NoExpAffiliates); Shawn Collins (@affiliatetip); Rae Hoffman-Dolan (@sugarrae); Jeremy Schoemaker (@shoemoney); Geno Prussakov (@ePrussakov); Zac Johnson (@moneyreign); Steph Lichtenstein (@MicroSteph); Jonathon Volk (@jonathonvolk); Matthew Wood (@matthewwood); Affiliate Summit (@affiliatesummit); LeadsCon (@LeadsCon); ad:tech (@adtech); PubCon (@pubcon);

AM Days (@AMDays); Commission Junction (@CJnetwork); Clickbooth (@clickbooth); ShareASale (@shareasale); Rakuten LinkShare (@LinkShareBlog); buy.at (@buyatUS); ClickBank (@ClickBank); XY7 (@XY7); Affiliate Window (@AffWin); Convert2Media (@convert2media); AvantLink (@AvantLink).

CONCLUSIONS

Affiliate marketing is NOT easy. You will see all manner of hype implying otherwise. Don't believe a word of it. It takes real work to make real big money. You need to learn the products, learn the market, do extensive research, and employ the right tools to make it wildly profitable.

Choosing an affiliate program to promote takes a lot of research and study but is the most important time you will spend. The affiliate choices you make will be offered on your websites, in social site marketing, on eBay and other classified sites, and in everything you do to advertise your existence to the world and make serious money.

What makes the task much easier is the **huge** number of affiliate programs available to you in virtually any niche you can imagine, and the help merchants and the networks offer to insure your success.

AND IT CAN ALL BE DONE FOR FREE. JUST GO FOR IT!

CHAPTER 11
AFFILIATE RICHES WITH EBAY CLASSIFIEDS

When most people think of eBay they think "auctions". There is no question that the eBay auction paradigm can be used very effectively in internet marketing.

But there is a lesser known way for infopreneurs to cash in on eBay that has nothing to do with auctions. It is called "eBay Classified Advertising". It is God's gift to the affiliate marketer. It can be used to generate direct sales, and to build a massive double-opt-in mailing list.

Advertising off-line, in publications that accept classified ads can be very profitable and should not be overlooked. But all but the very smallest off-line ads are quite costly, so most use the minimum-size two-line ads to generate leads. These ads are priced by the word, offer little in the way of "selling", and are generally squeezed together with dozens of competitor's ads. Their effectiveness is limited.

EBay Classifieds, on the other hand, can be huge and bold and include hundreds of words and many pictures. An equivalent size off-line ad would be prohibitively expensive, costing hundreds if not thousands of dollars. The eBay cost? Zero for "local classifieds", around $10 for a 30-day exposure across the entire eBay site!

The KEY to using eBay Classifieds profitably is the fact that these ads respond to searches made by eBay shoppers who you can target 100%! Everyone searching for your type of offer is a potential buyer. Your job is to create a KEYWORD RICH AD, starting with the title of the ad.

With eBay Classifieds there are no final selling fees to eat into your profits. And probably most important there is no "feedback" provision which precludes the habitually-unsatisfied or outright fraudulent buyers from leaving negative feedback about you and your products.

Unfortunately there exists a universe of idiots out there in cyberspace who get their jollyies castigating innocent sellers just for the fun of it.

Most of the successful eBayers I know use this format to build their mailing lists. They offer a free report and send the visitor to a website where they sign up for the freebie and can be directed to an affiliate offer, killing two birds with a single rock! But there are many others who skip this process, which admittedly takes more steps and more time, in favor of simply sending the visitor directly to an affiliate offer. Personally I use both.

A word of caution. EBay's "Rules" can be very confusing and ambiguous, and even worse, change frequently. What is true today is not necessarily true tomorrow. Until fairly recently fortunes were made selling digitally-downloaded reports through eBay auctions until this was outlawed. Now the same report can only be sold as a mailable CD or DVD. It's still profitable, but a bit of a pain. (Check out Kunaki.com which makes this requirement very doable and still very profitable.)

To check on eBay's latest rules, go to pages.ebay.com/help/sell/f-ad.html. It is a good idea to click on everything and read it all. It takes a few hours but could save you serious grief.

Also do the same at: pages.ebay.com/help/policies/listing-links.html. Irrespective of the "letter of the law" it is quite apparent from all of the ads on eBay that they do not rigorously enforce their restrictions. Pull up lots of ads and see for yourself.

It is a good idea to check out other classified ads to see what eBay is permitting (or turning a blind eye towards, rules-against notwithstanding) at any given time. If you see many ads doing exactly what you want to do (e.g., sending visitors away from eBay to non-eBay email-boxes or to affiliate websites or to your own website or email autoresponder) it is a pretty safe bet you can do the same.

One word of caution. EBay does not look favorably on sellers who use free email sites such as Yahoo! and HotMail and Gmail. If you register a domain name (URL) you can easily and quite inexpensively (usually FREE) set up email boxes at that URL. It is reported that eBay does not scrutinize sellers as closely when using URL-specific email addresses. Don't ask!

Under "What Is Not Allowed On eBay Classifieds" is a list of almost fifty "no-nos". Read it, and abide by it. This is actually a pretty good list for you to follow in all of your internet marketing, because most of the items would be prohibited in any medium you might choose. I strongly disagree with eBay's present exclusion of "e-cigarettes" because that is a very profitable affiliate category and seems to me to be in the public good.

I also have no personal moral problem marketing "nude art" as long as it is non-pornographic, but apparently eBay sees all nudity as bad. Affiliate programs for any sort of weapons are also specifically excluded, as are all "adult" products.

You can post 25 local ads per day, all FREE! Each ad can be posted in only one category, and in one chosen ZIP code. Posting that many ads daily, and doing it properly, is quite a chore, but if you could somehow end up posting 750 ads a month it is quite likely that you would generate a significant affiliate income!

There also exists in eBay a different level of Classified ad that is not quite free but offers some serious advantages. This is running Classified Ads directly on eBay.com. If you access pages.ebay.com/help/sell/formats.html you will see a detailed comparison under "Selecting A Selling Format". In this option you state a price, the buyer contacts you, and you handle the transaction personally, for example, on your website.

Most ads run for 30 days, although there is a "Good Until Cancelled" option. Either way you are charged a small "insertion fee" every 30 days. The fees charged are based on the category of product selected. You are NOT charged a final value fee, primarily because eBay has no way of knowing how many of something you may have sold.

Classifieds on eBay are a serious bargain! Each 30-day period presently costs only $9.95. The first picture in the ad is free. This would be your killer book cover. Additional pictures cost only $0.15 each. There are a number of "upgrades" that can add an additional $6.10/30-days, or $16.05 total, still a major bargain over off-line classifieds. A big ad with ten pictures keyword-targeted to a specific niche audience costing under $18.00 is a bargain.

These upgrades are intended to make your ads stand out in a crowd. I can't make a strong argument for using them, because it is the wording of your title and ad that drives visitors to your site, but using upgrades can't hurt either.

With eBay Classifieds you can sell on any ebay country site regardless of where you reside or from what country your eBay account was initially registered. Just note that fees and allowable products do vary country to country. Digital products are the most relevant example of this. They are AOK in the UK but theoretically a NO-NO in the US of A!

The same is true for outside linking. In reality you will find countless ads running with outside links featuring affiliate products. So join the crowd until such time as Ebay decides to tighten their rules or better police them.

Many marketers will post classified ads linking to their own paid-for listings on eBay. They set up identical Classified

Ads ending by the hour and linked to the paid-for listing giving the product a high profile. Though you are keyword-limited to 55 spaces in your eBay "Buy It Now" titles, you are not limited in putting keywords and phrases throughout your classified ads. You want to appear once for as many search terms as possible.

EBay Sales are shown to improve when you create an "About Me" page. Putting a "face" behind an anonymous offering makes many bidders more comfortable. Make it an attractive face, preferably female. Both men and women prefer to buy from women. Don't ask!

You can put virtually anything on this page, including a link to your website. The only restriction here is that any products you offer on your website that you are selling on eBay must be priced $1.00 higher than on eBay.

CONCLUSION

Regardless of costs and restrictions, selling through eBay Classified Ads represents perhaps the single best internet marketplace. Promoting your affiliate offers, or your own product website, using eBay Classifieds to drive traffic is by far the easiest and most cost-effective way to earn a very significant internet income.

CHAPTER 12
FREE CLASSIFIEDS TO ENHANCE YOUR PROFITS

Now here is a real NO BRAINER. It costs exactly zero run your affiliate ads on free classified advertising sites. Nothing. Nada. So why not go for it? No reason whatsoever. It also costs nothing to join a public affiliate network such as ClickBank. Nada. Just do it. **Nothing plus nothing equals pure profit potential!**

Are you going to get very rich doing this? Maybe. Can you make a lot of money with relatively little effort? Absolutely!

By far the most useful FREE advertising site is: usfreeads.com. They have been providing services for over a decade. What makes this site special is that you can link to your affiliate vendor directly from your ad, a **HUGE** plus.   Not all ad sites permit this. Some will require a link to your website squeeze page or pre-sell content.

CRAIGSLIST

Let's look at the well-known "Craigslist". This was the brainchild of a San Francisco computer programmer named Craig Newmark. A single guy, he wanted to keep track of what was going on in his home city. After letting a few of his friends in on it, the idea became a viral sensation! The area of focus became the entire Bay area. It became an internet bulletin board, with evermore categories added.

Soon other cities wanted "in", and the site expanded nationally then internationally. It became a place for people to offer their services, hire employees, meet other people for discussions, and buy and sell various items. It has evolved into a very powerful marketing tool for your earning pleasure!

Many internet marketers are discouraged by the Craigslist culture. Members who contribute to the community bulletin board police the "Rules", some written, some not. Any member can complain about an advertiser and Craigslist will remove the ad.

Craigslist's community is chock full of anti-capitalists who see themselves as champions of anti-commercialism and will complain about any ad that they feel might be, GOD forbid, for profit! You see, Craigslist is NOT in the ad/marketing business. They are a sort of ".org" non-profit group community bulletin board as opposed to a commercial marketplace.

But advertising here is a "numbers game". According to their website they get twenty <u>BILLION</u> page views a month! More than fifty million people in the United States use Craigslist. That's one in six Americans! (More like one in four if you take kids out of the calculation.)

They have almost a hundred topical forums on the website, and claim one-hundred-twenty-million monthly forum postings. Each month they get <u>fifty million</u> new free classified ads. These are massive numbers.

You have two possible approaches to earning on Craigslist, direct advertising, and forum participation. Let's look first at direct free advertising.

For starters, set up an account at craigslist.org (not .com). Just fill in your email address, copy the anti-fraud symbols shown, and click "Create Account". You will be sent an email message with a special link. Click on the link and you are taken to a page to create a password. Do so, and Bingo!, you have an account. You do not actually <u>need</u> an account to post ads, but it is helpful in keeping things organized. It is also needed to access details of forum posts.

Spend some time carefully searching all of the categories and subcategories available to you and choose some subcategories that relate to one of your niches. There are so many choices it should not be difficult to find matches.

Incidentally, running the same ad (with very different wording) in different subcategories exposes it to entirely different universes of potential customers. (If you run exactly the same or closely-similarly-worded ad it will probably get removed as a rules violation brought to the attention of Craigslist by the army of self-appointed profit-hating censors.)

You will be asked to choose a city for display of your ad. It takes a bit of time to hit all of the individual major markets, because you need to go through the entire posting procedure time and time again. And here again you need to re-word your ads for each post lest the anti-capitalists score again. The good news is that it only takes a couple of minutes per city. And you can even go for international markets!

Strictly by the rules you are NOT supposed to post multiple ads in different categories, or ads in more than one city. You are actually not supposed to be a professional marketer selling anything! The site is intended for rank amateurs selling "yard sale" and "garage sale" stuff. This is why you need to carefully study other ads that are being run and get a feel for what does and does not pass muster.

Properly worded, you should at least be able to direct individuals to your website to sell them something, squeeze-page them into collecting their email address, or have them click on an affiliate link. (Here again, affiliate marketing as such is against the rules.) Just learn the Craigslist culture well and you are on your way to placing profitable free ads any time you choose.

The second approach to marketing on Craigslist is through their forums. The Craigslist forums are sort of a free-for-all, with lots of threads completely off topic. But there seems to be no rules regarding posting website URLs and affiliate links, which makes your job easier. And being FREE makes it painless!

My suggestion is for you to check out forums on something close to your niche. They have forums for "fitness", "food", "garden", "money", "health", "sports", "music", "pets" and a host of others. Try to see if you can find logical places to post short blurbs about your product or your affiliate offers with appropriate links. I've done this, and gotten some click-throughs and revenue. This is not always a huge moneymaker, but it is pretty darned easy cash, and again, FREE..

OTHER ADVERTISING SITES TO CONSIDER

Aside from Craigslist, which many consider a pain to use, there are many other classified ad sites that are worth using as well.

You can find a long list at: thefreeadforum.com/ads/page/list-of-high-traffic-classified-ads-websites.html.

Here are some I suggest you use:

The number 2 classifieds site behind Craigslist is **backpage.com**. This site is primarily for sexually oriented material, so you probably won't use it. Then again.......

Kijiji.com will take you to eBay Classified ads. (This is an entire world unto itself.)

Gumtree.com is a busy UK classified site. Do not overlook English- language sites that happen to be located overseas.

Classified ads.com is an English-speaking world focused classified site.

Inetgiant.com is a great place to advertise your green products.

Adpost.com is an international site with a mostly English-speaking audience.

Adlandpro.com has very busy business opportunity and pet sections.

Classifiedadsforfree.com is a well-organized worldwide site.

Pennysaverusa.com/classifieds/usa/index.html is the online version of the old Penny Saver newspaper.

Epage.com has been in business since 1994, which tells me something positive. It even pre-dates Google! You get excellent exposure here because of their large affiliate program.

Recycler.com is an easy to use classified ads site.

Webcosmo.com is US focused but with opportunities for overseas ads.

Hoobly.com has had 15,000+ people have clicked their "like" button, so they must be doing something right!

Freeadlists.com is US based and very comprehensive.

Sell.com probably has one of the most valuable domain names in existence! In business for over a decade, it gets great exposure.

Bestwayclassifieds.com is a fast growing site with decent traffic.

Choseyouritem.com if nothing else has a very high opinion of its own site! Worth listing here.

Wantedwants.com also consider themselves to be the best in the world! Decent traffic and worth posting ads here Freeclassifieds.com is a mobile-device friendly site worth listings.

Businesslist.com/post-classified-ad/ is a US targeted classifieds site. All your ads are automatically tweeted to their twitter account.

Theworldwideclassifieds.pressmania.com/ has the feature of having never -expiring ads. Free ads get live links and even the ability to add a YouTube video to your ad.

Blujay.com is worth a long look. They submit your ads to Google Product Search shopping, which opens your offerings up to massive traffic. And you get a free online store to list all of your products under one roof if you so desire.

Ecrater.com, is very similar to BluJay. It also gets placement in Google searches. Title and word your ads to be rich in key search terms and you have a good chance of making sales at zero cost to you. They also provide a free store for you to stock.

Create free advertising on "Yahoo!Classifieds" through the Yahoo!Directory at:
dir.yahoo.com/business_and_economy/classifieds/.
Obviously they get massive traffic, and keyword-rich ads with the right headline will get seen. Go for it!

Ablewise.com will place your free ads worldwide! (Ten countries listed, mostly English speaking). They claim over 128,000,000 visitors!

Internetbusinessmoms.com has blog posts and forums that can be used for subtle advertising

Inetgiant.com offers free classifieds with a paid alternative that claims a 20x better response. Try it for free.

Adlandpro.com will run your classified ads for free. Study their site. They **have an interesting affiliate program.as well.**

ClassifiedAds.com is location-specific, which can be limiting (though you can run the same ad in large metro areas using different accounts.) Here again, nothing ventured nothing gained. Check it out.

Backpage.com gives you a massive number of choices for you to pin-point match ads to your potential customers.

Nationwidenewspapers.com offers access to a massive number of all sorts of publications that accept classified ads. They do not specifically offer free ads, but some of their ad packages are inexpensive and offer great exposure. Well worth a look.

Homebusinessmag.com is a widely circulated magazine dedicated to franchise offers and all manner of home-business opportunities. You can pay for their ads, both display and classified formats, but it is possible to get freebies if you meet certain criteria. "Free Listings are reserved for companies that offer substantial home-based businesses" or so states their website. If you have such a product, go for the freebie.

There are over a hundred-fifty specialized article directories which you should not overlook. These cover a massive range of niches. For example, if your product relates to dogs you have: **bestdogarticles.com**. Targeting golfers? Try: **golfmastery.us.** Horseback riding? See: **horsebackridingarticles.com**. Google "Specialist Article Directories" for a list, or just try (your niche)articles.com and see what pops up!

One of the other FREE sources of traffic to view your affiliate ads are "Traffic Exchanges". You simply enter your website domain name or an affiliate link and it will be displayed in rotation with other members of the traffic exchange. Here are the three I find best, though as with any major topic in this ebook doing a Google search will turn up many others.

TrafficSwarm at: **trafficswarm.com** offers free website traffic and free ads in their website directory.

HitPulse at: **hitpulse.com** offers free unlimited traffic to you affiliate ad websites.

InstantBuzz at: **instantbuzz.com** states on their website: "This breakthrough new patent-pending advertising technology will send targeted visitors to your site **today**. That's right. Install it right now (it's free and takes only a few seconds), and we'll start sending you targeted high quality traffic to your site today. Not tomorrow. Not next week. **Today.** 100% FREE - Installs in Seconds." That sounds like an offer that you simply can't refuse!

The free classified advertising sites are all absolutely flooded with ads, but you cannot beat "FREE". It is up to you to make your ads better than your competition's ads, or to write ads in niches where there is little or no competition.

Just look at free classified advertising as another of the many possible ways to insure multiple streams of internet income. Over time your various streams can flow together to create a massive river of profits!

Free (and paid) classified advertising is by far the easiest way to promote anything you are selling. Whether it is your own report or book product, a CD or DVD or video, or an affiliated vendor's product, exposing it to targeted buyers for little or no cost simply cannot be beat. Adhere to this one business model and profits are sure to follow!

JUST DO IT!!!

CHAPTER 13
RICHES FROM YOUR *OWN* AFFILIATE NETWORK

As we discussed above, representing vendors as their affiliate has proven to be a wonderful way for you to generate internet cash. The large number of possible programs, and the large number of ways to promote them, makes this income stream particularly attractive to newbies and experienced internet marketing pros alike. It is the perfect way to start your internet profits adventure.

Your product website, which the visitor is directed to by your advertising or by links posted in various places, will have a few short relevant articles on-topic. It will also have an eMail-collection form and your affiliate link. If you give the visitor a reason to give you their email address (a free report or whatever) they very often will. This is how you build your all-valuable double-opt-in email list for future marketing efforts. If they choose not to do so they can decline with a click and then hopefully click over to your affiliate's offer.

If your vendor does a good selling job your visitor will provide some personal data. This data can be as simple as a ZIP Code or an eMail address, all the way up to name, address and telephone number, and even better, an actual purchase. And you get a commission that is based in general on the depth of information collected. This is Affiliate Marketing 101, where you promote someone else's product.

But wouldn't you like to have hundreds, maybe thousands of affiliate marketers offering **YOUR** products? If you can create a complete affiliate package and present it to the most successful affiliate marketers for them to offer on your behalf, you can make a fortune without doing any marketing yourself! They do all of the marketing work, and you collect money for doing absolutely nothing on a day to day basis except watch your bank balance grow!

You could create the greatest book or report or training course ever seen on earth. You could simply expose it to a zillion potential affiliate marketers with a letter saying: "Here is the greatest product ever. Here's the website URL. It sells for $147.00 and I'll pay you a 70% commission. Please add it to your product mix." I can assure you that you will get a very large number of drooling affiliates. **I can also assure you that they will all be almost worthless.**

There are countless affiliate promoters out there who will join every affiliate program they see with a fat commission, toss it against the wall and see if anything sticks. Most do not have a clue how to market, and all they will do is waste your time with endless questions and ultimately with complaints because they are getting poor results. Any affiliate marketer that you would want to represent your product will want a great deal more than a simple description of your offer and a pat on the back. To attract the highest level of affiliate marketers you need a full-blown package of marketing materials for your affiliate to use in their marketing efforts.

This is the sort of package *you* should look for in any vendors whose affiliate program you choose to represent. Never try to market a vendor's product if they simply give you the product, tell you how great it is, offer you a fat commission, and then hands you the ball. You want a lot more than the ball!

Once you have created this affiliate marketing package, (and I can assure you it will take a great deal of your time and effort), not only will you be able to attract the very best affiliate marketers, but you will be able to turn the average or even sub-average marketer into a superstar!

To attract the most experienced affiliate marketers, the "super affiliates" as they are called, you must not only be able to prove your own great statistics but also must have a great affiliate marketing package. You need to SELL your program, explaining why they should become your affiliate.

Here are the steps you must follow in creating your **"Total Affiliate Marketing Package":**

For starters you must have special software to track and pay your affiliates. This is rather expensive, but well worth the cost if you have a good saleable product. You can do a Google search for "affiliate program software" and you will find a large number of choices to compare. Buying the software outright can cost $1,000 or so. Some have monthly rental schedules of from $25/month to $150/month depending on traffic. All have FREE trials. There is a nominal fee for installing the software on your server.

There are a number of programs available for creating your own affiliate army. One of the best known is the OmniStar Affiliate Software available at osiaffiliate.com. It costs $27/month for up to 200 affiliates, and has a FREE trial. (Also $47/month for 3,000, and $97/month for unlimited affiliates). Noting that they have clients such as Macy's and Cisco I assume they must be doing something right!

Other Programs that I would suggest you compare are: clickinc.com; affiliateshop.com; affiliatewiz.com; simpleaffiliate.com; and affiliateebooks.com.

Choose the compensation you plan to pay your affiliates. You can choose to pay for clicks, for leads, or a offer percentage of the sale. Unless you have been promoting your product for some time and have a very good handle on your conversion rates, stick to "% of sale", which is generally set between 35% and 70%. The higher % you offer to pay the more and better affiliates you will attract. Paying 70% may sound like a lot, but remember, this gives you 30% of a sale you would not have made at all without the affiliate. It is pure profit with zero effort. Program your affiliate compensation into your software after it is installed on your server.

Now for the time-consuming part, which you only need to do once for each product you offer to affiliates. You must create the advertising materials for your affiliates to use. These are the materials they will be putting on their websites and sending out to their email lists. If you have been selling the product for some time without affiliates (highly recommended) you should already have most of these materials created. You will need some banner ads, text-based ads, short articles, headlines, descriptions (all keyword rich), and photos.

Create a five to ten part mini-course about your product that your affiliate can use in his autoresponder email sequencing. Each chapter of the course need only be a single page.

TRAIN YOUR AFFILIATES! Teach them how you market your product. Be sure to teach them how to navigate your affiliate software to get their unique affiliate links.

Make certain your product website itself is optimized. When an affiliate visits the site he must be dazzled! He must believe that your sales letter will lead to a sale more often than not. And of course you should give him a free copy of whatever it is he will be marketing.

Attract potential affiliates by submitting your offer to affiliate directories. Go to: AffiliateAnnounce.com, and also do a search at Google for "affiliate directories".

Be certain that you have links on every page of your website that says: "Become An Affiliate". This should appear in your search bar at both the top and bottom of EVERY page, and on your site map. Make it as easy as possible for affiliates to offer to join by linking to a simple sign-up page. You can use this page to obtain information about the potential affiliate, so you can weed out the losers, which will predominate.

Consider buying Marlon Sanders "Affiliate Dashboard". It will be a great help to you in structuring your complete affiliate program package.

If you are selling from your own website, you should have a sign-up page where you turn your buyers or visitors into your personal army of affiliates. Get their information needed to identify and pay them their commissions. Let them know that they will receive their unique affiliate ID in an email. Remember, when you set up your own affiliate program you are giving regular computer users a chance to have their own home based business based on your product. That's pretty cool!

In this way some very clever marketers make each buyer of their product instantly into an affiliate! (They figure an army of average to poor affiliates will get them more income than a small squad of super-affiliates.) If they just bought your product they can surely picture someone else buying it through **them**. Make it as easy as possible for them to sign up. Get their personal information as needed to identify them and pay their commissions. Let them know that they will be receiving a unique affiliate ID.

When someone becomes your affiliate they will expect to receive some bonus that you will in fact promise on your website. When you provide the bonus, provide one or two additional "unadvertised" bonuses. **Always under-promise and over-deliver**. This is equally true when selling **any** product. British internet guru Avril Harper has developed this technique into an art form!

It is a good idea to keep in <u>constant touch</u> with your affiliates, especially the better ones. Depending on the success of your program and the amount of profit you are making, you can reward them with additional commission when they reach various sales levels. Competitive contests work well too.

Of course, you can have your own army of affiliates selling your products **WITHOUT** creating your own personal affiliate program **or even having a website**. Simply list your product sales-link directly with ClickBank (assuming it is a virtual product) or any of the dozens of other Affiliate Networks. (Google search "Affiliate Networks" for a list.) The downside here is that you will be paying some part of your potential profits to the affiliate network as opposed to keeping 100% for yourself.

And remember, when you set up your own affiliate program you are giving regular computer users a chance to have their own profitable home based business based on **YOUR** product! That's pretty cool.

Once you have a universe of capable affiliates fully trained and well-armed with your Affiliate Marketing Package you can sit back, relax, and count your money as sale after sale after sale comes in to your account. This is internet marketing nirvana!

Just DO IT!

CHAPTER 14
THE RIVER TO INTERNET WEALTH

THE AMAZON. The huge, mysterious river in South America. **AMAZON**, the huge internet presence that offers an amazing number of ways to cash in on their universally known brand. Many internet fortunes are being made with total focus on this one business model alone.

Amazon has become the number one fixed-price buying site on the internet. Starting out as "just a huge bookstore" it has become an immense all-around retail portal. Many eBay auction sellers find Amazon to be the perfect complement to their on-line businesses. There are definite practical differences between marketing on eBay and marketing on Amazon. Both grew up together, and have great brand recognition and massive traffic. Neither has any significant competition. Both have loyal buyers who return over and over again. But it is generally believed that Amazon marketers are more affluent. Average selling prices tend to be higher than on eBay.

Amazon buyers tend to be much easier to interface with. Their shopping experience is more "product oriented". You have far less interaction with your customers with Amazon. And there is no such thing as a non-paying Amazon customer!

There are at least six different ways you can weave Amazon's mighty river into your multiple streams of internet income. One of these, Kindle Direct Publishing (KDP) at kdp.amazon.com. But there are others that can be a valuable source of internet income. Consider these four business models:

You can become an Amazon affiliate, marketing their products through your website and earning affiliate commissions.

You can set up an "Amazon aStore" and use their clout to help market your products.

You can advertise your own products on Amazon, and pay only if they sell;

You can sell your products with Amazon doing the fulfillment and shipping on your behalf.

To expand on the above:

The Amazon affiliate program. To participate fully, you need to have your own website. You place Amazon ad links on your website, entice visitors to click on them, and earn commissions depending on the actions they take one they get to the Amazon offer.Go to the amazon.com home page. Click on "Shop All Departments" to see the categories of products they offer. Pick one, and then pick a sub-category, in some product area you find interesting. Register a URL that contains the words that would be appropriate to attract a visitor looking for the sort of item you have chosen.
Now go back to amazon.com and click on "Selling With Amazon". Click on "Associate Program" in the dropdown menu. This takes you to the Land of Plenty! You will be presented with three affiliate marketing choices: Links/Banners, Widgets, and aStore. Study them all. They offer a very wide variety of ways to present your affiliate links to your visitors.

If you do not wish to choose products on your own Amazon has a "Google Adsense-like" feature where they will place ads on your site that relate to the content on your site. For content you should have a few relevant short articles as you would for any website you build. At some point you will click on "Sign Up Now" to create your affiliate account. Just fill out the requested information to obtain your unique affiliate code.

The Amazon aStore. You can link to this on-line store directly from your website, or you can actually have it as an integral part of your website. Now you will have a dedicated shopping area where visitors can shop many different niche-related products. There is even a shopping cart that processes all transactions through Amazon.

To make the aStore a part of your website you will click on "Embed my store using an inline frame". You can make the store a distinct separate web page from your home page by clicking "Embed my store using a frameset". To link to your store as an off-site stand-alone, you will click on: "Simple link to my store as a stand-along site". It costs you nothing to sign up for a sellers' account and nothing to list products. You only pay a very fair fee (somewhere between 8% and 15% depending upon the product) when the product sells.

There are three ways to get started marketing on Amazon.. You can click through the "Amazon Catalog", find a related item and click the "Sell Yours Here" button. You can go to amazon.com home page and click on "Sell Your Stuff". Or you can first open up a "Seller's Account" and go to "Manage My Inventory" to list your products.

There is one other way to earn money through Amazon and that is setting up a **"Pro Merchant Account".** This is to provide you with an "Amazon Store". There is a monthly fee, plus a fee for every item you sell.

They also have an Amazon Services Product called "WebStore by Amazon", a complete e-commerce solution. To see the details of this option, check out: webstore.amazon.com. To set up an account click: "WebStore Self Service Registration". They offer a "Template Manager" that is a great aid in designing your Amazon store.

Last but not least, (the fifth business model), not to be outdone by Google, you can do the same sort of niche keyword focused pay-per-click advertising with Amazon. Although Google gets far more PPC traffic, it is certainly a good idea to do some Amazon PPC to see how your results compare.

Go for it!

MODULE FOUR
YOUR WINNING WEBSITES

CHAPTER 15
GET RICH WITH YOUR *OWN-PRODUCT* WEBSITES

Much of the money made by internet entrepreneurs is made selling information products, "How To....", or other specialized information not easily found or readily available quickly. Of course you can sell large physical products (TVs, etc.) if you wish, but if you decide to go that route you are getting into inventory and shipping and huge-store competition, ugly things that are completely avoided by selling "virtual" downloadable products.

The kind of visitors you seek want fast results, fast download, immediate delivery, all of which provides instant gratification. Quickness, quickness, quickness....the three most important factors in your virtual-product internet marketing. Your goal is to instantly gratify your visitors. For example, if they sign up for a newsletter or purchase a product, you must autorespond instantly congratulating them on their brilliant decision to acquire whatever it is they just bought.

"Rinse and repeat", as they say in the detergent-marketing arena. If they buy something, instantly surprise them with a first-time-buyer gift (a free report or whatever). Soon after reward them again for their wise decision. This is how you create lifetime loyalty.

It is not uncommon for single virtual reports to sell for anywhere from $9.97 to $19.97, and short information courses (basically groups of reports) to sell for $97.97 or more. Longer courses on eight or so CDs or DVDs commonly sell for $497.00 and up. Group telephone mentoring programs often sell for many thousands of dollars (I know of at least one that is $35,000!). Keep in mind that all of this represents virtually 100% profit, once your product is created.

You also have two opportunities available to you that you do not have on an affiliate site, the "back end upsell" offer and the "one time offer", the latter known in the trade as the OTO. These are somewhat advanced techniques, but once you are set up to sell something and have found a way to get visitors to your website these will greatly add to your income.

An upsell, which shows up on your site after the customer buys something from you, is normally an enhancement to what was just purchased. It can be the same exact information but presented on a physical CD or DVD. It can be additional "secret whatever" enhancements to what was just bought.

It can be the special "Platinum Professional Edition". If someone just spent $49.97 on something he perceives has that value, it isn't difficult to get the buyer to part with an additional $14.97 for whatever special enhancement you can dream up. Actually, I just recently saw a $197 upsell on a $19.97 purchase! I passed.

It is also common to see a page magically appear after you have said "NO!" to a $97 product offering you that exact product for $47 if you act immediately! It is preceded usually by a blurb about how the seller realizes that times are tough and it is understandable that you might not have $97. Sometimes the "reduced price bargain" is the same item originally offered, but without some minor piece of it. I suspect that there is no "lesser version", and if you go for the reduced price you get the full price item.

Want to create **real** urgency? Try a countdown! "Offer expires in sixty seconds" might just inspire a fast click-through! Check out **imtriggers.com** to apply this technique. Just be sure to give the visitor enough time to read your offer and react positively. You don't want to cut them off just as their finger descends on the "BUY" button!

Very effective is the <u>O</u>ne <u>T</u>ime <u>O</u>ffer (OTO): "WAIT: BEFORE YOU CHECK OUT I HAVE AN AMAZING DEAL FOR YOU. YOU WILL NEVER SEE THIS OFFER AGAIN ONCE YOU LEAVE THIS PAGE. WE HAVE A LIMITED NUMBER OF (use your imagination) AVAILABLE AT THIS TIME ONLY. FOR JUST $xxxxx".

Very often your OTO will be priced higher than the initial product, and you must write a convincing second sales letter for visitors to buy it. I know it works, because my bookcase is filled with gurus OTOs!

There are other advantages to having your own site. The most important is the ability to offer a FREE (the magic word) something (newsletter, report, course, whatever) to be sent directly to the customer's email box in exchange for the visitor simply providing you an email address. This is how the all-important all-valuable "Opt-In Email List" is created.   Having your own list of visitors interested in whatever it is you have to sell allows you to keep in touch with them, offer various freebies to secure their loyalty, and then occasionally offer them something relevant to buy. Very often they will, especially if they found your earlier offerings to have provided them some value.

You can also include a few affiliate offers on your website, but you always run the risk of the visitor leaving your site for the affiliate offer without buying your product. If it is a really high-paying affiliate with a great conversion rate that might not be a bad thing! Otherwise, common knowledge is to offer no alternatives to your offer.

There is one basic way to increase the frequency of orders. The key is continuous communication with people who have either bought something from you, or at least accepted some freebie from you. . A nice lady named Avril Harper in England is a master at this. Google search her and you will find an internet guru who really knows how to apply all of the proven website marketing techniques. No matter what report you buy from her you end up getting continual communication with all sorts of useful free stuff until she has something new to sell, which I almost always buy because she has been so darn nice! She has programmed my mind into her long-term marketing strategy, and it works.

Communication of this sort greatly diminishes the chances of someone deciding to opt-out of your email list. I'd certainly never opt out of Ms. Harper's. Retention of people on your list is a key to long term success. Communicate **and** "over-deliver". She does both.

Exceed your customer's expectations and you can have a customer for life. And remember; when you give out a freebie people feel a subtle obligation to return the favor. As in "buy something"!

If your site becomes very popular and gets a lot of visitors you can sell advertising space on the site. This can be very profitable if done correctly, but it also can diminish the sales of your own product. There are many companies that you can find in a Google search that can assist you in selling ad space on your sites.

GET A DOMAIN NAME AND CHOOSE A WEB HOST

Of course the first thing you must do is get a domain name through any of the domain name providers. If possible ONLY get "dot com" domain names. The entire internet industry is often referred to as the "DotCom Revolution". Simply, .coms are trusted. Having one implies that your site has been around a long time. They are worth more and bring in more revenue than other dot somethings.

Personally I use GoDaddy.com for my domain name purchases because they are less expensive than anyone else I would trust. There are literally hundreds of companies selling domain names as a simple Google search such as "purchase a dot com domain name" will attest. These names cost around $10 each for a year, and must be renewed at the end of each year for the same amount.

It is possible to pay for up to ten years, sometimes at a discount. Paying for longer terms can help you avoid losing a precious URL because you forgot to renew it after the first year. Believe me, it happens. I know. First hand. Very painful. It is also believed that Google's website rating algorithm may reward a domain name that is registered for a long time period. Apparently in their minds it implies permanence.

PLAN YOUR WEBSITE

You do have to make a choice between two basic "types" of website. The easiest, the one that requires the least maintenance, is a static site which you can tweak as often as you wish but need not do so if you are happy with your results. I would recommend this for any beginner.

The other type is a "Weblog Site" or "Blog Site" for short. Here you will be using a free program such as WordPress, and loading it into your host's site-building program. Once your site is created and on line, frequently posting information and changes to your site (your blogs) is the key to being viewed favorably by search engines. Posting content once or twice a week is ideal.

There are entire books written on the merits of each type of site. The blog site takes a lot more work to maintain, but is looked upon more favorably by Google and other search engines. They give you credit for changing content often. This can result in higher ranking in the search engine, and in theory ultimately more business.

One of the advantages to using WordPress is the number of extremely helpful plug-ins that are available. You must consider employing the following:

REVISION CONTROL: Allows you greater control over revisions than is inherent in WordPress itself.

GOOGLE XML SITEMAPS: This valuable plug-in automatically prepares your sitemap.

SCRIBE SEO: This plug-in helps with your website search optimization by suggesting useful keywords.

GRAVITY FORMS: If you want to create forms on your website you will find this plug-in to be invaluable.

W3 TOTAL CACHE: If you want to optimize your website's loading speed this plug-in will help accomplish that goal.

SOCIAL METRICS: If you want to monitor social media traffic on your site this plug-in will do it.

BACKUP BUDDY: Automatically backs up your site safely to any location you choose. You NEVER want to lose your site information.

YOAST SEO: For advanced site optimization to help search engines find your site easily you need this plug-in.

YOAST BREADCRUMBS: This plug-in facilitates your visitors in navigating your website.

WP-OPTIMIZE: This allows you to easily remove unwanted comments and post revisions.

In order to be highly successful with **any** website it is important to keep updating your content. Without doing so there is no reason for customers to make repeat visits. Customers love it, and so does Google. This is especially true with blog sites. There are many ways to acquire new material for your website:

Follow news and trends relevant to your industry. Do so by subscribing to relevant newsletters. You should also subscribe to RSS feeds from bloggers in your niche. Setting up "Google Alerts" for basic keywords will also supply almost endless content.

Monitor the social networks. Study questions and conversations. You can save a lot of time and effort by using tools such as tweetdeck.com and hootsuite.com.

Rework old content. You can modify almost anything you created in the past to create a new ebook or report, or even a video or CD. Compile and publish "best of" material periodically.

Consider conducting customer surveys using surveymonkey.com or surveygizmo.com. This can provide lots of material for blogs and site updates.

Keep an ongoing file of relevant articles plucked off of the many news services, msn.com and bbc.com being my two favorites. A properly categorized compilation of such material over time will give you tons of material for those times when you are at a loss to come up with exciting new content.

One very simple way to create a FREE website is to go to whypark.com and follow their very simple instructions. There will be some of their ads shown on the site. (WhyPark can't be expected to give you a free website, with hosting, out of the goodness of their heart. That's not a particularly viable business model!)

There is another "free" website creator that I would recommend you experiment with. You can only use it for your own products but cannot use it as an affiliate site with links away from the site. In order for this provider to be able to offer the site to you at no cost, including hosting and site creation tools plus a shopping cart, they reserve the right to place their own ads on the site. This could be a distraction for your visitors, but you can't beat the price!

Avoid "shouting" on your webpage. Consider your Heading as 28 point, subheading 16 point, and body 12 point fonts. Use 35 – 55 characters per line, and **always** left justify.

With that said, it is a great site to "practice" your internet commerce at absolutely no cost to you. Just go to VStore.ca (not .com) and sign up. You can create as many free sites as you wish. Your job is to come up with a product to sell, sign up for a free PayPal account, and create your site using Vstore's very simple step by step instructions. They will provide you with a unique web address: www. (whatever name you choose).vstoresite.com. You can always cloak this lengthy website if you wish.

If you want potential customers to see a simpler web address you can register any available dot com (.com) you want (e.g., myproduct.com) and point it to the longer Vstore compound-address. Most domain providers make this very easy to do with a couple of mouse clicks. Your potential buyer sees only your shortened address in your ads. Having you own unique dot com (.com) domain name serves two purposes. First of all, it should be chosen to be more memorable than the free address provided at VStore. Secondly, it has been shown that customers prefer the simple dot com to the compound one which to some buyers signals that it is an "amateur" site and perhaps not to be trusted.

To create your very own website with nothing on it but things you put on it, and with no revenue sharing with any third party, you must have your domain "hosted" at a company that has specialized software designed for that purpose. These hosts, for a modest monthly fee, provide you with the tools to create your own website without you needing any knowledge of computer programming codes whatsoever. Most hosts have excellent tutorials, and also have live support if you get stuck on some aspect of your site creation. One such host is doteasy.com.

Also check out: Joomla.org; Drupal.org; and webs.com. Web.com, a huge company, is now the sponsor of the former "Nationwide Golf Tour", which is now called the "web.com Golf Tour". They will create very fine websites for you, but they are not inexpensive. (I do, in fact, use them.)

TRUST AND TESTIMONIALS

Trust is important. Many visitors will not buy anything unless they have a high degree of trust in the website. Go to: trustgauge.com and study everything in the site. Install the trust gauge at: browseraccelerator.com. The more trust symbols, VeriSign, Better Business Bureau, Chamber of

Commerce or whatever you can legitimately add to your website the better.

Having testimonials on your website are very important to instill trust in your visitors. Of course at first, with a new product you have not sold, you have no feedback from real buyers. This should not prevent you from sending out ten or twenty free copies of your offering to friends, family and associates and asking them for honest appraisals of your work.

After adding a testimonial to your "sales letter" on your website don't just put initials such as "RJ" or "RJ Tucson" under it. Always use the individual's full name, and as much of a full address as they will allow, even including an email address. This makes the testimonials far more believable.

When soliciting the testimonials always ask permission in advance to add this identifying information. With unsolicited testimonials always write or email for permission to use their information on your website, paraphrased in any way you see fit. **NEVER FAKE YOUR TESTIMONIALS!** You can even have your testimonials "Authenticated". Check out: **authenticatedtestimonials.com**. For $35 year one and $25/year thereafter (for two verifications with additional ones at $13 each) they will contact the people whose testimonials are shown on your website. Once the testimonial is verified they allow you to place a verification seal alongside each testimonial. I strongly suggest you ask the permission of anyone who will be contacted to submit to this process.

HIRE A WEB HOSTING COMPANY

No matter how your site is created it must be "hosted" by some company that has specialized computer equipment designed for the purpose of seeing to it that anyone looking for your web domain name will find it. Virtually all of these hosting companies have simple ways for you to be able to create your own custom website using pre-programmed templates. Truly, even a computer-literate child can do it. You do not need a special ability to write computer code. Just follow very simple instructions.

Two hosting companies many top internet entrepreneurs use are HostGator.com and 1and1.com. Both allow you to create a perfectly functional site, and both have a variety of hosting plans, often with a free trial. Always start off with the least expensive hosting program until you are comfortable with the entire web creation/hosting process. We are talking under $10/month to get started.

There are literally hundreds of web hosting companies out there, and it is critical to your long-term success that you choose your host carefully. There are many variables. Two basic features are important to you: band-with (the amount of traffic you are allocated), and disc space (how much space your website's code occupies).

Do not be misled by companies stating on their website that you have "unlimited" disc space and bandwidth. You do not. How the FTC lets them get away with this blatantly false advertising I have no clue. If you take the time to read the hosts' "Terms and Conditions" you get the true poop. (And you should always read any Terms & Conditions to which you are "Agreeing").

The fact is they give you a lot of disc space and bandwidth, more than you will probably ever need until you become very successful. But once you begin to use more of either than they deem "safe" (your high usage puts others on the server at risk) for the server you are sharing with many others they will shut you down!

If that occurs, they will ask you to place your website on an expensive server dedicated to you alone. If you do have this "problem" it probably means you are making a ton of money anyway, so it isn't the worst thing that can happen. But neither you, nor the host themselves for that matter, has truly "unlimited" anything.

How much "space" do you actually need? Most websites you create won't use even 50 megabytes. Most hosts offer at least a gigabyte (a thousand megabytes). And as far as bandwidth is concerned, to exceed 15 gigabytes, which is below what most hosts offer, you would need an extraordinarily successful site with hundreds of thousand page views. You won't be there for a while.

Some hosts also advertise "unlimited domains", which means for one monthly fee you can set up as many different websites with different domain names as you choose. This is also absurd for the same reasons as unlimited disc space and bandwidth is absurd. But for all practical purposes, though you have nothing that is truly "unlimited", you are quite safe for a long time if you stay within the above space parameters.

To digress for a moment, it is never a good idea to have one single hosting company host more than two of your websites. Crap happens. Companies go out of business. Servers get infected with viruses. Hurricanes and ice storms take out power lines, and back-up generators if present may not provide a complete fix.   Your website is your business, and when it is off line you lose money. You are out of business 100% unless you have part of your business, your other websites, hosted elsewhere. This may seem a bit paranoid, but I have heard so many horror stories that it is clearly a precaution worth taking.

Another reason for having multiple hosts is that links between websites you own, but are hosted separately, count more in the eyes of the search engines. Links between websites at the same web host may be viewed by search engines as "link spamming", which can lower your ranking. This can result in fewer visitors seeing your website.

Pricing is not a big consideration, because most hosting companys' prices are quite competitive with each other. **NEVER** even consider for an instant using a "free" host, and there are many of them out there. **THERE IS NO FREE LUNCH EVER**. You get what you pay for, and "free" in hosting equates to "worthless". When you use a free host you have zero control over anything to do with your site. And they generally OWN your content. It's a rip-off.

At any hosting company you have a choice between shared hosting and dedicated-server hosting, the latter being far more expensive. Shared hosting is fine for your purposes. You could also buy your own server and have a host install it, but why anyone would want to do this is beyond me, though some paranoid folks do.

You may also see a choice between "Linux" and "Microsoft" servers. You want the more versatile Linux servers. You also might prefer a host who provides a "cPanel" for your own website creation. It is a great help in getting your site up and running as quickly as possible.

Do NOT even **bother** to check out "host-review" sites. In some of these, good reviews are literally purchased outright! In others, host company employees and relatives post glowing reports. Conversely, some negative reports you might see are posted by a host's competitors, or by a disgruntled ex-client whose problems probably had nothing to do with the hosting company itself. These sites tell you nothing useful.

It is difficult for you to thoroughly evaluate certain other important hosting factors. These include: ease and speed of contacting customer service; ease of setting up a website (though most have great tools and tutorials); and the size and resulting redundancy of their infrastructure (greater redundancy equals less potential downtime for your websites). This is where recommendations are helpful.

I have personally used many hosts. Even a good host can go sour for any number of business-related reasons. I have found that the most heavily-advertised hosts (the ones you see on TV a lot) are not by any means the best hosts for a variety of reasons. Someone has to pay for all of that expensive advertising. Guess who?!

Take a long comparative look at the following six hosts and decide which you believe best fit your needs. I use some of them, and others come highly recommended by a few serious internet gurus:

Arvixe at: arvixe.com;

HostExcellence at: hostexcellence.com;

LiquidWeb at: liquidweb.com;

HostICan at: hostican.com;

Avahost at: avahost.com;

BlueHost at: bluehost.com (My particular favorite.);

Many of the above have been providing services for a decade or so which tells me they are doing something right. It is also worthy of note that they all have very nice affiliate programs for you to join to earn additional monthly cash. And none of them advertise on TV!

There are three very popular hosting companies that in my opinion have certain shortcomings. I believe they all suffer from "over-popularity". Somehow somewhere someone has to pay for all the media ads. That's you and me. And they have to be cutting corners somewhere to save money.

Just for kicks check out the time it takes to access technical service on a free 800# at the above six. Do the same for the following three (do they even have an 800# direct to service?). Also compare the generosity of affiliate programs. I think you'll see my point:

GoDaddy at: godaddy.com (their website builder almost drove me nuts the one time I tried to use it!)

Host Gator at: hostgator.com;

1 & 1 at: oneandone.com.

Many internet entrepreneurs use these three and seem to do well with them. I'm just more comfortable with the above list of six.

When considering a web host one consideration is the security of your website. Simply having your domain host forward your URL directly to your product sales page allows the raw affiliate link to show in the visitor's browser. This makes it easy for a hijacker to steal your link and thereby steal your commissions. You can, however, see to it that your affiliate link does not show anywhere. The process is called "forwarding and masking".

Forwarding and masking of your affiliate link is available from most, but not all, hosting companies. They can forward raw affiliate links from your domain name direct to your affiliate vendor. For example, godaddy.com has an easy to use "Forward/Mask" facility which completely disguises your affiliate URL throughout the viewing and ordering process. You should always mask your affiliate links.

CREATE YOUR WINNING WEBSITE
We have not yet spoken about how to actually create your own website. This can cost you anywhere from zero to thousands of dollars. Zero is better! The interesting thing

is that the very expensive sites are not necessarily going to bring in any more money than a free or almost-free site.

In fact, a lot of your local website creation specialists, usually college computer-science students, who charge $50/hour or more, don't have a clue how to create the kind of simple "sell something" site you must create to sell your own products. They often try to impress you and your visitors with absolutely self-defeating "bells and whistles" that in reality detract from your goals. While inflating their techie-egos they diminish your profits.

The fact is they are not marketers. They're the geniuses we used to make fun of in school, the pocket-protector beanie-propeller-head types! They love animation and flash and dazzle and are really great at creating this stuff. Simplicity of design sells products. Flash and dazzle distracts. Go simple, period. The hosts mentioned above, Doteasy, Joomla, Drupa, Web and Webs all offer easy site-building capabilities.

No matter how you create your website there are certain elements that you must be certain are present. Some of the < > notation is HTML Code (**H**yper **T**ext **M**arkup **L**anguage") which is used to construct most websites. You will never need to learn to write this code, but a general familiarity is very useful.

"Meta Tags" are keyword-rich code read by search engines to classify your site. Go to: metatags.info/wizard for a free meta tag generator and analyzer.

Include only your main keywords in your page title, the fewer words the better. Use the "/" symbol to separate title words. Use only your main keywords, and "/" in place of filler words;

Use an <h1> header tag with your most important keywords. Be certain to place it as far towards the top left hand side as possible. That is what Google reads first.

Create an <h2> sub-header with different keywords.

Write your copy evenly sprinkling keywords throughout, but not too many. It is reported that 6% maximum by actual word count should be keywords. Bold, italicize or underline some keywords, once each;

Place your main keyword both at the very end lower right of the page. This is best done by putting your <h1> keywords in the copyright footer: ©2012 (your URL) (your keywords) If you have a graphic header at the top of the page Use an <alt> image tag. The HTML code would look similar to the following: <img src="(your graphic.jpg)" width="503" height="93" alt=("your keywords")>.

Consider changing the overall width of your website by making the white-space reading-area narrow (see love-poems-love-poems.com for an example of this format.) Many internet entrepreneurs selling their own products are going to this format, no side columns, just straight-forward easy to read text "down the middle".

Be sure to put navigation bars at the top and bottom of every page so that your visitor need not go back to your homepage to find another page they want to access.

In using color, keep to the theme. For example green for golf or gardening, perhaps pink and blue for a parenting site.

An important part of Google's rankings algorithm relates to your landing page, to which they assign a "Quality Score", or "QS". For starters, your pay-per-click (PPC) ad keywords must tie-in exactly with the landing page keywords. To obtain a high QS you must follow the guidelines below. There are "keyword hot-spots" that must be optimized. The keyword hotspots are: **domain name; title tag; headline; sub-headline; within the text; behind images; descriptions and keyword meta-tags; and a "sitemap".**

Domain: Best choice is: (your primary keyword).com
Next best: (your primary keyword).any relevant URL.com
Least best: any relevant URL.com/(your keyword)

Title tag: This is a simple piece of HTML code located at the very top of your webpage. The code looks like this:<title>(keyword-rich description)</title>. Google allows 70 characters, Yahoo 115. If possible, put the keywords in alphabetical order which actually has a small effect on rankings.

Headline & Sub-headline: You need to put a bit of HTML code around your headline and sub-headline. <h1> is for the headline, <h2> for the sub-headline. Thus: <h1>(keyword rich headline)</h1> , and for the sub-headline: <h2>(keyword-rich sub-headline)</h2>. You can use <h3> tags around any other less critical subheads used throughout the body text.

Content: You need keywords specifically in the first and last paragraphs, and a bit between, By actual count of words vs keywords you should be shooting for between 4% and 6% keyword density. More than that and Google will penalize you for keyword-spamming. And it is best to stick to only two or three of your optimum keywords.

Behind images: I'm not particularly fond of having any images at all, because they slow your download time. If you choose to use one or two, note that many webmasters overlook doing this. When you do, it gives the spider-bots even more keywords to help your rankings.

Normally, your image would show: <img src= "image .jpg" height="120" width="476">. This gives position and size, but nothing for a bot to index. You need to add an <alt> tag within this code. Your final code should read: <img src= "image .jpg" **alt="your keywords"** height="120"width="476">.

Description meta tags & keyword meta tags: Meta tags are background HTML that tells the indexing spider-bots what your page is all about. They should be positioned just below the title tag. They look like this: <meta name ="description" content=**"your full description">**. "Your full description" is the text included in your search results listing.

Directly below that is your keyword meta tag. This would look like: <meta name="keyword" content=**"your primary three keywords">**.
Separate your keywords with a comma.

There is no solid agreement that meta tags are any help in rankings. Search engines change their ranking algorithms so often that trying to out-guess them is futile. You certainly will not be penalized for using them.

Sitemap: You simply must have an "xml code" sitemap. Without one the indexing spider-bots may never see all of your pages. Bots need a trail to follow, and the site map provides it. At the bottom of every page of your website every page will be just two clicks away from each other. It makes the search engines happy. Google even helps you to build an XML sitemap. Enter your URL at: google.com/webmasters/sitemaps. Google will create a sitemap for you that you can simply paste into your website. You can also use snapsitemap.com.

Your visitors also need to have links from every page on your site to every other page. These are links created when you build your website, not the special XML sitemap created by Google. If you are using the WordPress blogging platform for your website there is a great Google plug-in available to automatically create your website sitemap mentioned above.

It also helps to put in links to .org and .edu authority sites related to your niche. Announce these on a page titled: "Other Resources". Google loves links to non-profit sites.

Following these rules will give you a website that is as friendly to Google's spiders (the electronic robots that find and classify your site) as it can be. Never lose sight of the fact that it is your Off-Site linking strategy (press releases, articles, blogs, etc.) that will ultimately determine your search engine positioning. This will be discussed in detail elsewhere in this book.

In creating a website do not forget about your secondary pages, which can rank as well as your main index.html page. Do NOT repeat the keywords on your index.html <title> tag on your secondary page <title> tags.

Do NOT use your URL in your <title> tags. If you MUST, place it at the END of the title tag. Use as many different keywords as you have without exceeding the 6% rule mentioned above.
It is virtually impossible to keep up with Google's site-ranking algorithm changes. An almost total flip-flop occurred recently when it was reported that what counts most now is the immediate availability to a viewer of relevant information. Ads should now appear somewhere below this content. This is definitely worth at least a split-test.

Using the tools available at your host's website all of the above website creation happens without any HTML code input on your part. Just follow the step by step instructions they provide. You should familiarize yourself with HTML code. Note I did not say "learn". To see the complete HTML code used to create any website go to that site and the click on "View" in your browser menu bar. Then select "Source" or "View Source" from the drop-down choices. For example, the Title Tag will appear at the top inside the <head></head> tags. It is all pretty logical when you look at it a while.

Aside from the programs provided by web hosts there are many on-line tools available for you to use to create your websites. For example, BlueVoda.com has an easy to use website creation program. They claim four-million downloads of the program. You can't beat the price…it's FREE! "Build Your Website In Thirty Minutes" is their claim. The one problem I have with it is that you must use them alone as your web host.

Another site worth visiting is **wix.com**. They offer an intuitive video tutorial.

Excitepro.com is a $147 website building program with a 30-day money-back guarantee. Worth a try.

You can also find good website creation templates at the following:
Freewebsitetemplates.com; Freewebtemplatews.com; Freesitetemplates.com; Templatesbox.com/templates.htm.

Be certain to carefully read the Terms and Conditions of any of the above, because some may not allow you to use their templates for commercial purposes.

A big plus in the eyes of search engines is the use of video on your website. This is not as difficult as it might seem intuitively. Many newbies shy away from putting audio and video on their websites. In fact, adding these could make your site load more slowly than you might like. If you are familiar with YouTube, you can put YouTube videos directly on to your website. Go to: dvdvideosoft.com. Linking to YouTube videos is simple. Try using instantvideositecreator.com, or instantvideosites.net.

For using audio recordings, check out byoaudio.com. Always use a decent microphone for creating your .wav audio files. For as little as $33 you can purchase the "Blue Microphones Snowflake" on line. If cost is no object you can blow $170 on Marshall Electronics "MXL Studio 24 USB". I find that an inexpensive microphone is fine.

ANALYTICS

Want to know who visits your website, where they came from and what they are looking for? Starting at $69/month visistat.com (and many others) will be happy to provide you with that information. Do you need this sort of intelligence when starting out? Is it useful? Absolutely. Necessary, not. There will be plenty of time for that sort of information once you are earning enough money that it no longer matters as an investment.

There are many programs that you can employ to analyze the effectiveness of different elements of your website. Listed alphabetically, you might consider:

ADOBE TEST AND TARGET: This is found within the Adobe Digital Marketing Suite. Rather complex, but allows you to design tests and target content.

AMADESA at amadesa.com: With its "Pick The Winner" technology you can test various combinations of page elements.

GLOBALMAXER at globalmaxer.com: Allows you to test various combinations of page elements.

GOOGLE: Their "Site Optimizer" also allows you to test combinations of page elements indicating which combinations should lead to the highest conversion rates.

MAXYMISER at maximiser.com: Customers offer feedback that can help you increase your conversion rates.

MONETATE at monetate.com: This software creates a control group for every one of your campaigns and allows comparisons of key metrics.

OFFER MAXIMA at officemaxima.com: Allows you to test and optimize various website designs, ads, and marketing campaigns.

SITECORE at sitecore.net: With its in-line editing interface you can compare your entire site or any individual page within your site for split-testing.

SITESPECT at sitespect.com: Fast to apply and evaluate results, you can test a number of changes simultaneously.

VERTSTER at vertster.com: Allows you to test unlimited numbers of page designs simultaneously!

WEBTRENDS at webtrends.com: Offers a step-wise approach of general testing against all traffic followed by a tightly focused approach.

You may also eventually want to study how your visitors actually view your site. Check out: crazyegg.com; clicktale.com and pagealizer.com. You can also Google-search for "Website Analytics Programs" from which you can determine anything imaginable about your website traffic. There are many from which to choose.

PRICING YOUR PRODUCT

Now let's talk about how you decide on a selling price for your report or book. For starters, look at what is being sold by other internet marketers within your niche. Research is your principal ally in all of your internet endeavors, but especially in pricing. See what the competition is charging for similar information.

Go to their sales pages and see what they are offering and for what price. If possible actually buy the product and see if you feel it is worth the asking price. Then you must decide whether to create and offer a better product at around the same price, or a better price for a very similar product, or something in between. Perhaps you can offer better or more bonuses.

I will re-emphasize a helpful hint that has stood the test of marketing time since the early days of mail order shopping: <u>ALWAYS END YOUR SELLING PRICE WITH A "7".</u>   Your price is $3.97 not $3.99. It is $9.97 not $9.99. It's $49.97 ont $49.99 and certainly not $50.00. There seem to be countless internet "how to get rich" products out there priced at either $9<u>7</u>.00 or $19<u>7</u>.00. Training courses are usually $99<u>7</u>.00.

I have split-tested on a number of occasions and have proven to myself that this conventional "end in a 7" wisdom is real. (It's origin is reportedly *Life Magazine's* original subscription price of $7.77).

If you are ever quoting provable earnings, always provide exact figures, such as "$7,356.27". Saying: "I earned $7,356.97 last month" is perceived by readers as far more credible than " I earned $7,400.00 last month".

GETTING TRAFFIC

Once you have your site created, and are making money with it, you can **explode** your business by having your **own** team of affiliates sending buyers to **your** website. You will need to help your affiliates as much as possible by giving them all sorts of advertising copy for their use in their marketing of your website.

There are many software products available to help you create affiliate materials packages. There is other software that enables you to track your affiliates and automatically pay them their commissions.   Here again, simple Google searches for "create an affiliate offer package" and "affiliate tracking software"   will give you a variety of products you can purchase and utilize.

Your website, which the visitor is directed to by your advertising or by links posted in various places, should have a few short relevant articles on-topic. It will also have an email-collection form. (This is known as your "squeeze page" because it is designed to squeeze information out of your visitor). If you give the visitor a reason to give you their email address (free report, newsletter, or whatever) they often will. If they choose not to do so they can decline with a mouse click and then hopefully click over to your report or ebook offer or to a commission-earning affiliate link.

Creating your own products and marketing them with your own unique website takes a good bit work. It is not the easiest way to earn internet income. **That** distinction goes to "Affiliate Marketing". Promoting affiliates is by far the easiest way to make fast internet money. Chapter 10 covers Affiliate Marketing in detail.

Most affiliate commission payouts are relatively small compared to what you can charge for your very own products on your very own website. Most highly successful internet entrepreneurs make the bulk of their money from their own websites selling their own virtual .pdf file-downloadable books and reports.

But you can have your own-product website and also do affiliate marketing from it. You can still have a squeeze page to gather those valuable email addresses, the individuals you can sell to in the future.

As with using a squeeze page on a website selling your only your own products, if the visitor chooses not to provide you their email address they can decline with a click and then hopefully click over to your affiliate's offer. If your affiliate does a good job on their website the visitor will provide them with some personal data. This data can be as simple as an email address, all the way up to name, address and telephone number, and even better, an actual purchase. You get a commission that is based in general on the depth of information collected.

Another technique some infopreneurs use to attract visitors is offering polling opportunities on any imaginable topic. People love to tell their opinion and "stand up and be counted". They love polls. Check out misterpoll.com, micropoll.com and surveymonkey.com.

CONSIDER A MEMBERSHIP SITE

There is yet another great way to make income from your own website. By far the most potentially profitable business model is one where you achieve a periodically-recurring income. Give me just 500 loyal customers each paying me a mere $10.00 a month, every month, and I've pocketed $60,000 a year! Now suppose I have three such income streams. Just do the math!

The best answer to this profit model is to create a "Membership Site". You
find a customer once and they continuously send you money automatically! Is this simple? Well, not really. Is it worth the effort? Hell yes!

A membership site has great perceived value. Instantly downloaded .pdf books do not. If you have created a good book you can easily break it up into many pieces to offer periodically. The sequential chapters, sent to members weekly, monthly, or whatever (through autoresponder pre-programming – see aweber.com) for a fixed subscription rate, can earn you far more money than the individual .pdf book ever could.

It also keeps you in constant contact with your clients, so you can offer related products every so often "available exclusively to my subscribers", as well as providing the occasional freebie. Just to get started with a Membership Site takes a good bit of effort. You need to stockpile twenty or so good pieces of original content. You need to set up a forum. You need to create the website, and offer a library of freebies. No small task.

You need to set up your site to manage customers' passwords, and to prohibit continued membership of those who fail to pay or opt out. And drop out they do, regardless of the quality of your posts. After a while, with no end in sight, people apparently get bored or indifferent.

Therefore it is a constant battle to retain members and make up for those who depart. You need to continually create new material, no small task in itself. Overall, just managing the membership site can be very time consuming.

But there **is** a way that can be accomplished quickly and requires very little maintenance, and no password-related software. This way is to create fixed-term memberships. All you need to accomplish this is a website and sales letter, an autoresponder, and a recurring-billing processor such as PayPal.

Your minimal costs involved are buying your domain name, hosting it, and having an autoresponder do all the work. If you cannot write, then add the cost of outsourcing your writing. No need to buy costly membership-site/password-enabled software.

Let's say you have a twenty-week program, which can be twenty chapters of your book. You pre-write twenty content-rich articles and load them into your autoresponder. The end of each article should be something of a "cliffhanger". Your customer just can't wait to see the next installment. There is a definite, unambiguous "finishing line" that they will likely stay the course to reach.

Members are far more likely to hang around the program than with a traditional no-finish-line membership site. They know they will "complete" the series and then no longer have to pay. The closer they get to the end the more "I'm almost there, so I'll stick it out" comes into the picture. Done correctly most members will continue to the very last installment.

You can offer a three to five page "Weekly Lesson" in downloadable .pdf format. There will be specific "homework" to be completed before the next lesson. Everything short and concise and building to some short-range and final conclusions. Your autoresponder takes care of everything.

Create scarcity in your membership site sales letter. Set a limit to the number of members you will "accept" and stick to it. Something between 1,000 and 2,000 is a good limit, and either $7.00/month or $17.00/month is a realistic price (though I've seen some a lot higher). Advertise the membership as you would any other product.

Remember, once you have loaded your autoresponder all you have to do is get visitors to your website. Once there you get their attention with a killer headline inducing them to read a convincing sales letter and then subscribe to your program. You drive traffic to the website in all of the ways, free and paid, that I've shared with you elsewhere in this book. Once this is all set up it runs itself! You just sit back and count your monthly income!

There is a wealth of software available for creating and managing a membership site. Consider: amember.com; membee.com; yourmembership.com; memberclicks.com; memberzone.com. I suggest you check out each of these to decide which one looks best for you to use.

THE MINI-SITE

There is a type of website known as a mini-site that can be a maxi-profit-center! A "mini-site" is a one-page website comprising a headline, sub-headline, a one-product sales letter, and an action button. Alternately, they can also be set up to have a few very short niche-focused articles and a few Google AdSense ads. They are quick to make, a few hours at most, simple to construct, and makes sales and list-building very fast. Because they are so easy to create some internet marketers have a hundred or more mini-sites, each earning a few dollars a day. Do the math. This can create a huge income over time.

Just find any popular niche. Go to: google.com and search "Google Keyword Tool External". Key in subjects that interest you. Google will provide you with suggested keywords and phrases. Chose keywords and phrases that have a minimum number of sites competing against you for those keyword phrases (called "long-tail keywords"). To determine this figure, just enter the different keywords and phrases between parentheses "xxxx" at google.com. The number of sites competing for those keywords appears at the top. Anything under 25,000 is a winner (for common terms the figure will be in the millions!)

Find a matching product at amazon.com or clickbank.com or Google AdSense. Then write, buy, have ghostwritten (fiverr.com is best for this), use public domain, or get a private label product, of at least three short (300 words is fine) keyword-rich articles.
Create a landing page, or squeeze page if you want to try to create a mailing list. On a squeeze page you offer

some incentive, a free report, newsletter, etc., in exchange for a visitor's email address.

One very effective technique used by experienced internet marketers is to focus on actual products and brand names. (You need to be certain that you can actually use these product names on your website. Check the affiliate's "Terms and Conditions" to be sure.) Then in parenthesis in a search engine enter your product preceded by the word "buy": "buy [your exact product name]". You want to find product names that are searched for thousands of times every week. Then see how many, as explained above, people are competing against you, the fewer the better.

Become an amazon.com associate (what they call an affiliate) find the link to your chosen product, and see if it has a really large image link for you to place on your website, the larger the better.

One quick and easy strategy is to buy a domain name based solely on an affiliate product's key words. Then create a simple one-page site with keyword-rich content and add the affiliate link. Nothing else. Then drive traffic with PPC and/ or article marketing. Sit back, and collect commissions!

One good place to access simple, easily created mini-site templates is:
diyminisite.com.

Landing pages designed specifically for that one device will need to be created alongside the landing pages created for desktop and laptop computers. I am not aware of any internet marketer who has totally solved this problem. My only advice to you is to create some VERY simple landing pages and VERY simple calls to action. This may be the year of the mini-mini-site!

THE BLOGGING PLATFORM WEBSITE

One way of making the mini-site work is using Google's free blogging platform at: blogger.com. Click on the button to start a free blog, chose a template, and strip it totally bare, all white. Then open the "html editor" and paste in your large Amazon image link at the top in the middle.

At your blogger.com account create a few short articles, referring to the exact product several times by name and brand, preceded by the word "buy". You can "swipe" the wording from the Amazon information about the product, but be certain to rearrange the wording as much as possible.

Remember, by using Blogger you are using a Google product, and they really prefer this and it greatly helps your search engine ranking. They like it even better if you make a new blog post to your site at least once a week. They reward changing content.

A popular alternative is to create your website at wordpress.com.

One way to find places to post comments is by using the free software "Blog Commentor Lite". A Google search will provide a number of places from which to download this software.

Try creating a few niche-focused mini-sites, and when you see the results you can obtain with relative ease you run the risk of becoming a mini-site addict! It's fun and profitable.

GETTING GOOGLE TO FIND AND INDEX YOUR SITE QUICKLY

Using Google AdWords pay per click advertising, or using Google's Blogger platform, will get your site indexed quickly. But if you choose to do neither you can still get indexed quickly.....for a price.

The Google website has a form on it for you to fill out that is meant to tell Google that your website exists. **NEVER** fill out this form! If you do that and nothing else it will take four to six weeks for them to index your site. This is also true about the forms found on other search engines.

There is, however, a way to get indexed in 24 hours! You simply purchase a backlink from a Page Rank 7 website. This can often be rented for a month for under $200. Once you are indexed you can cancel the link. Is it worth it? Perhaps. What is six weeks of potential traffic worth to you? Hard to say.

There are companies who broker backlinks. Check out:

Text Link Brokers at: textlinkbrokers.com
Link Adage at: linkadage.com
Text-Link-Ads at: text-link-ads.com

Somewhere **FAR** down the road if you can create a website that earns itself a Page Rank of 6 or 7 you can make a lot of extra money by selling or renting your backlinks to others! This is just another of the many possible multiple streams of internet income available to you down the road.

MAKING EVERYTHING WORK RIGHT

You must periodically check the viability of every link on your websites. This includes the internal links from your sitemap, page to page, links to other websites, the links to your order page, links to blogs and social sites, and all affiliate links. Website links do break occasionally, for reasons known only to computer geeks and God. Maybe only God!

If you have only one or two websites you can easily do this yourself every week or so. You can pay a local college kid to do it, or enlist one of your own kids. If you have ten, or fifty or more websites, which you might very well eventually have (I have well over 300) you can also pay professionals to do it for you. Google "Website Monitoring Services" and you will find many. Check out internetsupervision.com. They will monitor a single site for FREE, multiple sites for a modest monthly fee.

AVOIDING FAKE VISITORS

At some point in time you may encounter a problem with computer generated "visitors" trying to join your list or access your information or fill out some form on your website for nefarious reasons of their own. As you surf the web you will come upon many websites that have solved this problem with a type of "challenge-response" test called "CAPTCHA".

This is a short acronym for the rather cumbersome: "Completely Automated Public Turing test to tell Computers and Humans Apart". It consists of a line of text contorted in a way that a human can read and copy it (barely) but a computer-robot cannot. Free CAPTCHA plugins are available at: captcha.net.

STUDYING THE COMPETITION

You can let your competition show you exactly what you must do to create a website that will rank higher in the search engines than theirs!   It takes a bit of work, but the results should be positive. Every website is created using a programming language called HTML. When you create your website using your web host's simplified "click here" WYSIWYG" (Pronounced "whizzeewig" , What You See Is What You Get) site creation tool, the resulting website is created in HTML even though you didn't write a word of the code yourself.

You can actually view the exact codes used for your website, or for any competitor's website, by viewing the "source code". In your browser where you see: File>Edit >View Favorites >Tools >Help. Click on "View". From the drop-down menu choose "Source". As if by magic the entire HTML code for the site in question is displayed! Now by looking at the code you can tell whether your prime competitor, the one in the top position, is actually building his website optimally. This is called "On Page Optimization".

Look for a number of key things that you can do better than they did to better optimize your website and be on your way to having it rated higher than theirs by the search engines. Check to see:

Are they using an <h1> header tag?

If they are using a header tag, are they placing their keywords in the tag?

Are they using an <h2> sub-title tag?

If they are using an <h2> tag does it contain keywords?

Are they using their main keyword in the <title> tag?

Are there any images?

If there are images, are they using <alt> image tags including "(keyword) image"?

Have they bolded (or italicized or underlined) their keywords anywhere within the body text copy?

Have they placed their keyword one time at the beginning of their copy?

Have they placed their keyword one time at the end of their copy?

Did they include keywords in the copyright "©" footer?

Have they achieved Google PageRank 4 or higher?

If your competitor has not done any one or more of the above, just be certain that you do and it will go a long way to ranking higher. But do not lose site of the fact that, no matter how well you do your on-line optimizing, it is ultimately your off-line optimizing that will determines your search engine ranking.

This is where your SEO, **S**earch **E**ngine **O**ptimization, comes into play. Creating backlinks to your website through a variety of techniques is the #1 means of getting high search engine results.

WHAT ABOUT TARGETING OVERSEAS MARKETS?

It has been reported that only a bit over 50% of all online content is in English. I find this a bit startling. Even more significant for your future marketing efforts is the fact that, according to a study by Smartling, 90% of all web users live **outside** of English-Speaking countries. With a billion or so new internet users added every four years, it is pretty obvious that translating websites and books into other major languages is almost a necessity even today.

When you are beginning your internet marketing adventure, focusing on English speaking countries is all you need to do. Somewhere done the road if you want your entire website, or some article or book, translated into a foreign language, you have two choices.

The correct way is to hire a professional translator. This can be very expensive, but with your guidance it can create an end result that will offer a satisfactory experience for your overseas visitor. As with other outsourcing, you can use elance.com and rentacoder.com. My favorite is fiverr.com, which has dozens of translators eager to work for five bucks a pop! Go to fiverr.com and enter "(language) translations" in the search box. The primary language to consider is Spanish, followed by French, German and Italian. Virtually every person in the developed world speaks at least one and more likely two or three of these. That is, except most Americans who struggle mightily with English!

Keeping everything in American vernacular English is fine for sales to American customers, as well as Canadians, Kiwis, and Aussies. In fact, you will find that many Europeans will buy English-language books as well. Somewhere down the road, however, you should at least experiment with foreign-language books and websites.

The **wrong** way, in my never-humble opinion, is to use one of the on-line translation programs that are available. You can TRY: translator.go.com; dictionary.com/translate/; voila.com/services/translate/.

If nothing else reading your poorly-translated site creates great comic relief for your overseas visitors! You never know. You just might make a sale or two out of pity. Mostly you will just look as an idiot.

THE NEW WORLD OF MOBILE READING DEVICES

Every day an increasing amount of web commerce is completed from mobile devices. Because mobile devices enjoy a very wide variety of different screen sizes, resolutions, operating systems, memory and processors it is a huge challenge to design a website, mini or otherwise, that will be fully functional for every mobile device. You need to determine which one device is most popular with the visitors you hope to attract and optimize websites for that one device.

Today it is reported that thirty percent of all web surfing, and an unknown amount of web buying, is done on mobile devices, cell phones, Blackberries, Androids, and the like. These devices cannot at present process data at anywhere close to the rate that today's laptops and desktops can. Because of this, conventional websites, with their complex re-directs and fancy computer codes simply take far too long to download on tiny portable devices. We are in an age of "instant gratification". Very few will wait even thirty seconds for a website to download for them to part with their money. The challenge is to create relevant content, offer a product and the means for someone to pay for it, and then to deliver it, all within, say, thirty seconds (as can be accomplished on a desktop computer).

The solution today is creating Responsive Web Design (RWD). It enables websites to adapt to the differences in screen sizes between personal desktop and laptop computers, tablet readers, and smartphones. Website Magazine August 2012 offers the technical coding steps to accomplish this using "CSS" that is beyond the scope and intent of this book.

I suggest you visit the following sites relative to studying mobile device websites: Mobilestorm.com; mobify.com; dudamobile.com; usablenet.com; jumptap.com; flurry.com; wakanda.org; localytics.com.

Having your own website gathering email addresses and selling your own products one at a time or periodically is the classic business model that has made more internet entrepreneur millionaires than any other. It may not be the easiest of the multiple streams of internet income to establish, but it is a sound, long-term business model that can create an enormous residual income for life.

CHAPTER 16
LANDING PAGE MAGIC

So you've acquired your domain name, and decided on a hosting company. You now have at your disposal a host of website creation tools, and a wealth of instructions on how to proceed. But proceed to where? And for what end?

The two basic parts of your website are the **landing page**, and the **sales letter. The landing page is the first page of your sales letter.** It is the foundation upon which all of your book or report sales or affiliate selling efforts rest. Without a killer landing page your internet marketing efforts are zilch. You won't make a dime.

YOUR LANDING PAGE

Once you have your keyword list segmented you have a decision to make. Your choice is "direct linking" or "landing page". In affiliate marketing you do not need to have a website ever. Linking to your vendor's website directly from your ad is quick and easy. It does, however, have some negatives.

First of all, in the long run having a double-opt-in mailing list is one key to success in internet marketing. With direct linking you have no way to achieve this. Even more important is Google's "one-URL" rule. If two or more affiliates are direct linking only one ad will be displayed based primarily on which bidder is paying the highest price. This results in a bidding war that no one wins.

Lastly, some vendors will not even permit direct linking. Because of all of these negatives, I recommend that you ONLY go the landing-page route.

Here again, you have two choices. You can create a short landing page with an opt-in freebie offer and perhaps three short articles relating to the best keywords, OR, you can create a full-blown search-engine-optimized website.

The shorter landing page is the way to go for any newbie because it is easy to create, and takes little time to get up and running. On the other hand, a true website is a valuable property that can be sold at some future time for a substantial sum. Such a site also gives you the option of running other ads (both AdSense and contextual), and getting free traffic through high search engine positioning.

There is only ONE purpose of a landing page. **It is to pre-sell your visitor to click on your affiliate link and do what you want them to do when they finally reach the vendor destination.** Any tiny little thing that distracts your visitor from that one single goal can kill your conversions.

It is nice to have an attractive landing page, with pleasant colors and readable type fonts. But the prettiest website ever created is worthless unless it has two basic factors: **Extreme clarity, and relevance.**

The very instant your visitor "lands" it must be **instantly** clear to them what the site is all about. Instantly. No thought required. No exception.

Once they decide to stay (a decision which takes which takes about a mili-second) they must be exposed to nothing but relevant content. Your text must closely replicate your ad copy and the keywords your visitor used to get there.

CREATING THE LANDING PAGE FRAMEWORK

Back in the "old days" creating a website was a giant pain. Either you learned to write computer code, or you purchased one of two available expensive software programs. The learning curve for any of these three choices was pretty steep, so most of us just hired a college computer geek to make us a website. Unfortunately all these kids knew how to do was create odd-looking, flashy, totally non-commercial sites.

The actual mechanics of building a landing page today is greatly simplified by the availability of many different totally-intuitive website-building programs. Every web host provides one for FREE. All one needs to know is what is desired to appear on the site, type it out in plain English in any word processor (e.g., Microsoft Word) and upload to the host server.

There are two basic types of landing pages, the direct sale, and the review-comparison. The direct sale has always worked well for me, and it is a lot easier to create. You must write compelling copy articulating the benefits of the product. Then you send the visitor to the vendor's website.

If you can write very compelling copy, send them directly to the vendor's order page. If you believe that the vendor does a great job on their sales page, and your blurb is not as strong, send them there.

The other type of landing page is the review site. You present comparisons, the great benefits and the lesser benefits and some minor deficiency of each.

You must be an affiliate of each of the three, so that no matter which one the visitor chooses you earn a commission if the vendor's site converts. One can look at this as what is known in Marketing 101 as an "assumptive close". "Sir or madam, do you want the red one or the green one?" People love to make choices, especially if your comparisons are believable.

WHAT GOES ON THE LANDING PAGE? AND WHERE?

For starters, it has been tested and confirmed that most visitors will spend ten seconds maximum at a site. For this reason alone ALL of the critical copy needs to be ABOVE THE FOLD. This is the point where a visitor must begin to scroll down, analogous to the bottom portion of a folded newspaper. Three key elements go above the fold:

A strong headline containing the major benefit;

A summary, which can be bullet points explaining what the offer is all about. If appropriate a small image off to the left can be useful;

A call to action in the form of a big green "Click Here To Order" or "Sign Up Now" button. One above the fold and one below is appropriate. Other buttons that might be appropriate depending on your offer: "Click Here Now"; "Search Now"; "Click Here To Discover More"; "Visit Site Now"; "Click Here For More Info".

Your headline is critical. A strong headline puts the visitor in a buying mood. Matching your headline to your Google ad works very well because they already clicked on your (hopefully) killer ad to get to your headline! You need to present the biggest benefit at a 3rd grade reading level. The benefit is the visitor's net positive result from buying the product. If necessary, the headline can be three or four lines long.

Your summary copy must be benefit oriented. It should be short and to the point. It should be benefit, benefit, benefit. The higher priced an offer the longer the copy should be. Very short copy is appropriate if the vendor is only going to be asking for a name and email address. Other short copy could be your headline followed by bullet points. In any event, keep any paragraph to three or four lines maximum.

If your vendor has won any special recognition be certain to show this above the fold as well.

Never make the visitor scroll down to figure out what your site is all about. You must be certain everything important falls above the fold for the common screen resolutions: 640x480; 800x600; and 1024x768. You can check this out at browsershots.org. You only need to be concerned about versions of InternetExplorer, Firefox, and Google Chrome, though you can also check out about fifteen other lesser-known browsers.

Your call to action can be the big green button described above. It can also be buried within your text inside of a benefit statement. For example:

Click HERE to (benefit, benefit, benefit);
Order Now to (benefit, benefit, benefit);
Secure your copy NOW so that (benefit, benefit, benefit).

All links should be in the normal "link blue" which turns to "purplish" when clicked. Having a link near the top, in the middle, and just before the fold is best.

Below the fold is extremely important space. Here you will mention some features associated with benefits. A visitor usually will only browse this. At the bottom of the first page you MUST have links to four additional pages pages. (You will create these pages one time and use them for all of your offers.) These pages are: "Privacy Policy", "About Us", and "Contact Us".

In addition, to make Google happy, be sure to include a "site map" that links every page to every other page for the benefit of their spider-bots and to enhance your quality score. To make them even happier, include another page called a "Resource Page". This will contain a list of .org and .edu sites that relate to your niche.

No matter which of the two basic types of landing pages you choose, you should consider an opt-in choice for the visitor to exchange their first name and email address in for some freebie you offer. The freebie should be a relevant report or course or newsletter, and should have high perceived value.

Two features are important: a "No Thanks" button that immediately makes the opt-in box disappear and a statement at the bottom that says: "We respect your privacy and never sell OR share your email address with anyone".

The "sales letter" is the body of your " landing page" and it can be a page or two, or well over a hundred pages! We'll explain all of that later on in Chapter 13.

Let's first look at a landing page for an affiliate program. **The sole purpose of this landing page is to pre-sell your visitor to click on your affiliate link so you have a chance to earn an affiliate commission.** You must focus your landing page on this one goal. Nothing on the page should distract your visitor from taking **that one action.**

You need two qualities on your landing page, **clarity and relevance.** The instant your visitor sees your landing page it must be abundantly clear what the page is about. All content on this page must be directly relevant and focused on the single goal of getting the visitor to click on your affiliate link.

There are three general types of landing pages depending upon what action you want your visitor to take:

The single-product **direct sales site page**. This pre-sells one affiliate offer and links the visitor either to the affiliate's website or directly to the merchant's order page. (Make it original. Do NOT copy the affiliate's website material. Google hates that.)

Review page. Here you provide the visitor with a detailed review of several different related-type products, with ayouraffiliate link to each.

The opt-in page also known as a "squeeze page". Here you offer the visitor some freebie such as a relevant special report or free ezine (email newsletter) subscription in exchange for the visitor's email address. This is in conjunction with either the direct sales page or the review page. This is how you create a mailing list for future marketing to that visitor. In general it will not detract from the visitor from clicking over to the affiliate because if they can easily decline the opt-in by simply hitting: "No Thanks".

It is always a good idea to check what other affiliate marketers in your niche are doing. Don't copy them, but try to learn from them. There are various ways to identify affiliate's sites. You will find that review sites are almost always affiliate sites as opposed to a merchant selling their own product. Most affiliate direct-sales sites are just one to a few pages.

And most affiliate links have a domain name that has lots of dashes (-- ---) or weird symbols (e.g., "??hop=abc" or "?aff=xyz?"), things like that after the primary domain name. Though many affiliate marketers foolishly do not go to the trouble of doing so, you can shorten any long link with special software provided by companies such as: shorturl.com;   budurl.com ; ittybittyurl.com; and littleurl.com;

There is one school of thought that says visitors are much more likely to click on a shortened URL. I have found that to be true. It is worth doing a a split-test somewhere down the road. (That's a test with parallel identical sites. One with the long affiliate-generated URL and the other with the shortened one.

ALWAYS keep all of the critical elements of the landing page "above the fold". Check that this proves to be true for your website at all common screen resolutions used by your visitors: 640x480, 800x600, and 1024x768. This is the part of the landing page a visitor sees **before** he has to scroll down. Then be certain to:

Have a very strong headline that addresses the major BENEFIT of the product. (Capitalize the initial letter of each word only.) This is by far the most important element of your landing page. Try to match the headline exactly with your Google ad headline.

Have a brief summary ABOVE THE FOLD. You want the visitor to see your headline and summary at the same time. explains the offer's benefits.

Keep all paragraphs short, four to five lines at most. Make the first paragraph the strongest because it is probably the only one the visitor will actually read. The less expensive the product generally the shorter the copy needs to be.

Consider using bullet points for clarity, as I am writing here.

Have a CALL TO ACTION. A "Sign Up", "Click Here NOW!", "Click For More Info", "Visit Site Now" or any equivalent button must be clearly visible. For whatever deep psychological reason it has been found that a GREEN button converts better.

Have three such buttons: one above the fold, one in the middle, one at the end.

If appropriate a small image of a major benefit of the product is useful. Have links at the bottom of the page to your "Privacy Policy", "About Us", and "Contact Us". Google also wants to see a "site map" page with links to all of your other pages.

If your affiliate vendor has won any awards, has strong testimonials, and/or a 100% guarantee ask them whether you can use these on your landing page.

It is important that the landing page be as readable as possible. Follow these guidelines. Simple is best. <u>Pretty and cutesy and colorful sucks.</u>

Use only a sans-serif type (sans="without" the little tips on letters such as the "T" in Times New Roman, as opposed to the "T" in Ariel).

A font size of 12 is easiest to read. Use font size 10 if you need some additional space.

Black text on white. Period.

Keep columns to a maximum of 60 characters across.

Preferably use a single column.

Always use the familiar BLUE underlining of your text links. And make certain it turns purple once it is clicked on.

Use larger font, **BOLD** for text links.

When placing ads on your landing page, it is a good idea to follow the advice that has been derived by studies of site-visitor habits. For instance, top right above the navigation bar; and lower right at the bottom, are considered the worst ad locations. Anything top left and center above the nav bar; right along your content, and lower left along the bottom is acceptable.

Better though are the upper right, a center space below the nav bar, and the bottom center. The prime real estate is considered the center above your content but below the ad directly under nav bar.

It is very advantageous to have social site media sharing buttons on your landing page. If someone buys your offer you should invite them to share your content with their Facebook friends and Twitter followers, their LinkedIn connections, and any other social sites where you have established a presence. You can use the "official" icons, or you can create your own including some message pertaining to why they should visit your social site.

Linking to social media is an especially valuable t echnique if you are short on testimonials but have a large following on some social site. This is a way to instill confidence in a hesitant visitor.

Overall, don't try to reinvent the wheel. The above general rules are followed almost to the letter by every successful internet entrepreneur I know.

JUST DO IT!

CHAPTER 17
KILLER HEADLINES FOR VISITOR ATTENTION

The secret to a successful ad is the **headline**. It is reported that studies show you have **three seconds maximum** to keep a visitor sufficiently interested in your ad to actually read it! If the headline fails to get attention, no matter how well-crafted your ad might be it is useless unless your visitors actually read it.

It is also reported that **five times** as many visitors will read your headline as will read your copy. The headline is the ad for your sales letter that follows. In general longer headlines are known to out-pull short ones.

To be successful your website must address four competitive aspects: **PRICE, QUALITY, SERVICE ,** and **EXCLUSIVITY**. Buying your product is their best bet, perhaps ONLY bet, to getting what they want. You promise this, plus quick results, in the **headline.**

An effective headline forces your potential customer to learn more. It must instantly ignite an emotion that fascinates them into reading what follows. It must address one or more of **five very basic human needs**. It has to make it difficult for the prospect to ignore what follows. If the headline fails to get attention, you are wasting your time and money. These five basic needs are listed below in order of importance:
PSYCHOLOGICAL NEEDS: These are the very basics of thirst, hunger, shelter, clothing and sex.

SAFETY & SECURITY NEEDS: The need for physical, emotional and financial security.

SOCIAL NEEDS: The need for affiliation, love, affection, companionship and acceptance.

ESTEEM NEEDS: Self-esteem, recognition, attention, respect and achievement.

"SELF" NEEDS: Known as self-actualization, it is the need of an individual to reach their full potential as they perceive it.

Your job is to "feel" your customer's needs, wants and desires and write your headlines accordingly, with as much passion and emotion as you can.

Here are some emotional triggers that successful internet marketing entrepreneurs address in their headlines:

People want to: live as long as possible; make and save money; save time; give and receive love; learn new things; be popular; look their best, physically & clothing-wise; eliminate the negative things in life.

People want: comfort; "inside information"; salvation. "Accentuate The Positive, Eliminate The Negative, Latch On To The Affirmative, Don't Mess With Mister In-Between" " were the words to a 40s' song written by Johnny Mercer that applies perfectly to writing headlines. In creating products and choosing affiliate programs to represent, consider those that eliminate the negatives:

Eliminate/Reduce: hard work; stress; risk; guilt;

Eliminate/Prevent: embarrassment;

Eliminate/Relieve: pain;

Eliminate/Ease: doubts;

Eliminate/Free: from worry; from fear; from anxiety.

Always remember that people want to be thought of as: smart; successful; attractive; expert; influential; creative; important; knowledgeable; efficient and sociable.

And they want the personal freedom to be independent, to travel, to resist being dominated and pushed around, to control others, and to have their own business. Address these issues for certain success.

Products addressing wealth, love, health and beauty, and safety have proven over time to be the best for generating affiliate and report profits.

There are at least ten different and distinct "types" of headlines. These are:

Headlines beginning with "How To" (e.g. "How To Train A Doberman");

Headlines that pose a question (e.g., "Are You Sick And Tired Of The 9 -5")

Headlines that make a command, and focus solely on the your offer's most important benefit (e.g., "Triple Your Income Next Year");

News Headlines, written as an announcement (e.g. "Announcing A New Breakthrough In Dog Training");

The Headline Offering A Solution: (e.g., If You Have Trouble Training Your Puppy This Report Will Make You An Expert".)

Headlines offering a benefit: (e.g., "Make More Money With My System".

The Personalized Headline: (e.g., "Here's How **You** [if possible insert actual name from a mail-merge program] Can Earn More Money").

The Testimonial Headline: (e.g., "[recognized name who has liked the product] says that [product] is the best"; OR signing your own name at the end: (e.g., "I found this report to be the best! [signed]").

The Guarantee Headline: (e.g., "Announcing a report guaranteed to help you train your dog!").

The Discount Sale Headline: (e.g., "Get up to 70% Off Our Widget If You Act Today").

Remember, it is not only the headline words that are important. The font style, the font size, and the font color all help your visitor form a snap opinion to read your ad.

Make it easy to read. Avoid fonts with "serifs", those little end squiggles such as at the two top ends of the bar and at the bottom "T" in Times New Roman font. Much better is a "sans-serif" (without squiggles, such as the "naked T" in the Ariel font.)

Avoid dark and drab colors and backgrounds. Dark and drab colors create a depressing mood; bright and clear colors are uplifting. Try to uplift. Black print on qa white background is almost universally considered to produce the best results because it is the easiest to read.

Black color can be associated with death, depression and unpleasantness. Red denotes passion, sexuality, power and strength. White is associated with purity, goodness and clarity. Orange can be interpreted as cheery and warming. Yellow can signal caution, but it can be attention-getting and signify energy. Use yellow to emphasize certain words, but use sparingly.

Green is generally thought of as pleasant, harmonious, and elicits feelings of security (e.g., money). Purple can be associated with justice and royalty, and can signify mystery. Blue is calming and cooling, inducing tranquility to most, though some find it "over-tranquil" bordering on depressing.

I have found that either red or dark blue against a white background makes the best headlines. Making it a different color from your sub-title tends to draw the reader into the ad below.

Some say to use all capitals, but ONLY in a headline. You must include targeted key words in your title, together with "power words" that have been proven over decades to increase ad results. Some say never use all capitals, just capitalize the first letter of each word. You could split-test an ad too see if it matters.

The key power words for your headlines and sub-headlines are: **FREE**; **YOU**; **YOUR**; **HOW**; **WHO; and NEW.** Less important but not to be ignored are: PROVEN; SECRET(S); EASY; GUARANTEED; POWEREFUL; SHOCKING; DISCOVER; BREAKTHROUGH; LOVE.

Others are: ULTIMATE; INCREDIBLE; MASTER; REVEALED; UNCOVERED; RESULTS, PROFITS; MONEY; HIDDEN; SHOCKED; SCIENTIFIC; DISCOVERY; AMAZING; NOW; SHOW; SIMPLE; CONFIDENTIAL; REVEALS; GIANT; YOU CAN; METHOD; PEOPLE; WANT; and WHY.

The first five words in dark above appear in almost 75% of all successful headlines. Be certain to use them liberally. Also refer to Chapter 5 for a more extensive list of power words.

There are a number of general rules that have proven to be effective in writing headlines. Include as many of these as possible::

Promise a benefit;

Length is not critical. 15 word headlines get the same results as four word headlines, all else being equal;

Add some "news"…new product, new improvement, etc.;

No gimmicks or "tricky" words. Use plain English;

Make certain your headline "says it all" with no need to read the ad to get the message.

And most important, TARGET YOUR MARKET. Aim at the bulls-eye, those people who are most likely to be interested in your offer.

Offer instant gratification.

For whatever reason headlines that ask a question seem to command the most attention. Once the reader sees the question it is natural for them to read on to find the answer! The best headlines challenge the reader, involves their self- esteem, and does not allow a simple mental "yes/no" response.

Your Sub-Headline follows exactly the same rules for keywords and power words, fonts and colors as the headline. It is often a bit longer, with more keywords. Do not use words you used in the headline. Explain nothing here. That follows in the body of the ad. Try to create a sense of mystery or secrecy so they read on to the body of the ad.

There is a very interesting free tool for evaluating the "emotional" value of your headlines from 0 to 100%. It rates your headline on three bases:

Intellectual. Ads effectiveness where your product requires reasoning or careful evaluation.

Empathetic. Ads to bring out positive emotional reactions in your visitors.

Spiritual. Ads to have the deepest emotional appeal.

This interesting tool is found at: aminstitute.com/headline/index.htm. Apparently they employ a scientifically researched algorithm to create an EMV rating (**E**motional **M**arketing **V**alue). I certainly do not use it to entirely guide my headline creation, but it offers some very interesting insights into the emotions induced by certain words that may trump the actual dictionary meaning of a word.

It is reported that a 50% EMV is minimum for a good headline, and that "headline pros" achieve between 75% and 100%. It is well worth your consideration. You can't beat the price! A list of your keywords having both a high EMV and a high KEI is a great starting point in your quest to have your headlines provide the optimum conversion of visitors to buyers.

Do not shy away from being a "copycat", and learning from the pros. You need to look at examples of good ad copy. Look no further than the cover of the *National Enquirer* or *Cosmopolitan* magazine. You can also see some professionally crafted headlines for product offers at: otsdirect.com/products.html; trsdirect.com/product.php; and also
ohpdirect.com/product.php.

Spend a disproportionate amount of time creating your headlines. They are fundamental to your success, whether used on your website, in your blogs or in your advertising. All successful internet marketers become proficient headline writers. Study this chapter, and work towards making headline writing a primary skill.

Your banker will thank you!

CHAPTER 18
KILLER SALES LETTERS FOR MAXIMUM SALES

Your sales letter, the body text of your website, appears directly below your headline and sub-headline. Obviously if your headline doesn't get them to keep reading <u>you can have the best sales letter ever written and sell nothing, ever.</u> Assuming that you have enticed the visitor to read on, the wording of your sales letter is the difference between your success and failure in internet marketing.

Before I go into detail about how to write a sales letter to optimize your results, I have a strong suggestion. Check out the one-product sales letters of some of the most successful internet gurus. Famous infopreneurs such as Marlon Sanders, Jim Edwards, John Reese, Jonothan Mizel, Brian Terry, Mike Filsame, Avril Harper, Anthony Morrison, Dr. Jeffrey Lant, Armand Morin, Alex Mandossian, Mark Joyner, Robert Allen and John Thornhill come to mind, but all of the famous internet millionaires follow pretty much the same formula.

Google search any of them and study their sales letters. I suggest you print them out and create your own file of killer sales letters. I have printed out dozens over the years. Some are short, four or five pages. Some are extremely long. I have seen 150+ page sales letters selling a $19.97 ebook product! I've seen five-page sales letters offering a $997.00 virtual training product! There are no hard and fast rules.

THE STRUCTURE

It is common knowledge that the <u>longer</u> the sales letter the better, as long as it is well constructed and well written. That may seem counter-intuitive, but it has been proven again and again by many of the most successful infopreneurs.

You will find that ALL the guru's sales letters have a few basic concepts in common:

The sales letter follows a dynamite headline and sub-headline;
Their copy draws you deeper and deeper into their sales letter;
There are "Buy Now" buttons throughout the sales letter;
They stress benefits;
They sell results, not products;
There is ample white space;
The paragraphs are short';
They italicize, colorize, or underline a word here and there;
There are sub-headlines sprinkled throughtout the sales letter;
They offer some sort of "proof" and/or testimonials;
They offer a guarantee;
They offer bonus incentives;
They end the sales letter with their personal signature;
Most use "P.S." and "P.P.S." messages at the bottom;
Most offer PayPal payments;
Many display "authority symbols", such as Verisign and Better Business Bureau (BBB) logos;
There is almost always an upsell after you buy;
There is almost always a "one time offer" after you buy;

Beyond the OTO there is frequently a "takeaway". This might be a time limit after which the offer disappears, or a limit as to the number that will ever be sold.

Do not underestimate the power of "urgency", which is created by the "takeaway". The buyer who "is going to think about it and come back later" **NEVER BUYS**. They **MUST** buy now!

Here are a few "takeaway" ideas you can tailor to your product. Always include a REASON for the takeaway:

"Remember, you must act by Friday midnight in order to get my seven bonuses. These bonuses are provided to me by third parties and I cannot control availability."

"I regret that I can handle only 67 new clients. My plate is too full to consider taking on more, so contact me immediately or be left out of this amazing opportunity."

"We are only offering 750 of these reports. When they are gone they are gone. We do not want to oversaturate the market in fairness to everyone."

This special pricing cannot be guaranteed beyond Friday. Because of increasing demand and limited supply it is likely the price will double after that.

IMPORTANT: Absolutely carry out the "threat". Kill the offer after the set time period. Don't take on a 68th client. Stop selling after 750 are sold. Actually raise the price on Friday! I know that I have personally hesitated to buy something I knew I wanted and when I went back a day later to buy it I was unable to do so. I was really ticked off, but If nothing else that marketer earned my respect, and I jumped at his next offer!

There are, however, countless slimeballs who make various pull-back threats and clearly do not abide by them. They never had any intention to do so. Their offer prices never rise. They never disappear. I lose all respect for these unethical marketers.

In regard to testimonials, it is imperative that these be legitimate. At first asking friends and family for their honest opinion can be a good start. Once you do gather testimonials always use the full name and city address of the person writing it. If possible include a small thumbnail photo of the person and a professional title if they have one.

It is also a good idea to put a thumbnail picture of yourself somewhere at the bottom near your signature. **People like to deal with a "real person".** You will find that every internet guru has his or her picture plastered all over their website. By the time you get to the bottom of the sales letter you feel as if you know them personally! You are buying from a trusted friend.

YOUR SOLE OBJECTIVE

You have one and only one objective. **You need to elicit a positive response and sell your product**. If that takes one page or a hundred, that is your one objective.

Every word and phrase in your sale letter must contribute to that objective. No fluff. If a word or phrase or entire paragraph does not help make the sale, eliminate it. Use the shortest words possible to convey a thought. Keep sentences to one and a half lines total. Keep paragraphs to five lines maximum.

Remember, you are not writing to impress Ms. Boring your High School English teacher. You want your Sales Letter to be read and acted upon, not read and admired. And never lose site of the fact that **people do not buy what they need. They buy emotionally what they want**. At the very beginning of the sales letter state the major benefits. This is in   the first few lines. Make an emotional connection to your visitor as fast as you can.

All visitors tune ONLY into one station, WIIFM. If you cannot answer their question: "**W**hat's **I**n **I**t **F**or **M**e", you cannot sell anything. Also in the back of your visitors' minds are such profound thoughts as: "So what?" and "Who cares?" You may be convinced you have the greatest product in the world but your visitor is very far from convinced of this. **Your sales letter must do the convincing.**

Every successful sales letter is focused on **emotional appeal**. You must identify the underlying emotional needs satisfied by your product. Make your visitor believe that you understand them and their need, that you've been there, and done that, and finally found the <u>one</u> solution, which just happens to be the one you are asking them to buy!

Certain of the various so-called "deadly sins" are a critical matter of focus in your sales letter writing. Why? Because even the most Godly amongst us are, by human nature, susceptible to one or more of them (if not ALL!). Take a long hard look at:

Human **greed** is a powerful motivator. How does your product address this need for wealth or power? A copy of Gordon Gecko's "Greed Is Good" monologue from the movie *Wall Street* hangs over my desk! Its real meaning is often misunderstood as being negative. Taken in context it is a very positive statement of reality. Good power words to use in this sort of sales letter copy are "amass", "money", "millionaire", "monopolize", "proven", "big bucks", and "cash".

Ah, **lust**! The pleasure emotion. Play to it in your sales letter if it somehow fits your product. Who doesn't want pleasure? Who doesn't lust over something? Great pleasure power words are "love", "attract". "entice", "charming", "tempt", "seduce", and "sexy".

Envy is another "deadly sin". Many of us see things that others have that we want. My first wife would freak out if a neighbor built a pool that was six inches longer than our pool (which is one of many reasons why she's an ex!) Envy in the extreme.

Anyway, you need to promise fulfillment of your visitor's need to have something bigger or better than their friends or neighbors. Or something they wish they had but do not.

"Your friends will glow with envy when xxxxx (your product makes them glow!)". Power words could be "desire", "covet" (with due respect for your neighbor's ass), "secret", "begrudge", "extraordinary", "amazed", and "people just like you…".

Let's focus too on **vanity**. People care about others' opinions about their appearance, abilities and achievements. Some power words to consider are "beautiful", "attractive", "magnetic", "younger", "stronger", "genius", "confident" and the ever important "**YOU".**

The need for instant gratification, quick and optimal results with minimum effort, defines the emotion of **laziness** (sloth)**.** "Avoid xxxxxxx (your product) mistakes that waste your time". "Do (whatever) in three days instead of seven". Get the idea? Good power words and phrases to interject into your sales letter copy are "easy", "fast", "instant access", "lightening", "blueprint" and "save time".

Pride is another strong emotion you can address in your sales letter. People want to feel good about their accomplishments. Psychologists call this "self-actualization", and it has nothing to do with what other people think. Good power words in your sales letters include: "accomplish", "master", "envy", "best", "greatest", "biggest", "transform", and "wealth" all can work well.

Make note that **fear** is probably the strongest human motivator. Fear of loss is a powerful motivator of action to buy something from you. For example, "Avoid The Five Biggest Mistakes That Can Cost You Thousands Of Dollars In xxxxxxxxx" (fill in your product that addresses this fear). Get the idea? Good power words in this sales letter copy could be "save", "secure", "safety", and "defend".

Depending on your product, you may well be able to address more than one of the above emotions. **The more the better.**

OTHER CONSIDERATION

Remember, it is not only the sales letter wording that is important. The font style, the font size, and the font color all help your visitor form a snap opinion to read your ad.

Make it easy to read. Avoid fonts with "serifs", those little end squigglys such as at the two top ends of the bar and at the bottom "T" in Times New Roman font. Much better is a "sans-serif" (without squigglys) such as the naked "T" in the Ariel font.

Different visitors will approach reading a sales letter differently. Some will start at the beginning and read word for word. Some will read the headline and skip to the signature to see whose offer it is, and then may go back to the top.

Others will scan the entire sales letter, taking note only of the sub-headlines you should have scattered throughout. These folk then may or may not go back over the entire sales letter. A few will look **only** at the testimonials! If you are lucky, and it does happen, some will look for the first order button and not read anything!

The key to addressing these behavior patterns is to **WRITE FOR ALL OF THEM**. For example, pretend you are the visitoronly reading the sub-headlines. Would you be convinced to buy your product?

To summarize, never lose site of the need to address basic human emotions in all of your sales letter copy. Failing to do so, and failure to relate to your visitor, is certain doom in your internet marketing adventure. Following the simple guidelines shared above will give you the best possible chance for a winning and profitable conversion rate of readers to clickers.

CHAPTER 19

WINNING BIG WITH SEARCH ENGINE OPTIMIZATION

Any website is virtually worthless if you are the only one who knows it exists. If you simply build it they definitely will NOT come. This is not *Field Of Dreams*! This is contrary to the implications in TV ads from various website purveyors: "Have your own website with us and everyone will find you". A very big misleading lie. Not quite the whole story. When people search the internet they enter their search term and are a click away from getting a list of thousands of websites that have the information they seek. Why would they happen to find yours?

Incidentally, in this Chapter we are talking about fully-developed multi-page multi-function Google-friendly websites. These are NOT mini-sites.

SEARCH ENGINES

There are actually dozens of different search engines. It is reported that Google gets 75% of all searches, Yahoo 15%, Bing 5%, and all the others combined a mere 5%. You really only need to focus on Google and Yahoo. These are all known as "relevancy based search engines". They use a remarkable assortment of computer programs to "mine" data. Their operative programs are called "spiders", "crawlers", and "robots".

A search engine basically consists of three distinct software programs:

Spider Software requests pages from websites. It "sees" text and links and the URL. It does not see images, logos or videos, unless you include a text "alt tag" associated with these elements. It especially loves links.

Index Software contains an algorithm that takes all of the spider software information and analyzes and stores it.

<u>Query Software</u> checks through everything in the index software and responds to searches by <u>matching search terms with relevant websites.</u>

KEYWORDS CONSIDERATION

The reason keywords are so important is simply to insure that the query software sends searchers to your website in

deference to your competitor's websites.

One can think of keywords in three ways:

Keywords that bring in great traffic but poor sales. These are words people use when they are researching, "just looking".
Keywords that bring in good traffic and decent sales. These are words people use when they are in a buying mood.

Keywords that bring in low traffic but huge sales. This is the buying behavior in a tightly-focused niche market.

There are supposedly **2,000,000,000** (yes, that's two <u>billion</u>!) people, more than one-quarter of the people on the planet, accessing the internet! It is quite impossible to market to all of them at once. We must market to a small segment, known as a niche as discussed in Chapter 4. You want a targeted <u>bulls-eye</u> group of internet searchers. We do not even need a tiny slice of that two-billion visitor internet pie. We only need to lick the crumbs off the knife!

There are many books written on the nuances of Search Engine Optimization, or "SEO". This term means getting your website considered more favorably than other websites, so much so that your rise as cream to the top of unpasteurized farm milk! There are many SEO courses offered. There are companies who will do SEO for you, often for outrageous sums of money.

The simple fact is that SEO is actually rather simple for you to accomplish yourself. You have one goal and that is to have the search engines **FOR FREE** place your website in the **TOP THREE** searches when a potential visitor enters a particular search term.

Any other search engine position has almost zero value. People are inherently impatient and often lazy. (It has been documented that position two and three, which are often much less expensive to buy if you are paying for placement by bidding high are as effective in getting clicks as position one.) With literally millions of websites out there this high positioning might seem impossible. It isn't. It just takes an understanding of how sites are rated, and then takes some research and effort.

You build your "findability" in many ways: To achieve one of the first three search positions you have two choices (actually three choices, as you will see later). Either you create a powerfully optimized site as described below, in which event your top-tier positioning is free, OR pay for positioning.

You literally bid on the position you want. (This "highest-bids-rank-highest" model previously worked 100% of the time, but Google also at present takes into account how relevant the content on your site is to the search term that found it).

When someone enters a search term in Google the first page that comes up has a couple of websites at the very top within a special box (how did THAT happen? See below.) Then there are the SEO ranked sites. On the right side there is a column of paid sites.

To eventually rise to a FREE top rank position there are four key elements that you must consider as you are creating niche-focused campaign websites. Let's look at these in the order of importance:

KEYWORD DENSITY is critical. This is the number of times your key word or key word phrase (known as a long tail keyword) appears on your basic home page, your LANDING PAGE. You literally have to count the number of words. Unfortunately the rating algorithm is not static, but varies between three and six percent.

I try to stay around 4%-5% keyword density. That means if I have four-hundred words on my landing page around sixteen to twenty words need to be my keywords (a long tail keyword counts as one word for % sake). Fewer is not considered dense enough, much greater is considered keyword spamming and is penalized. I never cease to be amazed how few sites adhere to this critical formula.

THE DESCRIPTION, your AdWords ad, is also very important. This is the blurb that a visitor sees first for each of the websites that their search returns. Three are three key rules: **a.** Use 25 words or less; **b.** Use all possible keywords; **c.** Make your EXACT keywords the FIRST words of the description. Never deviate from these rules.

IMPORTANT: NEVER end your description with a period. Create a "cliffhanger". End with: [description] "and…." The "…." leads visitors to click to "see what's next" when they visit your site.

Write your description try to make it emotional. Use action and "feeling" words, for example" FREE (the most valuable word); Save; Limited Time Only; While Supplies last"; Discounted Price; Wholesale Price; Dominate …..(whatever).

THE TITLE is equally important. Just two rules here: **a.** six to twelve words; **b.** Use ALL KEYWORDS in the title.

THE DOMAIN NAME (URL): Two rules**: a.** get a .com only;   **b.** Use as many of your keywords as possible. These keywords must be in your URL and the name of your landing page. Here is where your keyword research comes into play. You want to find a multi-word search term (known as a long-tail keyword) that gets between 3,000 and 10,000 hits per month, and then register a URL with this exact long-tail keyword.

If you are carful to do all of the above you will be well on your way to a top-three position. You have done your search engine optimization. If you do not achieve it at first, take a critical look at the sites rated above yours, and then try to tweak yours in ways that slowly raise your ranking. I believe you will be very pleased with the results you achieve, at zero cost.

KEEP GOOGLE HAPPY (You want a happy Google!)

Here are some additional tips that will help keep you on the best of terms with Google in your affiliate or product marketing:

You MUST have **unique** content on your website. Do not copy content from your affiliate vendor's site. Google can determine if you do, and penalize you for it.

Try to have at least five, preferably ten pages of unique content.

Have a Privacy Policy page;

Have an "About Us" page;

Have a "Contact Us" page;

Have a FAQ (**F**requently **A**sked **Q**uestions) page;

Have small links to the above three pages at the bottom of your landing page;

Have an "Additional Useful Information" page with links to various other short articles. (Remember to put the links to your affiliate at the end of each article);

Include a "Site Map" page, with links to every other page. This allows Google to easily spider your entire site. **<u>Very important.</u>**

Your landing page content must be targeted and relevant to the keywords on which you are bidding.

Consider including a Resource Page with a link at the bottom of your landing page. This should contain a list of any .edu or .org sites related to your niche. This scores big points with Google.

Of course the search engines need to FIND your site. You CAN manually submit your site to every search engine. Not to worry! Here is a word of advice about manually submitting your website: FORGET IT! There are actually companies that <u>charge</u> you to do this. Forget them too!

The fact is that the moment your website is live the electronic robots mentioned above will eventually find your site and rank it based upon how well you have done your Search Engine Optimization.

Using keyword statistics analyzers, discussed in an earlier Chapter, you will be finding:

The number of times your EXACT keyword or keyword phrase was searched over the past month.

The number of website pages that contain that exact keyword, a measure of your competition.

A "Keyword Effectiveness Index" (KEI, found in WordTracker) which is a numerical representation of how effective your individual keywords may prove to be.

Headlines are one key to search engine ranking. Once you have a list of the best prospective keywords, create some headlines using those keywords. Earlier we spoke of the free tool for evaluating the "emotional" value of your headlines from 0 to 100%. It rates your headline on three bases:

Intellectual. Ads effectiveness where your product requires reasoning or careful evaluation.

Empathetic. Ads crafted to bring out positive emotional reactions in your visitors.

Spiritual. Ads designed to have the deepest emotional appeal.

The program is found at: aminstitute.com/headline/index.htm.

Many internet marketers choose a browser called "Firefox" instead of the ubiquitous Microsoft Internet Explorer. Just Google search "Firefox Download" and follow the instructions. You can have any number of browsers on your computer and use them interchangeably. You will need to designate one as your "default" browser. That's the one that shows up first when you awaken your computer from its "unconscious mode" (I'm sure teckies have a different term for computer beddy-by!)

Many consider Firefox to be more reliable and faster. Personally I kept IE and use both interchangeably. I also use the "Google Chrome" browser which I can convince myself is at least a micro-second faster than the others.

Firefox has an EXTREMELY valuable plug-in called "SEO QUAKE". It's free, and it is a great time saver. Using your shiny new Firefox browser Google search" "Install SEO Quake for Firefox", follow the instructions to download the program.

What SEO Quake gives you is a toolbar in Firefox that automatically provides a wealth of information on any website you enter in the browser. It enables you at a glance to see some very important facts about your competition. These include:

Google PageRank. On a scale of 0 – 10, even a rank of 1 shows some traffic. A 4 rank is very good and indicates very decent traffic. A page rank of 5 or more is great. The higher the number you see the worse for you as a direct competitor.

Google Index gives an idea of the size of your competitor's website in the number of pages it has kept in its index. This can be from one to many thousands of pages.

The MSN Index of the actual number of pages in the site today.

Yahoo!'s assessment of the number of links pointing to the competitor's home page. Your hope is to exceed this number.

The Alexa rank of the site, a measure of search engine traffic the site is receiving. Anything below 1,000,000 is very good.

The age of the website. Google does rank older sites better, all else being equal.

You can click on any of the above items and get a wealth of additional information, including the "meta tags" and "meta description" your competitor is using, as well as all of his keywords and their density!

According to Google there are over 200 (!) factors in the algorithm that determines PageRank, and these are tweaked continuously. No one outside of a few Google insiders know the details, sort of like the formula for CocaCola of Dr.Pepper! (Can you believe there are 23 DP ingredients?!) This is why SEO can be frustrating. Your best bet is to study what is working for your top competition any try to emulate it.

You can check the PageRank of any website by browsing to:
google-page-rank-check.com, or:
prchecker.info/check_page_rank.php.
The latter will even provide you with a FREE page ranking code for your website.

There are MANY free keywords tools. A Google search will reveal them all. They have various limitations, but there is no harm in playing with a few to see what you can come up with. Many have free trials before you would need to pay for anything.

LINKING STRATEGY

The most powerful way to raise your ranking in the search engines is to get as many backlinks (links coming in from other websites) as possible. The higher ranked the site from which the link comes the better. Google ranks sites on a 1 to 10 scale. (You can get the page rank of any site by installing the Google Toolbar at toolbar.google.com.)

You can create the best, most keyword rich website with a dynamite headline and a select URL and find that you are having trouble getting a high ranking by the search engines. You can be trying to sell your website and find there is very little buying interest. Well, have you looked at your link status lately?

Many internet entrepreneurs spend a great deal of time getting their websites "just right", but neglect to initiate a strategy to create valuable incoming links, the valued backlinks. Having a large number of links coming in to your website from other websites that <u>have content relevant to yours</u>, and have a <u>high ranking</u> in their own right is a website enhancement you must not overlook. Links from sites that have no relevance to your site whatsoever are worthless.

Backlinks do more than merely grow a site's value to the search engines. Once your website visitors trust your advice and recognize your URL or company name they will probably recommend your site to others. This creates even more backlinks for you.

Every incoming link to your website , regardless of the actual quality of that backlink, has potential to drive traffic to your site. Every visitor counts. No matter the source, the more traffic arriving at your site, the higher it can climb in the search engines.

There are many ways to obtain great links, some cost money, some do not. Let' s talk about the costly ways first. You can get what are called "Authority Links" by getting listed in "General Directories", for a price. The Yahoo! Directory and the business.com directory each costs around $300/year. Authority Websites are sites having high Google PageRank (6+), show near the top of search results, and have <u>lots</u> of relevant content.
At a lower cost, GoGuides at: goguides.com, and JoeAnt at: joeant.com, cost well under $100/year. These are all well worth the price, once you are making some internet cash and can afford them. Another worthwhile site to study is linkworth.com.

Backlinks are a real commodity. They are regularly bought, sold and traded. Check out: textlinkbrokers.com and: linkadage.com. Studying these sites will give you a very complete picture of what backlinks cost to buy. It will also show you the potential you have yourself to sell backlinks once you have your own high PageRank sites created over time.

You should periodically check the viability of every link on your website. This includes the internal links from your sitemap, page to page, links to other websites, the links to your order page, links to blogs and social sites, and all affiliate links. Website links do break occasionally, for reasons known only to computer geeks and God. Maybe only God.

If you have only a few websites you can easily do this yourself every week or so. You can pay a local college kid to do it, or enlist one of your own kids. If you have ten, or fifty or more websites, which you may very well have eventually (I have well over 300) you can also pay professionals to do it for you. You can Google "Website Monitoring Services". Check out internetsupervision.com. They will monitor a single site for FREE, multiple sites for a modest monthly fee.

SELL "HIGH-PAGE RANK" LINKS AS A BUSINESS MODEL

It is a fact that some internet marketers set up websites specifically for the purpose of growing their PageRank and then selling links. They make no effort to sell any product, employ AdSense, or use affiliate links. This can be very profitable if done right. As a business model you can simply sell links from your site through a link broker.

With this business model you don't care whether you get any visitors or actually sell anything ever. No search engine optimization. No tight niche focus. No keyword research. No analytics to find where your visitors originate. All you do is build links to your site. If you already happen to have some high PageRank sites you link them to a new site for instant backlinks. The idea of this business model is to make money with the absolute minimum of cost and effort.

With this business model you will be focusing on huge general markets such as "Weight loss", "finance", "food", "hobbies" etc., as opposed to a focused niche. Do not worry about niche keywords when registering your domain name. Work in such words as "about", "guide to..", "news". "Info", etc. in the domain name. You build your backlinks in exactly the same way you would for any commercial website. You simply delete any need to spend time and money optimizing the website to make money in more conventional ways other than selling links.

FREE BACKLINKS

EVERY OTHER WAY TO GET BACKLINKS, EVERYTHING BELOW, IS <u>FREE</u>! It just takes some work on your part to make it all happen.

There is a FREE very important General Directory called "The Open Directory Project" at: dmoz.org. Your site is reviewed by real human editors, and unless your site has very high quality relevant content it will not get in to the DMOZ directory. Submit and pray!

Look to the many "niche directories" that focus on the specific industry upon which you are focusing. These directories will generally allow you to use page-focused anchor text links, where the general directories will not. You can locate niche directories with a Google search of: "(your keyword) directory".

When submitting to any of these directories be certain to get listed in as many relevant categories within the directory as possible, and get listed in any regional categories as well.

There is one very useful way to find websites for linking. Go to Google and search exactly as follows: (your keyword) "please also suggest my link to the linkpartners.com directory". When you click "Submit" Google will reward you with a list of websites that have link submission forms. Go to these websites, fill out the forms, and you will have many new links rather quickly.

Beyond directories, creating social media profiles can get you links, but most social sites do not register in Google PageRank. One social site that does is meetup.com which links to your site with the anchor text of your choice.

Blogs help add backlinks in a big way. If you are creating your websites in the WordPress blogging program it can be a big help in this regard. There is an interesting program that works with WordPress data to help you accomplish getting valuable backlinks. Go to CommentHut at: commenthut.com. Download their FREE "Lite" version. It finds WordPress blog-websites using your chosen keywords and phrases. It only indexes those websites that accept comments. You can even specify that the program only spit out high-page-rank websites which are most important to your search engine optimization link strategy.

Visit the websites that the program comes up with and post **relevant** comments on the site. Put your URL link (or preferably anchor text) in the "Your Website" panel. When your comment is published, presto, you have your one-way back link!
The upgraded (read "pay for it") version of CommentHut expands the search to many more blog platforms other than WordPress. According to their website this upgrade gives you 90% more results!

As it frequently does, Google apparently has rather recently changed the manner in which it considers the value of links. Where keyword-rich links seemed to be the best choice, the old, simple URL may in fact now be preferred. Trying to out-guess Google is a fool's errand. For now I'm going with simple URL links. If nothing else, it's easier!

Here is another approach: Do a Google search and note the top 50 or so ranking websites in your general niche. Starting with the top site, which probably has the highest Google PageRank, see if they have a "Links" or "Resource" tab. If they do, click on it and request a link. If not, look under "Contact Us" and write to the webmaster to request a link. If your site is not in direct competition you have a fair chance of getting the requested link. You might offer to write guest blogs or contribute articles in an effort to establish a long-term relationship with the webmaster.

Google sees websites linking to your websites as casting a "vote" for your site. If your site is good enough for a webmaster to recommend your products to their own visitors, Google loves it. The higher ranked the website linking to yours is the MORE Google loves it. You can check the PageRank of potential link sites at: google-page-rank-check.com or at: prchecker.info/check_page_rank.php. The latter even provides a free page ranking code for your website.

A WORD OF CAUTION: Google HATES links obtained from sources that are specifically created to provide you with links. Your site can be downgraded or banned entirely. Do not be tempted by the ads you will see promising great SEO results. These companies are referred to in the industry as "link farms", "link exchanges" and "pay-for-link". No, no, no! Got it?

Google also hates "keyword spamming", cramming your website with a massive number of keywords and little valuable content. When Google sends a searcher to a website they want that searcher to have a satisfying experience.

Links are extremely important to the search engines. Most webmasters seem content to use their just URL, their exact web address, as their link to their site. This is OK in that it will get some incoming traffic.

OPTIMIZE YOUR LINKS

But to optimize the value of your links you want to create keyword rich links. This requires messing a bit with HTML code, but if you can fill in your information in the following code you will be fine (omit the brackets):

<a href=http://www.[your exact URL]>[your keywords]</a>

Use this enhanced link wherever you can, such as:

In your PPC advertising where you are allowed to use any link of your choice.

Embedded within your press releases. You may pay a small extra fee for this. It's is worth it.

In all of your signature boxes.

In the blog posts you make to other websites.

In your social media marketing.

In articles and blog posts on your own website.

Once you have established good relationships with other website owners and they are linking to you, suggest that they link to you using your keyword-enhanced link.

Do not request this same "anchor text" (the keywords in your link request) for every incoming link. And match the anchor text to the keywords you are targeting to point toward a specific page of your website. Avoid linking to your exact domain name. Try to get incoming links directed to keywords and keyword phrases.

Do NOT send all of your incoming links to your main index.html page. Create a balanced link program to include your secondary pages IF the secondary pages contain useful relevant content, as they should.

Once you gain experience and know a little about HTML code (or you are advising someone who is creating your site for you) use **absolute** links: href="http://www. (your domain name).com/page.htm"></a>, as opposed to using **relative** links: href="page.htm"></a>.

I suggest you visit the following linking tool websites: ontolo.com; raventools.com; buzzstream.com; ahrefs.com; siteexplorer.co (not.com); majesticseo.com.

THE "DO FOLLOW" WEBSITES

Links come in two flavors, one-way and two-way. One-way links taste better to Google. They imply something other than "I'll link to you if you link to me". Your goal is to have links placed on high-ranking websites without you having to reciprocate the gesture.

You will find that some websites are easier than others from which to obtain links. Some actively encourage links by inviting freelance contributions and allowing those contributors to place backlinks. Some refuse to allow backlinks of any kind. The key here is in the coding of a given site. A site can be coded "NoFollow" or "DoFollow". The former of these two codes instructs a search engine to ignore links.

It is a waste of time to contact the NoFollow sites, with a few exceptions. Huge traffic NoFollow sites such as "Yahoo! Answers" and "Wikipedia" are fine to spread your articles to because some of their many visitors will go to the trouble of copying your link data into their browsers and you will get traffic that way.   Traffic is traffic!

You can find "DoFollow" backlink-friendly blog sites at: dofollow.info. Also check out: techtipsmaster.com/do-follow-forums-and-blogs.html, and: robdogg.com/wordpress/2008/02/10/7-high-page-rank-blogs-that-dofollow/

Another great way to get backlinks is by creating articles (your own writing, private label rights (PLR) articles, or public-domain extractions) and submitting them to "Article Directories". Of course you will include your appropriate links at the end of the article. Chapter 37 covers article marketing in detail.

Doing a Google search for "list of article directories" will present a mind-boggling number of choices. You want to use those with PageRank 5 or higher. You will find that ezinearticles.com, goareticles.com, helium.com and isnare.com fall into this category. Check others at: vincesamios.com/internetmarketing/50-high-page-rank-article-directories

Another way to get backlinks is by submitting press releases of anything you can create that is newsworthy. We will look at press releases in detail in Chapter 34.

AVOID BEING "GRAY BARRED" BY GOOGLE

Here is a very important tip. It is something to which very few webmasters pay attention. **PERIODICALLY CHECK YOUR BACKLINKS.** There are two reasons for doing this.

First of all, over time some of the websites with which you had reciprocal links may no longer be showing your link, even though you are still showing theirs. This hurts you in the rankings because Google's ranking-algorithm factors in the number of links you show outgoing. The more such links the <u>lower</u> your ranking. So immediately delete any links on your website that are no longer being reciprocated.

Secondly, and most important, that quality backlink you had last week could very well, for whatever reason, been penalized or black-listed by Google. You will suffer terribly from guilt-by-association. You could drop hundreds of places and not have the remotest clue why. You took no action that would upset Google, but your back-linked website did.

What might the offending website been caught doing? Anything contrary to Google's Terms and Conditions qualifies. For example, using text the same color as a background to make it invisible to the eye but "seen" by the web spiders. This text could contain a massive number of keywords. Big no-no.

Keyword spamming, or "stuffing" could happen not only in the text copy but aslo within the meta-tag, title-tag, and alt-image.

How do you get protection from this seemingly unfair downgrading of your website? There are two ways, manually for FREE (rather time-consuming) or using a program you can buy. How do you monitor your links to avoid this problem from happening? For one, you can do an individual Google search for each of your linked websites.

Download the Google toolbar from: toolbar.google.com. If you enter a website URL and the toolbar results come up in gray color that site is banned! This is known in the trade as being "gray barred". <u>You never want to be gray barred!</u>

But you definitely do not want any of your linked websites to be gray barred either. Immediately remove any such link from your website. No permanent harm done.

Doing a search for rotten backlinks one by one can be a time-consuming pain. This can be greatly facilitated by purchasing a program called "SEO Elite". It costs under two-hundred bucks, and is well worth the price. Check out: seoelite.com. Aside from making backlink-checking a snap, you will discover that it contains many features that will help you in all of your search engine optimization.

There is one linking aspect that many webmasters overlook. Google sees all links as "votes" for your website, But they even count votes for yourself, from right within your own website! It is important to create links from each page of your website to your home page. The more pages that link, the better.

Your "Off-Page" optimization is the single most important factor in achieving high search engine ranking. All of the factors mentioned above must be addressed if you hope for serious internet marketing success:

You must have lots of quality links pointed back to your website. Your links must include your keywords within the anchor text. Try to obtain links from the same websites from which the top websites in your niche got theirs;

Try to get links from as many different IP Addresses (specific unique computers) as possible;

Try to have the same % of keyword-specific links in to your website as the top competitor has;

If necessary you can buy backlinks;

Write articles with your website in the footer of the article, and submit these to article directories;

Post blogs often.

By following the above procedures you will have a leg up on the vast majority of websites against which you will be competing. Spare no detail. Every click counts. It's a pure numbers game, and the more visitors who see your offer the more sales you will make and the richer you will become.

To summarize, quality backlinks add tremendous value to a website. They help grow your site's resale value as well as increasing advertising revenues. You can expect a higher resale price for a website with good quality backlinks than a similar site without such links. And if paid ads are a source of revenue on your website you will be able to charge, and get, higher prices.

CHAPTER 20
BIG BUCK BLOGGING

If there is any Chapter in this book that someone new to internet commerce should skip this is it! It isn't that the subject is unimportant. Quite the opposite. But unless you have already established yourself as a dedicated blogger and can immediately use that talent to enhance your internet business there are many other talents that you must develop first. Because blogging is closely associated with websites it simply fits better here in Module Three.

"Blogging & Pinging". Sounds like a law firm or a music group! It is in fact a great way to get search engine recognition and to attract visitors to your website.

"Blog" is short for "We**bLog**". It is your personal and often-updated journal (log) intended for public consumption. It's like keeping an electronic diary. "Pinging" is a method of informing others that your blog exists, and alerts them whenever you make a new blog posting.

When we talk about blogs here we have two separate topics to consider. One is creating websites directly with blogs using Google's "Blogger" program. The other is creating websites using a blog-based software program called "Word Press". There are other blog software choices, but these two have become industry standards.

GOOGLE'S BLOGGER PLATFORM

Let's first talk "Blogger". Your blog is a combination of a database and a website. You focus on written content, while Blogger dates and archives your entries any way you wish (or not at all). The website it generates can contain not only your latest blog, but links to all of your previous blogs. It can contain photos as well as written copy. It can contain videos. It can contain, if you wish, a mechanism for visitors to leave comments.

In general, creating a marketing website in the conventional manner, at your website's host's servers, as discussed in Chapters 10 through 14, can be a challenge. This is especially true the first time you do it. In time you will find that is not particularly difficult.

Although most web hosts have control panels (known as "cPanels") to facilitate site creation there is a rather steep learning curve. If you were to print out (as I have) all of the cPanel instructions you would end up with hundreds of pages of text almost an inch thick! A bit intimidating for someone new to internet commerce to say the least.

The key to creating websites quickly and easily is using Google's FREE blogging platform found at: blogger.com. Starting your blog is amazingly simple. Create your account at blogger.com by filling in some intuitive forms with basic preferences. Then chose one of their many templates, and you are ready to boogie! Or bloggie. Or whatever.

Blogger even hosts your website for FREE on its BlogSpot servers, in exchange for a small amount of their advertising being placed on your website. But you can host your blog at your own web host of choice if you prefer. Personally I want total control of my business websites now and evermore so I choose never to have Google as my web host. But that does cost me hosting fees, and you can't beat Google's FREE.

Blogger and BlogSpot are two different and distinct Google services. If the only purpose for your blog is to keep friends and family informed about your life then the FREE BlogSpot hosting is perfect for your needs.

Sign up at blogger.com. For starters you will want to strip the blog template totally bare, all white. Then you open the "html editor" and cut/paste in your message from your word processor (Microsoft Word or whichever). That is all there is to it!

You place your post in the main editing area. You can click "Preview" to see how it will look once published. It is automatically formatted with the template you chose. Their entire website is intuitive and easy to navigate. Once you have used it the first time, it becomes extremely easy in the future. Very flat learning curve compared to a cPanel.

Remember, by using Blogger you are using a Google product, and they really prefer it over other blogging software. Using Blogger greatly enhances your Google search engine ranking. Google likes it even better if you make a new blog post to your site at least once a week. All search engines reward unique, changing content. The big advantage of blogging and pinging is that it gets your website indexed by the search engines almost immediately. And again, it's FREE.

The above is an over-simplified overview of Blogger. If you are creating a blog simply for personal use between family and friends that is about all you need to know. But blogging for business purposes, setting up an effective marketing blog, is very different from creating a social blog.

Social blogging is sort of an extended version of the character-limited Twitter mini-blog. You do not have to be concerned about using the optimal user name and keywords, search engine optimization, or getting noticed and ranked by the search engines. It is extremely easy to create a social blog in Blogger.

Blogging for business purposes is NOT extremely easy to accomplish. But nor is it rocket science. It is almost impossible to get it right without some trial and error unless you have a good set of instructions. I hope to share with you here my experiences which hopefully will save you a great deal of time and angst.

START HERE

BEFORE you ever consider creating your business blog website there are many preliminary things you need to do. Without these initial steps you will find yourself going back and making changes in your entries in Blogger time and time again. In fact you won't have a clue what information to fill into many of the boxes.

If you are already running a non-blog-based business and have fully-developed products being marketed elsewhere you can skip to the highlighted paragraph below to where we first access the Blogger program.

You can use your Blogger website to market anything, from your own virtual products to affiliate programs. Start from scratch with a niche-centered search, Chapter 4. Choose your niches wisely. Then create a list of at least five virtual products or affiliate programs you want to represent, Chapter 16. Then for each of these programs, create a list of the ten best keywords for each program, Chapter 5.

Now you must register your keyword-rich domain names for the above five products. It can be helpful, but not critical, that all of the programs be in the same general niche but with each within its own sub-niche. Then choose a web host to accept your Blogger program. This host should (and most do) have a program called "Technorati" installed.

Next you need to pretend you are writing a classified ad. Create headlines, sub-headlines, and short copy. Chapters 17 and 18 should help you do this. Last but not least create a Google AdSense account .

NOW you have everything you need to begin to actually set up your Blogger website account.

Setting up this Google Blogger website correctly is a three-step process, Google is step one, Yahoo! step two, and other blog search engines step three.

Step one: Go to blogger.com. You can skip the "quick tour" until after you read this entire chapter, by which time you shouldn't need it! You will be asked for a "user name and password" and a "display name". This display name is shown at the end of each post you make.

For a social-only blog (family and friends) it is irrelevant what you fill in here. Not so for your business account. (Incidentally, you can change the "display name" for each and every blog you send in the future.)

Your "Title" should be short and sweet, three to four words maximum, and must contain your main keywords. (For a social blog it can simply be your name or nickname). Your URL will be: (your keywords).blogspot.com.

Use a REAL email address where asked, and agree to the Terms of Service. It is not a bad idea to actually read these!

Time to name your blog, in the "Blog Title" box. Use two to four of your best keywords. In the next box choose your URL with the same keywords. If the URL you choose is already in use Google will tell you this. Try the hyphenated version, or no spaces between words, or rearrange the words, or try different words. You will eventually find an unused relevant URL to register at godaddy.com or any other domain registrar. I find GoDaddy to be the easiest and least expensive in the long rum..

It is this URL that Google Adsense (Chapter 38) uses to decide what ads to place on your Blogger site. (This is just as Adsense does with your non-Blogger URL at your non-BlogSpot hosted websites.)

If you choose to use Google's free BlogSpot hosting option (which I suggested above that you not do for a business website) your BlogSpot address (URL) will be: (your keywords).blogspot.com. (At this point you can tell Blogger if you want to host outside of BlogSpot and they will explain how to accomplish this. It is easier for you if you just stick with Google, though you lose some control as I mentioned above.)

To tell whether you have chosen an AdSense-friendly choice for your BlogSpot-specific URL, go to: resultsgenerator.com/adsense and enter your URL. Click on "Show Me Sample Ads". If two or more sample ads appear that's great. Job done. But if no ads appear you need to choose a different URL. Slight wording variations, or hyphens between words, may well produce sample ads on the next try. Then you have to go back to Blogger to see whether this new URL is taken, register it, etc..

It is not carved in stone that you actually must <u>use</u> AdSense ads on your site. This exercise in URL keyword validation will in any event tell you whether your URL is search engine friendly or is not.

Once you have your blog title and blog address, copy the word verification letters (used by webmasters to weed out robot visitors) and click "continue".

You now choose one of a dozen or so ready-made templates for your blog.
Always clear everything extraneous off the template and start on a clean white page. For all practical purposes it makes no difference which template you choose. Pick one you like, then scrub it clean! Click "continue" and you are ready to blog! Do a test blog, titling it "test". Leave the link field blank. Put "test" in the body of the post. Click "Publish Post".

If you click "View Blog", up it comes with your blog body text "test". You will see four tabs across the top: "Posting", "Settings", Template" and "View Blog".

Click on "Settings". A number of sub-tabs drop down. You must make changes in some of these sub-tabs. Leave everything else alone.

Click on "Publishing". Where it says: "Notify Weblogs.com" you must make this choice: "Yes". Click on "Save Settings".

Click on "Formatting". At the bottom where it says "Show Link Field" you must make this choice: "Yes". Click on "Save Settings".

Click on "Comments". For "Who Can Comment" choose "Anyone". Under "Comment Notification Address" put any email address where you want notice that someone has posted a comment on your blog. (Incidentally, comments are great because they qualify as "new content" for the spiders.) Click on "Save Settings".

You want your blog to be archived daily. Make this change and click "Save Settings".

Under the "Site Feed Tab" make a note of your "Site Feed URL" which is your Blogger URL followed by "/atom.xml". Now click on the "Republish" button. Hopefully you will see: "Your blog published successfully." Everything is now set up properly for you to blog and ping!

Under the "Template" tab, your business blog template "Editor" entry each post should contain a keyword or phrase.

Under "Computer Security" you will see HTML code. Scroll down to: <p class="post-fiiter">. Below that, where you see the following code:

<aref="<$BlogItemPermalinkURL$>"title="permanent link>< $BlogItemDateTime$></a></em>. Replace ONLY the highlighted words with your keywords. You need to do this for every blog you post.

You will often be using "BlogThis! in Blogger to cut and paste whole articles or parts of articles that relate to your website's content. You can add text and remove text by accessing the "HTML" (**H**yper **T**ext **M**arkup **L**anguage) code (the body of the post) and making text changes within the code.

You do not need to actually know HTML code. Just look for the words you want to delete, or look for the position within the text where you want to insert additional words.

It is also important to have links on your blog, the more the better. Go to the "Templates" tab and scroll down to the HTML code for sidebar links. The yellow shaded code is the URL for the link. The green shaded code is what your visitor sees.

You want to have that green code full of keywords. You replace ONLY the words "EDITME" with your blog's URL (yellow area) and relevant keywords (green area).

You will see an "About Me" line in small type at the upper right. You will want to change the "Editor" in the sidebar to be the same as you are using when posting blogs. Replace: <$**BlogMemberProfile**$> with that name.

Last but not least go to the "Settings" tab and click on the "Basic" sub-tab. Put in a keyword rich description. Then click on "Save Settings" and "Republish".

All of this may seem like an awful lot of work, and at first it is. The more you blog the easier it all becomes, until it is second nature and takes relatively little time.

BLOGGING WITH YAHOO!

Now we come to the important **step two**, blogging and pinging Yahoo!. Setting this up properly is a bit tricky, and is where many Blogger sites go wrong. Yahoo! could well account for 30% of your website's income, so it is worthwhile to get this correct.

Go to yahoo.com and click on "My Yahoo!" at the upper right. Click on "Sign Up" and follow the instructions to "Create Your Yahoo ID". This will be the address for your shiny new Yahoo! email account (after checking the box "Create my free Yahoo! email account"). You will also create a case-sensitive password. (No need to mess with the "Customizing Yahoo!" option).

Copy the verification code. Agree to the Terms and Conditions (which I suggest you actually read). Once you click "I Agree" you are ready to link your blog website to your new Yahoo! account. The key is that Yahoo! allows you to subscribe to <u>your OWN blog "RSS feed"</u>.

FYI, "RSS", depending on who you ask, stands for "**R**DS **S**ite **S**ummary", "**R**ich **S**ite **S**ummary", or "**R**eally **S**wift **S**yndication". Whatever.

Once you see your "Registration Completed" welcome page, print out a copy for your records. Click on "Continue To My Yahoo!". Up comes your own personal landing page. It is unimportant how you wish to personalize this page.

Now the key step, registering for your own blog. Click on the "Add Content" button at the very bottom of the landing page. Up comes a "Find Content" box. At the far right in almost zero point type (!) there is a link that says "Add RSS by URL". Click on it. Enter your Blogger **site feed** URL address, which is your Blogger URL followed by "/atom.xml". Click "Add".

The test post "text" you did earlier allows your blog to become "active" as Yahoo! does a quick search to validate your address. You will now see a screen with a button that reads: "Add To My Yahoo!". Click on it. Once you see that your site feed URL has been accepted, click on the "My Yahoo! Home" button. You will see your blog listed at the bottom. Success is yours!!!

Yahoo! spiders have seen your site immediately upon receipt of your blog. They visited and indexed and you are on your way to search engine recognition with no delay at all.

Now let's ping Yahoo!. Right-clicking on the blog you want to ping to Yahoo! you will see a box that reads: "Properties for (your blog name)". There will be a filled-in "Location" field containing your actual URL. To ping Yahoo! you **must** add a string of text immediately before your URL in this box. Add the following code: "api.my.yahoo.com/rss/ping?u=", without the quotation marks. Ping Yahoo by clicking on the bookmarked link. Done!

You should see a message that says: Refresh requested: (your URL). To confirm that Yahoo! pinged the blog go back to your Yahoo! home page. At the bottom where you registered your blog earlier you should see the latest post. End of messing with Yahoo!.

In summary, every time you add content to Google's Blogger you will ping both Yahoo! and Ping-O-Matic (see below). You may also wish to add your blog to other sites for submission. A Google search for "Blogging Submission Sites" will turn up many. You might want to start with: blogarama.com, blogsearchengine.com, and globeofblogs.com.

AND THE OTHERS..........

Last **Step, Three**. Let us now ping other search engines by using Technorati. This is a real-time every-minute-update that keeps track of the entire world of blogs, which is known affectionately as "The Blogosphere". Go to technorati.com and click "Sign Up!". Fill out the intuitive form. Scan down to the "Your Blogs" section. Add your actual Blogger (or non-Blogger) URL

Next click on "Claim This Weblog". Copy the code you see in "Profile Link" and include it in a short blog post on your website. (The text in this case need not be for visitor consumption, but simply for pinging search- purposes.) Then click on "Ping Technorati" and wait for the "Ping Received" message, and you are done.

There is a time-saver available. Say you have several new blogs, and might find going through the above procedure for each one to be a pain, which it is. Enter "Ping-O-Matic". This service not only automatically pings Technorati but a dozen or more other blog search engines. Go to pingomatic.com.

Enter your keyword rich blog name created earlier, and your Blogger or non-Blogger URL. Check off every one of the "Services To Ping" and click "Submit Pings". Done. Bookmark this site and in the future return here to re-ping quickly.

To be certain your pinging is successful, and your website is being spidered by the web bots go to google.com and enter: allinurl:(your URL). If you get "no results" you are not yet being spidered. Check every day for three days, and if you are still not being spidered (unlikely) repeat the entire pinging procedure.

Remember, without pinging every time you blog it can be months before your website is found by the search engine robot spiders. Also, your website will only be re-spidered and updated maybe every three months. For optimum search engine placement pinging after each blog post **is critical.**

In the future you will be using the "Blog This" tab in Blogger. From the list of your websites at the upper right side drop-down menu you select one, and highlight some text. Paste it into the body of your blog template. Note that your title has appeared in the Title Field, and your URL appears in the URL field. Also, the text you highlighted will be seen in the body of the blog. That's all there is to it!

From a marketing perspective one key value of blogs is that you can easily place "contextual" (within your written copy) links in your blog. These can take your reader anywhere, including to a squeeze page on your website, your "buy now" website or any page of your website, or directly to an affiliate site (Chapter 16 through 20). You simply underline the text words that are the link, and tell Blogger what the URL is for that link.

You get visitors to you blog website in all of the ways you get visitors to any other conventional website.

WORD PRESS YOUR WAY TO SUCCESS

Now let's turn our attention to the other popular blog software, creating your marketing websites using a program called "WordPress". The advantage WordPress has over creating your websites within your web host's cPanel (or whatever site-creation program they may have) is a greatly flattened learning curve. And WordPress is FREE.

Just as with Blogger, you can have WordPress host your website, at wordpress.com. I do not recommend this. As with BlogPost, I greatly prefer to always be in full command of my website's future. I'm just more comfortable having my own host whose primary business is hosting.

WordPress is relatively easy to work with compared to a host's cPanel. The power of the program lies in the large number of available "plug-ins" that enhance the functionality of this blog-based website-creation platform.

Once you have your domain name set up at some web host. Be certain your host is WordPress friendly by having "Fantastico" software; most are. You will go to wordpress.org (not .com) website and download the software to your host server.

The WordPress folk pride themselves in the fact that the entire process takes less than five minutes. They claim to have served over 65 million downloads, so to say it is a popular website creation tool would be an understatement. It is reported that 22% of all active domains operate on the WordPress platform!

Here are some "must have" WordPress plugins that I strongly recommend. A Google search for "WordPress Plug Ins" will uncover many more. An extensive list can be found at urbangiraffe.com.

AddThis at: wordpress.org/extend/plugins/addthis/. This plug-in is for social site bookmarking.
Akismet at: wordpress.org/extend/plugins/akismet/. This helps to filter out spam comments if you have set up a comments feature on your WordPress website.

All In One Adsense & YPN at: wordpress.org/extend/plugins/all-in-one-adsense-and-ypn-pro/. This software code facilitates your Google Adsense commission program.

Lighter Menus simplifies the rather awkward basic WordPress menu system. Find it at: wordpress.org/tags/lighter-menu-plugin.

Google XML Sitemaps keep Google happy. You definitely want them to like your site. Happy Google, happy you! Download from: wordpress.org/extend/plugins/google-sitemap-generator/. This plug-in also alerts the major search engines whenever your sitemap has been updated.

Tiny MCE Advanced at: wordpress.org/extend/plugins/tinymce-advanced/. This is an enhancement to the WordPress editor.

HeadSpace2 facilitates adding your meta tags (site-identifying code words.) Download from: wordpress.org/extend/plugins/headspace2/.

WP-DB Manager at: wordpress.org/extend/plugins/wp-dbmanager/ is rather important. You DO want to be able to restore and back-up your precious files, no?

WP Super Cache is a very fast caching engine producing static html code files, at: wordpress.org/extend/plugins/wp-super-cache/.

Ultimate Google Analytics are great for all of your statistical analyses: wordpress.org/extend/plugins/ultimate-google-analytics/. This adds a Google JavaScript on each of your website pages.

WordPress Automatic Upgrade is useful for keeping the code in your account up to date. It is found within your account.

Technically (not that it matters!) CaRP is an RSS to HTML parser/converter written in PHP. Whatever. You will find the CaRP script for FREE at: geckotribe.com/rss/carp/.

Creating a WordPress blog-based website for business purposes is important because WordPress is search-engine friendly. It enables customizable permalinks, meaning that your blog posts automatically contain original descriptive keywords in their page names.

Backlinks, links coming in from other websites to yours are very important for enhancing your search engine ranking. There is an interesting program that works with WordPress data to help you accomplish getting backlinks.
Go to CommentHut at: commenthut.com. Download their FREE "Lite" version. It finds WordPress blog-websites using your chosen keywords and phrases. It only indexes those websites that accept comments. You can even specify that the program only spit out high-page-rank websites which are most important to your search engine optimization.

Visit the websites that the program comes up with and post **relevant** comments on the site. Put your URL link in the "Your Website" panel. When your comment is published, presto, you have your one-way back link! The upgraded (read "pay for it") version expands the search to many more blog platforms other than WordPress. According to their website this gives you 90% more results!

For all of the information you could ever want about WordPress go to: codex.wordpress.org. Prepare to be overwhelmed!

Aside from Blogger and WordPress, there are many other popular blog programs, most of them totally FREE. Be certain to check out:

Tumbler.com, a micro-blog. Easy to use.
Blogetery.com, a WordPress platform.
Typepad.com, very business focused. One of my favorites.
Blogster.com a social-site type community.
Hubpages.com is commercial-oriented.
LiveJournal.com, a social-site-type.
Xanga.com, you get a "site" not just a weblog.
Blog.com, integrates with many other platforms.

Wikispaces.com claims seven-million members.
Tblog.com, a social-site type.

Because they are FREE there is no reason not to try these
as well. You might just find they fit your needs even better.

LINKING CONSIDERATIONS

There is a point you need to consider in all of your blog
links. Instead of simply using your keyword-rich URL by
itself, consider enhancing the link with additional keywords.
This requires messing a bit with HTML code, but if you
simply can fill in your information in the appropriate code
you will be fine (omit the brackets [ ]):

<a href=http://www.[your exact URL]>[your added
keywords]</a>

Doing this is a big help in your ultimate goal of high search
engine positioning.

You can find "DoFollow" backlink-friendly blog sites at:
dofollow.info. Also check out: techtipsmaster.com/do-
follow-forums-and-blogs.html, and:
robdogg.com/wordpress/2008/02/10/7-high-page-rank-
blogs-that-dofollow/

Some high PageRank blogs to which you should definitely
post blogs are: bloglines.com; blogpulse.com;
blogdiffer.com; getblogs.com; blogorama.com;
blogcatalog.com; blogstreet.com; blogflux.com;
bloghub.com.

Here are some other websites I would strongly recommend
for posting short, concise blog posts that are very content-
rich: reddit.com; stumbleupon.com; xanga.com;
ehow.com; digg.com; hubpages.com.

You may be amazed at the response you will get from posting at these sites. Great for potential sales, for building your mailing lists, and for generating the backlinks that will help you achieve higher search engine rankings. And remember, all of this exposure is **FREE.**

Remember to close all of your blogs with your link, but make it a "cliff hanger". Don't just say: "To learn more about (your product) click here". Instead, say something like: "(There is one product that (whatever special benefit you product offers). Want to know what it is? Find out at (your website URL or specific page URL)." See the difference? On which link would you be more likely to click?

PODCASTING FOR THE TALKATIVE

No chapter on blogging would be complete without mention of a technique called "Podcasting". This is simply a self-**audio**-publishing medium. It is far beyond the scope and intention of this book to give you anything other than an overview of podcasting.

If some time in the future you want to get seriously involved in podcasting there are many fine books on the subject you can purchase or borrow from the library.

Podcasts are created by anyone desiring to share some passion or idea with the masses via any listening device. If one has the means to listen to a radio broadcast, they can listen to your podcast. This of course includes not only portable devices such as an iPod (or any MP3 player), but also desktops or laptop computers or tablets.

A podcast can be downloaded directly from a podcaster's website and listened to on your PC using any media player you choose. It is a way for people to fill their iPods and other media devices with something other than music!

Podcasts can be scripted or unscripted. They bring their listeners unedited, real, from-the-heart commentary on anything imaginable. As opposed to radio, there are no regulations as to content. It is a Libertarian's delight!

Technically there is a computer language called "XML" (Extensible Markup Language). A text form called "RSS" (Real Simple Syndication) links to an XML formatted file. RSS feeds enable you to share your verbal content across the internet.

One needs specialized software to receive podcasts. This software is referred to generically as "podcatchers" which in techno-geek speak are known as "podcast aggregators". This open-source (read "FREE and ever-evolving) software tool allows you to subscribe to and manage any RSS feeds you want automatically downloaded. Popular software for Microsoft Windows includes:

Doppler Radio at: dopplerradio.net/
iPodder at: ipodder.sourceforge.net/download/index.php
Nimiq at: podcatchermatrix.org/show/nimiq

I suggest you access each of these sites and click on all of the various links. Once you have studied these sites in detail you will have an excellent grasp of the entire podcasting realm.

With podcasts you are able to lie in bed and broadcast to the world! You choose a topic, decide on the length of your show, and decide how often it will run. Generally, your topic should be something you know well and are passionate about.

Clearly there is a potential marketing component here. While your visitors are seeking entertaining and informative listening, the opportunity to include a pitch for your website or book-publishing links clearly exists. But, as with maintaining a blog with frequent fresh content, podcasting can take a good bit of your time.

You should also realize that, unless you can produce a very special and highly-sought podcast on a regular schedule, it is unlikely that your audience will ever exceed a few thousand listeners. This is not a very large potential group of buyers for your products.

In order to produce podcasts you only need a computer, a website, and a microphone, plus some software downloaded from the internet. To be effective your computer should have a Pentium 4 or stronger central processing unit (CPU), one gigabyte of random access memory (RAM), four gigabytes of free space on your hard drive, and "line in/line out" connections for a microphone and headset.

You will need specialized recording software. I believe the most commonly used product is "Audacity for Windows", an audio editor/recorder. You can access this at: audacity.sourceforge.net/. The best part is that it's FREE.

If you already have an adequate computer your only additional cost is a decent microphone and headset from Radio Shack (now officially called, for whatever idiotic reason, simply "The Shack") or Walmart.

If you want to add podcasted RSS feeds to your website, use a website script called CaRP (not CrAP!). You will need a "File Transfer Protocol" (FTP) program to use in conjunction with CaRP. (I use "Cute FTP"at cuteftp.com). A Google search will turn up many ftp programs.   Filezilla at: filezilla.com is another popular ftp program.

There are, in my never humble opinion, lots of time-effective (and therefore cost-effective....time is money) ways to make money on the internet. Perhaps I have not given podcasting a serious marketing effort. I'm told by friends who get their jollies talking into a microphone in their pajamas that podcasing is great fun and can be profitable. I'm just too busy getting rich with other multiple streams of internet income to bother!

IN CONCLUSION

To summarize: Be certain you use your primary keyword(s) in your blog URL. Use your primary key phrase in the title of your posts. Use your secondary keywords in the body of your post. Tweak your default settings as described above. Update as often as possible.

So there you have it. Blogging can be a highly profitable, though a bit time consuming, way to market your products. Google's Blogger can get your marketing website up and running quickly. Pinging will get you noticed quickly. WordPress can make starting a marketing website a breeze. Podcasting is an awareness you can file away for the future.

Take the time to work with blogs. You may well find, as many internet infopreneurs have, that it is one of the most powerful of the multiple streams of internet wealth creation business models.

JUST DO IT!

MODULE FIVE
THE EBAY CASH MACHINE

CHAPTER 21: HOW TO CASH IN BIG WITH EBAY AUCTIONS

CHAPTER 21
HOW TO CASH IN BIG WITH EBAY AUCTIONS

Internet auctions started as a hobby for a few computer geeks in San Francisco. They wanted to create a virtual swap meet to dispose of unwanted items in exchange for items they wanted.

It took less than a decade for this idea to become a multi-billion-dollar worldwide enterprise. This is quite the same as the Social Media phenomenon. Put a couple of genius propeller-heads together in a garage and out comes magic!

EBay presents the internet marketer with the best low-risk option for making money on line. You simply **must** include it in your internet marketing mix. There are a lot of "get rich quick" scams out there, but eBay is a completely legitimate business that anyone can run from the comfort of their home.

EBay should become a key component in your overall internet marketing multiple streams of internet strategy. When you've got millions of shoppers looking for anything and everything imaginable (ten million or so at any given moment) there is almost always someone who says: "That's **exactly** what I want!"

There is a credible story of a teenager who started out auctioning a paper clip on eBay and through a long succession of auctions kept doubling his product's value until he was able to buy a house! [This closely follows the arithmetic mentioned earlier behind taking a penny, doubling it every day for a month, and ending up with millions of dollars.]

Never underestimate the value of eBay auctions once you acquire the "how to" knowledge I'm sharing in this book. I believe it was H. L. Mencken who first said: "No one ever went broke under-estimating the intelligence of the American Public". And of course P. T. Barnum is quoted as saying : "There's a sucker born every minute!". EBay is proof of both!

The fact is, many people buy items on eBay OFTEN for far more than they are worth or could be bought for elsewhere. Auctions are an addiction to many, just as are slot machines. This is to the advantage of those who know eBay profit-techniques and take advantage of the addicts.

In contrast, there are many real bargains to be had. You can even buy items on eBay (assuming you actually find a real bargain) and re-sell the same item on eBay for much more money than you just paid simply be employing better eBay marketing techniques! We call this "eBay Arbitrage", and it is quite easy to accomplish and a lot of fun. Many eBay sellers are clueless on how to optimize their auction sales' results for top dollar. There is one marketing key to making money in eBay Arbitrage. It also applies to any physical product you might want to buy outside of eBay and sell on eBay. It is quite profound.

Back in the early 1900s the wealthiest man in the United States was an industrialist named J. Pierpoint Morgan. He was so rich he once actually bailed out the US Treasury! Another financier asked JP for an audience to teach him the secrets of his boundless success. JP agreed to a $20,000 fee for the meeting, which was a lot of money back in those days.

They met at Morgan's posh office, sat across a table, and JP gave him 100% of his valuable advice in ONE

SENTENCE: **"Buy low, sell high!"** That was it. End of meeting. Thanks for the 20K! That sentence is as true today as it was back then. The point is, you make your money when you **buy**, not when you sell. Got it?

THE POWER EBAY AFFORDS YOU

EBay may just be the perfect business model. Consider:

You can sell to any one of the hundreds of millions of people worldwide who are connected to the internet;

Your geographic location can by dynamic. Work from wherever you live, work from wherever you travel, work from anywhere;

You do not need employees. Your computer is the only "help" you need;

You can choose to work part-time or full-time, any hours you choose;

You can "quit" any time you wish without penalty;

There is no barrier to entry;

You need no formal education;

The risks of starting an eBay business are almost non-existent;

You can buy and sell merchandise in the same place;

Record keeping is automatically done for you within your account;

You can perform market research for FREE before you post a single item for sale.

I challenge you to show me any business model on earth that even comes close to making a living on eBay. **There simply aren't any.**

HOW YOU MAKE MONEY ON EBAY

Actually, there are three separate and distinct ways to use eBay as a primary stream of internet income. From the viewpoint of attracting potential buyers, understand that people who search eBay are looking to actually BUY something. Visitors to Google are more likely to simply be looking for information. Google is larger, but eBay can produce much better targeted marketing results.

The first income stream which we will discuss is the well-known eBay auction platform. In fact, most people think this is eBay's *only* purpose. Not so. Later we will explore the other two eBay income streams, having your own "eBay Store", and marketing with "eBay Classified Ads". Once you have a product to sell you should utilize all three eBay income streams.

There are entire expensive courses on eBay marketing available. You will often see these offered on late-night TV infomercials. I own most of these, and there is certainly a wealth of information contained in them. They cost many hundreds of dollars.

The reality is that eBay is so easy to learn and to use that it is a pure waste of money for any newbie to buy these. My personal excuse is that I buy everything internet-income-related because I can occasionally pick up one item of information that I can profitably add to my years of hard-knocks knowledge.

As for the $97 and lower cost 50+ page eBay reports one sees advertised, again, nothing wrong with most of them. They are often filled with useless fluff and are vastly overpriced. Though touted as beginners' information, they can be more valuable to those already doing well on eBay.

We are focusing first on promoting virtual electronically-downloadable products. EBay has "forbidden" (ostensibly) selling such digitally delivered items, .pdf flles of your report or ebook, or .wav audio versions, when using their **auction** format. To comply with this relatively new rule you must now convert your reports and books into a physical CD and send the CD, beautifully packaged, to the buyer.

I say "ostensibly" because eBay does not seem to rigidly enforce this rule. Just look at all of the ads for digital products and you will see what I mean. EBay's rules are well-known in the industry as being very difficult to interpret. Contacting them directly reminds me of contacting the Internal Revenue Service. Ask three different people the exact same question and you are very likely to get three conflicting answers!

When rules are so complex and vague that company employees themselves cannot agree on their interpretation it is an invitation to do whatever you damn please! If you are in the mood to be frustrated, check out eBay's official rules at: pages.ebay.com/help/sell/f-ad.html. I can only guess what the "f" stands for! Find?

Be certain to check out such things as: "Can I add a PayPal button in my auction?"; "Can I link to my website from a Classified Ad?"; or "How can I promote my affiliate links on eBay?". If you can find definitive answers to these questions, and techniques that work 100% of the time, you have the makings of your own valuable report! I'll be your first customer!

But being forced to produce hard copies of your virtual product is not all bad. In fact, you can actually make more money because of a buyer's increased perceived value of a physical CD over a virtual ebook.

Thanks to Kunaki (at kunaki.com) providing CDs is a relative simple and amazingly inexpensive process. It is a fact that many buyers would prefer a CD over an ebook in any event. Further, you can still offer the buyer the digital download as a FREE incentive. Also check out Swift CD at: swiftcd.com. My approach to offering you multiple choices of recommended vendors for anything on the internet is to have you actually try them all over time. That way you will inevitably find one with which you are most comfortable after comparing prices and service. And you always have a back-up source if one goes belly-up!

You are, of course, permitted to send out printed copies of your reports and eBooks using the auction format. You can buy these printed copies of your books yourself at Amazon's createspace.com at a very reduced price (around five bucks) and resell them on eBay for multiples of your cost.

You can, however, still sell your digital products, as well as physical products on "eBay Classified Ads" which we will discuss further below. There are also many techniques to link eBay to your websites where you can sell anything at all, including your vendor affiliate links.

AUCTION EXCITEMENT!

Have you ever attended a live auction in person? If not, you should, even if you have no intention of buying anything. You will learn quickly that auctions are very seductive. You have eager buyers curious to check out the items being auctioned. The items being auctioned are (at least at that moment) one of a kind, a scarcity factor that is always important in marketing any product.

There is a key difference between live auctions, such as conducted regularly at Christie's and Sotheby's and countless local auctions, and an eBay auction. Ebay is a facilitator, a giant bulletin board. They do not take possession of the goods, and make no warranties about the quality of the item, as do the auction houses.

EBay makes no representation about the seller's or buyer's honesty, nor do they take any percentage of the payments, as do the auction houses. Auction houses get a fat percentage of the sale price. EBay exists by charging all manner of fees, but not a big piece of your profits.

EBay auctions are fun to follow, but there is something impersonal about the experience. I've never felt my heart pound watching a computer screen. Not so with in-person auctions. The live auctioneer, who is an expert at "working a crowd", creates a palpable urgency. Once the first bidder's number card is held up, others almost invariably follow. If the auctioneer can involve at least two people who really want the item the fun starts! It becomes a hand to hand battle, a competition for superiority. Mano a mano. If more than two bidders are involved it becomes a feeding frenzy. If you happen to be one of the bidders, you had better have a strong heart! And it is almost as exciting to be an observer.

I know, because I buy lots of things at auction, from art work to ephemera to rare coins to cars to houses. And believe me, there is a sense of euphoria when you are the last man standing (even if you know damn well you overpaid for something!).

And it can be quite deflating if the price is bid up to a level where you decide (and you have only an instant to make that decision before you hear "going…..going….go__") that bidding any further might well insure either a quickie divorce or at least a Spartan lifestyle in the near future!

RESEARCH IDEAS

The key to eBay success is the same as it is in all internet marketing, **research.** To attempt to sell anything on eBay without first knowing as much as possible about what is happening in a given niche is a waste of your time. It can also significantly lower your profits.

Your research goals are to answer these key questions:

What products are selling?
What products are not selling?
What are the *top* selling products?
How are my competitors selling their products?
What are the conversion rates for key products in my niche?
What is the average selling price in my niche?

There is an almost bewildering assortment of program tools to simplify your eBay marketing once you begin to sell many items. eBay provides a very comprehensive list of these tools which you may wish to study. Go to: pages.ebay.com/sellerinformation/sellingresources/sellingtools.html.

The good news is that there is a wealth of research information available on eBay itself. The most valuable tool is the "eBay Pulse Pages" at: pulse.ebay.com. Here you can locate all of the most popular keyword searches and the most frequently visited listings for every category.

You can also find "Hot Item Reports" here, showing items most commonly searched for, not necessarily sold, in the previous month. If you observe an item on this list month after month it is a good indication of unsatisfied demand. There is also a "Hot Selling Items Report" you can download for FREE:
pages.ebay.com/sellercentral/hotitems.pdf.

EBay has a catalog at: pages.ebay.com/sellercentral/catalog.html that will provide you with a good look at what products are in demand. This is set up specifically to facilitate the listing of certain kinds of consumer items in a standardized manner.

Certain products MUST be listed in the catalog. These include cameras, video games, cell phones, TVs, computers and a host of other electronic items. We are not concerned with any of this physical-product stuff in this book.

There are also endless "eBay Guides" that can be accessed for FREE by clicking on: Site Map>Buying Resources>Reviews & Guides. There are, in fact, almost 1,500 help reports within the eBay website! You can find the entire list at: pages.ebay.com/help/index/ALL.html. I suspect one could take a month to read them all! And it's not a bad idea to do so if you are serious about learning all you possibly can about marketing on eBay.

EBay also has a paid subscription service called "eBayMarketplace". For a reasonable price, and with very short-term options available, sellers can "Get an indication of demand for the items they're selling, at what price they should sell them for, and pick up selling tips from other members." Worth checking out.

You definitely should check out the list and access those reports that are relevant to the specific marketing you will be doing. You can certainly get started with eBay marketing without studying any of these, but knowledge is power.

Excellent research can be done by clicking on "Advanced Search" on eBay's home page. Then click: (enter your niche or keywords)>Completed Auctions Only. Here you can research categories sellers are using, their auction duration, and starting prices.

You can again go to Advanced Search and click: "a">Completed Auctions>Worldwide>Sort By>Price:Highest First". (Use "a" or anything you choose, and try: > Price Lowest First. This is yet another way to see where the action is overall.

To see which keywords are searched the most go to buy.ebay.com. For strings of common keywords go to: keyword-index.ebat.com/B-1.html. For specific product keywords search: product-keyword.ebay.com/PB-1.html.

Beyond eBay, Google has many very useful tools. For example, go to: groups.google.com. Type in your niche description, add a question in the question box, and you will get an answer that could be very useful. Give it a try. It's fun!

There are also excellent third-party research tools available. Check out HammerTap at: hammertap.com (best value in my opinion) and Terapeak at: terapeak.com. The latter is more expensive but has a few unique features. Both are monthly subscriptions, and each has a trial period.

FINDING YOUR PROPER AUCTION CATEGORY

It is absolutely essential to list your auctions under the proper category. Here is a list of generic categories often used to sell information products:

Books>Other
Business & Industrial>Businesses For Sale>Other
Business & Industrial>Businesses For Sale>Websites
Computers & Office Products>Software>PC>Other
Computers & Office Products>Technology Books
Computers & Office Products>Services>Informational
Everything Else>Services>Information Services
Everything Else>EBay User Tools

The key, however, is simply to find where on eBay buyers are searching for the products you are selling. You should always list in specific niche locations, but do not overlook the above generic location possibilities.

GET STARTED

Here are the simple steps you need to follow to begin your eBay marketing adventure:

Go to eBay.com and register for a free seller account which takes less than a minute.

Register for free on PayPal.com to process your eBay payments and receipts.

Return to your eBay account and link it to your PayPal account. (Incidently, eBay actually owns PayPal). Check out the PayPal fees (well worth the cost) at paypal.com/fees. Learn about the PayPal Seller Protection Policy at: paypal.com/securitycenter.

Set up your seller account, completing all of the personal information requested.

Under "Financial Information" set up your eBay payment information.

Go to ebay.com/idverify and complete the procedure steps.

Review the eBay selling fees. This includes Insertion Fees, various Listing Upgrades, and Final Value Fees.

Decide what to sell.

Decide on your auction format. Your choices are "Auction-style", "Buy It Now", "Fixed Price" (which eliminates all bidding), and "Best Offer". You can use combinations of auction and buy-it-now, or fixed price with best offer.

Create great pictures of your item or create appropriate book covers for reports or case covers for CDs and DVDs.

Write your ad title using keywords that a buyer might use when searching. You are allowed 80 characters, and should use them all. (See Chapter35).

If space allows add "Fast Delivery" to your title or sub-title, if appropriate and if there is sufficient space.

Write your item description, as you would any good advertisement.

Determine your shipping costs. See: ebay.com/shippingguide.

Now click "Sell" and enter all of your information.

Select your product category. Be very specific and tightly niche focused.

Launch your auction!

It is important to note that you pay final value fees ONLY if your item actually sells. It is FREE to list up to 50 auction-style listings per month that start at any price. You can add the buy-it-now feature to all of these listings for FREE.

TECHNIQUES AND NUANCES

You can learn all about the fees eBay charges for their many options at: ebay.com/fees. For fees charged for the convenience of using PayPal go to paypal.com/fees.

There are a number of special techniques and nuances that experienced eBay marketers use to enhance their profits:

Choose your "User Name" very carefully. This name becomes your business identification. You want a name that implies you are an expert in your field. This important step is often overlooked. This is your eBay business ID that people will search for when they want to see what you are selling. Idiotic names like "Snuffles4U" don't cut it! But if you are promoting health care products you might try "BestHealthCareGuru". Get the idea?

If you have a keyword rich URL for your product website, use it (without the .com) as your eBay user name.

If you are marketing in more than one niche choose a different user name for each niche. EBay permits this as long as all of your user names refer back to the same email address.

IMPORTANT: Try **not** to use a **free** e-mail service to manage your auctions (Yahoo! mail, HotMail, Gmail). For one thing eBay scrutinizes such accounts more closely than those with a "real" email address (one associated with a website). Apparently savvy buyers are more likely to buy from a seller who does not use free email.

This will require that you get a domain name (URL) and set up email boxes with the provider (at no or nominal cost). You will need at least four mailboxes xxxx@yourURL.com: orders, shipping, loss prevention and (your name).

Somewhere along the line you will need an autoresponder (such as aweber.com discussed earlier) for every possible response to common questions, such as: "When Can I Expect Shipment"; "How Do I Pay", etc. It is a great time saver.

Never forget that a buyer is not only sizing up your product but is also sizing up YOU! Make your listings sound light and friendly.

In the manner of Google Adwords, where you pay per click, eBay has an under-utilized keyword-purchase tool. When someone searches for that keyword or phrase you show up at the top above the search term! If you have done thorough keyword homework and the economics work for your particular item you should at least give this a test run.

YOUR AUCTION TITLE & SUB-TITLE

Your two most important features are the **TITLE** and the **PHOTO**. You
should also consider the "SubTitle" option which allows you to make an important statement such as: "Free Shipping If Item Sells For $X Or More".

Always use keywords in your descriptions to direct people who use the "search" feature. Use keywords in your title. This is critical. It is the most important aspect of your ad. Use "****" liberally. Do not use all capital letters. Capitalize only the initial letter of each title word. (Some disagree with this and advise all capitals).

If you need more space than the 80 characters allowed for a title, note that "_" and "~" do not count as characters, but a blank space does. Placing either between two words saves one character. You want to use every possible character allowed.

If you have a short title, use the underscore symbol, "___" between each word because it makes your title look longer and helps it to stand out from other titles.

In your title be sure to put the most important and most commonly-searched terms first.

YOUR AUCTION LISTING

A higher-priced item generally should have a longer description.

Write honest descriptions of whatever it is you are selling. Do not exaggerate anything. It is always better to under-promise and over-deliver. Point out any negatives.

Always add a "Gallery Picture". This small extra expense allows a photo of your product to appear when buyers are searching with key words or browsing your category. Additional pictures add a small cost, but pictures from various angles can help sell an item. So can a picture that has nothing to do with your product that somehow "says": "HOT", as lava flowing from a volcano might suggest.

Consider a picture of money, along with a picture of your cover, if you are selling a report on making money. The point is, a second picture can complement the first.

Avoid using words that no buyer would ever put in a search box, such as "rare", "beautiful", "unusual", "L@@K", "Super-duper", etc.

Consider using bullet points, bold text, color, or any other highlights that will make your listing stand out in a crowd.

Consider using animated "gifs" to attract attention to your listing. Do a Google search for "free gifs". Check out: wilsoninfo.com/email.htm.

Avoid bright colored backgrounds on your auction listing pages.

The use of audio in your listings will grab the attention of prospective buyers. So will the addition of video clips.

Always use the "**BOLD**" upgrade. It is cheap and effective. You must stand out in the crowd. The "Border" and "Highlight" options should also be considered. These can increase your odds for a sale. But you must be certain that your selling price can absorb the costs for all of these enhancements.

Use the "Highlight" option to stand out in a crowd of competitors. This is a rather expensive option so be certain your item is priced accordingly.

Listing an item in two categories increases is a good idea but it costs a bit more.

Consider the more expensive "Gallery Featured" listing if you are selling something that is high enough priced to absorb the extra cost but that has huge competition for a similarly-searched item. It greatly reduces the competition and gives you about a two to one edge in making the sale.

If you want to be certain your auction shows up near the top of its category it will cost you $19.95 for a "Featured Auction". This is good for high priced items in a general category. In tight niches bidders will hunt you down so this is a waste of money. New listings are only at the top of the first page for a <u>few hours</u>. Your Featured Plus listing stays at the top for the duration of the auction.

A clever use of a Featured Listing ad is to funnel visitors to your non-featured auctions for the same product. You could state: "If you want to buy this book now please visit my other auction which has a 'Buy It Now' button". "Home Page Featured" is great for exposure, but the cost is prohibitive except for <u>very</u> high priced items.

A "Fixed Price" listing format eliminates bidding entirely. The item is available immediately at the price you set. The duration of such a listing is 30 days. What you give up in exchange for possibly getting the price at which you will be satisfied is the possibility of a bidding frenzy driving the price much higher.

For an additional fee in a Fixed Price listing if you will accept a bit less for your item you can opt to pay for a "Best Offer". You are not obligated to accept any best offer. Strategically, making your Fixed Price higher than you actually want, you might actually get a Best Offer higher than you expected from a bargain-seeking buyer!

Use your word processor to spell-check everything. Nothing looks worse in a listing than misspelled words.

If you have multiples of the same item to sell try the "Dutch Auction" format. It saves multiple fees, but you could end up with less profit than running multiple separate standard auctions.

Cross-merchandising can enhance your profits. EBay has FREE tools for the purpose. At the bottom of your listing it will show four related items, rotated in order of expiration. Watch out for eBay fee breakpoints. For example, listing at $9.99 rather than $10.00 saves $0.20. This may seem trivial, but over hundreds of listings it can become significant.

If you have a number of the same item and you always want to show up in both "newly listed" and "ending soonest" list the item every day of the week.

Be sure to always create a link from your auction to your eBay store.

Always have the HTML feature on your eBay listing form turned "ON". This will automatically make your links "clickable" for the buyer.

Include shipping costs in your description.

State a return policy. Include a statement at the bottom of your listing such as: "You have (X…whatever you choose that you are comfortable with. I suggest 5, 7 or 10 days) days to return the product, no questions asked, for a full refund. The cost of shipping will not be refunded.".

You can put virtually anything on this page, including a link to your website. The only restriction here is that any products you offer on your website that you are selling also on eBay must be priced at least $1.00 higher than on eBay.

EBay's "Auction Launch" feature allows you to do all of your auction setup any time prior to starting the actual auction.

If your item receives no bids you can relist it one time at no additional costs. You can make changes in the listing. It is silly not to take advantage of this feature.

You can make changes to your item description during an auction under the "Revise Your Item" instructions.

If you find you have made an error of some sort in your listing you have the option of cancelling all bidders and the auction.

Never use a <u>visible</u> "visitor-counter". If you want a counter use a hidden one. It is one of the useful options eBay offers.

TIMING YOUR AUCTION

Experienced eBay marketers have found that the actual time of day to begin an auction is important. They say that experience has proven that the best time of day is to post is so that it closes at 11:30 PM Eastern time, 8:30 PM Western time. Don't try to reinvent the wheel. Go with the experts. Use this timing.

There are, however, exceptions. Auctions aimed at housewives might best end on a weekday morning. For opportunity seekers try ending your auction a bit later at night.
On what day should you run an auction? In general, the best day to post a 10-day auction is Thursday, because

you get exposure on two weekends, and end on a Sunday which experts consider to be the best day to end any auction. A 7-day auction should always post on Sunday to end on Sunday.

You will find that you get the most traffic on the first and seventh day. Some buyers choose to search by "newly listed". More often they search for those items "ending soonest".

PRICING YOUR PRODUCT

Once you have experience and have reason to believe that what you are selling will get a fair bid do not use a "reserve price" (a minimum below which you will not sell). If you are really concerned about getting what you believe you should then set up a reserve bid. But remember, a low opening bid and no reserve usually attracts more buyers. It's just a bit riskier.

Be very careful choosing your starting bid price. Many of the pros always start at $0.99. You can start at any price you want, but you want to attract bidders and hopefully start a bidding frenzy. You need to leave room for the price to be bid up.

When setting a "reserve bid", the price below which you will not sell, use an "off-beat" number (such as $47.43 as opposed to $49.95, $49.99 or $50.00). This foils buyers who make a game out of trying to guess how close they can get to a reserve price without triggering the auction.

If you are selling a 30 - 40 page report many find $19.97 to be a good reserve or Buy It Now option that generally sells successfully.

If your pricing allows for it, consider offering some sort of free gift with your items. This should be a small, lightweight item you can buy in bulk. Check out liquidation.com and overstock.com for ideas.

SHIPPING MATTERS

Do NOT try to make money on postage and handling. List a shipping price that honestly covers your shipping and packaging cost. People hate to over-pay "S & H" charges, and you will often get fewer and lower bids if your S & H seems out of line with reality. (Some pros prefer to use a flat rate for everything that makes them a small profit. $5.00, $6.00 and similar flat-rate numbers seem to work best.)

Use the US Postal Service (USPS) Priority Mail, with the extra for delivery verification, for anything under two pounds. They have fixed rates and excellent free shipping envelopes and boxes. Use United Parcel Service (UPS), for almost everything else. Delivery confirmation is free.

Don't overlook FedX ground shipment which is often cheaper than UPS.

No matter how you ship be certain to buy some sort of proof that your item arrived at the bidder's address. This can prevent infinite headaches later on.

Be sure to state the number of days after the order is processed that the item will be shipped. Every buyer unrealistically expects instant shipment, while your schedule might be once a week on Thursdays. Ill will can be avoided by employing this one simple step.

If you are selling something tangible, like a CD or DVD, ship it immediately upon payment. Keep an open communication line with your buyers, especially if you are waiting for a check to clear.

Consider offering free shipping only to Buy It Now customers. It is a fact that more eBay buyers use the Buy It Now feature than participate in auctions.

GETTING PAID

Accept payments in every possible way. Don't overlook "cash", "checks" and "money orders". I have never seen the need for having a separate credit card merchant account because PayPal also allows customers without PayPal accounts to use credit cards. Always use PayPal's Seller Protection policy.

(The only downside I see to using PayPal is that they insist you send items to the PayPal confirmed address, which may not be the address the buyer wants used. And PayPal does take a small part of your profits.

Be certain to add the PayPal icon to your auctions. In your PayPal account-overview page click: Profile>Selling Preferences>Auctions>Automatic Logo Insertion.

Some people like to buy on credit. When you use PayPal's financing option you get all of your money up front, can ship the item immediately, and PayPal accepts the risk of the buyer not making all of the payments.

If a buyer pays by check always wait ten days after deposit before you ship.

If you want to accept checks electronically, known as an ACH (Automated Clearing House) payment, check out 123ach.com. It is not cheap at $25/month plus $0.30/transaction, but if you do a large volume of sales it might be advantageous to offer your buyers this option.

OTHER ITEMS

Sales are shown to improve when you create an **"About Me"** page. Putting a "face" behind an anonymous offering makes many bidders more comfortable. Make it an attractive face, preferably female. <u>Both men and women prefer to buy from women.</u> Don't ask! I'm not a shrink. I do know it matters.

When writing your personal profile do not exaggerate or make yourself seem like more than you are. You want a brief snapshot of who you are, how and why you got into selling on eBay, and why they should want to deal with you.

<u>Always make customer satisfaction your #1 priority</u>. Send email #1 as soon as the auction closes. Send a second email confirming that you received payment, advising when you will ship the item. Send a third email immediately after you ship and include the tracking number. Keep you emails light and friendly. Never use all capital letters.

Always check the "Want It Now" listings where buyers post requests when they can't find an item they want. This FREE service gives you the opportunity to respond to the listing and offer your product if it fits the buyer's needs.

Do not overlook the opportunity to contact a <u>losing</u> bidder to see whether they might be interested in purchasing the same item if you have more than one of the item sold to the high bidder.
Save <u>all</u> of your emails, both sent and received. You may need them at a later date for dispute resolution.

Take advantage of eBay's "Store Referral Credit". If you send customers to your eBay store from your website or other outside link, and they buy something from the store inventory when they arrive, you get a full 75% off your Final Value Fees for every item bought!

Keep in touch with the reality of the many scams to which you could fall prey. Check out eBay's "Trust and Safety

Discussions Board". Also periodically look at: pirsquare.letzebuerg.com.biz/scams.html.

When using an eBay Store or eBay Classified ad, never send your downloadable product .pdf via email. Instead send an email directing the buyer to a site where it can be downloaded in a .zip format. (Use the FREE .zip tool at: winzip.com).

If at all possible register for eBay's "ID Verify" service. This just costs a few bucks, and you may need to make a few inexpensive purchases. This will help establish your credibility with buyers.

Do not exclude buyers outside of the USA. Just be certain you know and advise the shipping costs, and get paid in equivalent US dollars.

Include a short refund policy to add buyer comfort. "You have five days to return our product, as shipped, for a full refund (shipping excluded), no questions asked."

NEVER accept payment in cash. Even if the buyer sends it by Registered Mail you may receive an empty envelope from a buyer who swears there was money in it when posted.

It is OK to accept payment by Cashier's check or money order, though these are relatively easy to counterfeit. Seek the advice of a qualified professional (accountant or attorney) regarding what, if any, sales taxes to collect. The above factors are used by every successful eBay entrepreneur I know. It may look like a lot to learn, but after a while it becomes second nature and very simple.

TOOLS OF THE TRADE

There are many tools available to make your entire eBay marketing experience easier. You do not absolutely NEED any of these, but they can save you time and time is money,

The first eBay tool you will want to use is their "TurboLister". You will find this to be a great time saver and well worth the time to learn its nuances. It is FREE. You can store and organize all of your eBay auction ads, which can get quite confusing once you start posting many auctions.
A useful but rather complex tool called Shooting Star can be bought for around $100 at: softwaregeek.com/download/shooting_star.html. There should be a free trial available. It is another real time saver.

It is very useful to use pre-configured templates. Check out: linkfrog.com. They have over 2,000 templates from which to choose. Always use a simple template without a "frames" feature. Stay away from eBay's "border" option. Too many others use it. You want your listings to stand out as much as possible.

If you plan on using many photos in your auctions, you can avoid paying eBay's add-per-photo fees. They allow you to host pictures through any third party site. Check out: doteasyhosting.com; imagewiz.net; and andele.com.

A very useful $97 tool is MyDigitalDispatch. Go to mydigitaldispatch.com and check out the many valuable features. You might decide you cannot live without it!

WINNING STRATEGIES

It is best for a newbie to start with the auction format. Here you can set a "reserve price" below which you will not sell. This will protect you from selling any item far below what you need to sell it to net a profit. This price can be disclosed to bidders or kept secret. Disclosing it may actually prevent the bidding from ever starting. Not revealing it may annoy bidders who get repeat messages that there bid is insufficient. Personally I prefer reserves because I am never stuck with selling something far below its true value.

The eBay "Buy It Now" (BIN) feature is available in the auction model. It is in my mind sort of like placing a reserve. Either way it is the price at which I'd be comfortable selling my item. Using it in the auction format gives me a shot at a higher price. BIN is the model used in the eBay Store format. In the auction format, once any bid is placed the BIN disappears.

There is also something called a "Dutch Auction". If you have more than one of an item you take bids, but are obligated to sell to all of the bidders at the lowest bid price at the end of the auction. It saves the cost of multiple insertion fees, but to my mind it risks far lower profits.

You will find that many auctions have last minute, even last second, bid winners. The bidding pros wait until the very end, keep the price lower than it might have been had they bid earlier, and score at the conclusion. In fact, there are computer programs called "Sniping Software" that do this automatically. It's all within the Rules, so it is simply a fact of eBay life with which you must learn to live.

Perhaps your biggest problem with eBay auctions will be the presence of fake bidders. There are even those who will win an auction but never pay a dime. As a seller you do have the ability to put some restrictions on your buyers. For example, you can accept only high-feedback rated buyers (if buyer-ratings are still available) or only those who have a valid PayPal account. This will weed out a lot of fraud, but you can never eliminate it entirely. Seller beware!

One great feature of eBay is the ease with which you can see how strong the market is for your particular product.

Not only can you watch other auctions as they progress, but you can view everything that transpired within the past ninety days.

Consider using eBay's "Cross-Promotion" feature. You can study this at: pages.ebay.com/storefronts/subscriptions.html. You will need an eBay Shop to use this feature, which allows cross-promotions between your Shop and your Auctions.

Consider "pre-approving" your bidders. EBay allows you to do this in order to weed out buyers you consider undesirable. You can, however, use this to build interest in an upcoming auction. It is certainly a plus if you can have a list of pre-approved bidders salivating over the start of your next auction!

You set up your auction in the usual manner, but state clearly that anyone who wants to bid MUST email you to be pre-approved. Any bidder who tries to bid without emailing you first will be rejected by eBay and instructed to email you first. There is a link in your account that allows you to add "Pre-Approved Bidders/Buyers". You will need to obtain the bidders' eBay user ID.

If you really want to stand out from the crowd consider providing a personal audio or video in your auction listing. Many people find it easier to absorb information when they hear it or see it. There are many hosting services that will host your recordings and provide the links for your auctions. Check out:

Auction Video at: auctionvideo.com

I2iAuction Videos at: i2iauction.com

SellersVoice at: sellersvoice.com

VideoSnap at: videosnap.logitech.com

Properly executed audio and video can create a comfort level in a visitor that might help them decide to buy. Done poorly it could turn off some visitors. You need to monitor your conversion rates with and without the multi-media approach.

MONITOR YOUR COMPETITION

One thing about the Ebay marketplace is that it is impossible to keep a secret! **No good idea goes unnoticed or un-copied by your competitors.** If you find a great item to sell and it sells very well expect to see someone else selling it quite soon. If you come up with a creative strategy for marketing a product you can be equally certain that others will employ that strategy faster than you can blink. These are simple realities with which we must learn to live. You must learn to do likewise.

Many less-honorable sellers literally copy their competitor's wording in their own listings. They even steal the images used by competitors. Do not do these things yourself. Imitation may be the sincerest form of flattery, but it is both immoral and self-defeating. You want to differentiate, not copy.

This is not to say that you should not monitor your competition and learn from both their successes and mistakes. Let's call it "competitive research", because it sounds better than "spying"! There are a number of ways for you to accomplish this:

Sign up for any competitors' newsletter. You can be certain they will be signing up for yours!

Be sure to add all of your competitors to your "Favorite Sellers" list to monitor their new auctions. Don't be too flattered when you find that you are your competitors' "Favorite Seller"!

Check your competitors' feedback for likes and dislikes.

Study your competitors' auction details. You especially want to know how well their items sell and how much they get for their items.

Use eBay Search for your items to see if you have a new competitor.

Actually buy something from a competitor to see how fast they react, what their service is like, and what sirt of emails they send out.

This intelligence is not too unlike the research you should do prior to selling anything on eBay. Armed with this information you should be able to do enough things better than your competitors   to differentiate yourself from them and profit in your chosen niche.

SUMMARY OF SELLING STRATEGIES

To summarize, your overall eBay selling strategy should be:

Choose the appropriate listing category;

Create a great title and sub-title;

Set up high quality pictures;

Write a complete, well-formatted description free of spelling errors;

Determine the range of pricing that items similar to yours have historically achieved;

Start with low opening bids, such as the common $0.99.

Use a reserve if you want to be certain of getting at least what you believe you need;

Avoid bidders with no bidding history;

State reasonable shipping costs;

State clear Terms and Conditions;

Require a bidder have a PayPal account;

Use standard auction lengths, 7-day is best;

Set your auctions to end at strategic times;

You should start off with the auction format, but it will not be long before you will want to have your own store. The public is accustomed to buying from brick and mortar stores, and actually perceive "a store" to have more credibility than an auction.

Offer an overall professional look.

Do not ever accept a bid from outside the USA because of the high probability of fraud from foreign bidders (especially from Indonesia and African nations.

CREATING AN OPT-IN EMAIL LIST

EBay is one of the best ways that you can use to create your valuable double-opt-in email list. You must make it as easy as possible for your visitor to sign up, and you need to give them an incentive to do so. There are a number of places for you to accomplish this. I suggest you use ALL of them.

Include an opt-in form on your AboutMe page. You direct them to that page from your auction listing or from your end-of-auction emails.

Create a "further description" page on a website outside of eBay. Have the opt-in form at the bottom of that page. Have a link in your auction listing to that page,

Using third-party management software you can collect opt-ins during your customer's checkout procedure. Set it up so that receiving a newsletter or special report or future discount is the default option.

All of your end-of-auction emails should have a link to the opt-in form on your AbouitMe page.

Ask your buyers to add you to their "Favorite Sellers" list so that they will receive your new items listings direct from eBay.

Ask your buyers to add you to their "Favorite Stores" list

In general you want to make it clear to them that it is in their best interest to provide their email address. Build your customer list on your autoresponder, categorized by niche. You can periodically, automatically, send them an informal newsletter about that niche. You want to gain their trust so they will buy more from you in the future. Offer them special "subscriber-only" discounts. Advise them of upcoming auctions.

YOUR OWN EBAY STORE

If you plan to sell on eBay, be certain not to overlook the value in having your own eBay storefront. It is **virtual** brick and mortar! Properly run it should cover many times the cost to own it, and be a significant addition to your multiple streams of internet income. Having your very own eBay Store, when properly conceived and created, can be a huge money-maker. It isn't exactly inexpensive, but of course cost is only relative. In total, including the monthly fee, if one was to sell a single $9.97 from your store it would cost around $17.35...not a great way to make

money! (eBay takes an 11% final value fee for each sale).
But TEN sales of that same product would only cost around
$27 and show a return on investment of 200%, not at all
bad.   You can expand the arithmetic from there, but it is
clear that if you can sell many of an item the cost of the
store and final value fee become irrelevant.

The big advantage to having a store is the fact that you can
list as many products as you like, ten, a hundred, a
thousand! And you can sell those auction-banned
downloadable ebooks without being forced to create
physical CDs.

As with all eBay advertising, there are a host of
"enhancement fees" that can be added and are worth
considering but are not absolutely needed to attract buyers.
You should always link you auctions to your store.

Having an eBay store gets you access to advanced design,
marketing and reporting features. It also assures you the
lowest Fixed Price listing fees, substantially lower than in
the auctions.

By far the most important aspect of having your own eBay
store is the fact that you can send the search engines, or
any other traffic source. Directly to it just as you would with
any website. When you consider that your auctions last at
most ten days and the items in your store are perpetually
there to be bought, the advantage of having a store
becomes obvious.

On top of that, customers who arrived to buy one item
might very well view and buy other items from your
potentially-limitless store inventory. Plus you now have the
ability to offer freebies or send newsletters telling buyers
what promotions you are running and what new products
you will be carrying. If you employ the "Good 'Till
Cancelled" option an item will automatically re-list every 30

days or until you cancel the sale or the item is sold out.

BECOME AN EBAY AFFILIATE

There is another way to make money with eBay beyond selling your own products. Consider joining their affiliate program and promoting eBay itself through your own website or blog. It is FREE to join, and you benefit financially.

EBay pays you a sum (at this writing $45) for every visitor you send them who registers and bids on something within 30 days. You also earn around $0.25 for each subsequent bid or Buy It Now purchase made by that person. EBay provides you with marketing tools and training on how to maximize your affiliate income. Go to: affiliates.ebay.com to apply.

As an eBay seller you should be directing people to your own auctions. You should also direct people to categories in which you do not participate. If possible focus on high-traffic general categories such as computers, collectibles, clothing, antiques and DVDs.

SURPRISING EBAY ALTERNATIVES

Although eBay is the best known auction site by far, there are as many as four-hundred others! EBay gets well over half of all auction visitors which number in the tens of millions.

The Amazon.com auction platform at one time received almost as many visitors as eBay. In late 2011 they decided to shut it down. The same is true for the Yahoo! auction site, which closed late that same year. Competition from eBay is just too much for even the largest companies to handle.

One smaller auction site is Etsy.com. It is intended for auctions only of personally-made craft items. I have had good experience with their platform for appropriate items.

If you go to internetauctionlist.com you will find many hundreds of other auction choices. Most auction-oriented internet entrepreneurs I know stick with eBay, Yahoo! and Etsy and do very well with these and a few others.

Often overlooked but quite useful is "eBid" at ebid.net. It has been around for twelve years with offerings in fifteen or so countries. It has NO LISTING FEES! As with eBay you can have your own eBid store.....in fact you can have up to five of them. And they are FREE too! BUT, you cannot sell virtual products, or use the site to connect to third party affiliate websites.

For selling your hard copy CDs and DVDs and book printouts eBid is well worth trying. You can't beat FREE. There is a small final sale value fee, which is what keeps them in business.

"Online Auction", at online auction.com, charges a low monthly fee but has no listing or final value fees. This can be a very cost effective auction solution. They DO allow linking to your website, where you can sell your products or link to affiliates. The absence of a final value fee basically means that they don't give a rats petunia what you sell and for how much. All transactions are strictly between you and your buyer.

Another auction site that has been around for a decade or so is "CQOut" at cqout.com. They are pretty much patterned after eBay, with slightly lower fees. They also offer escrow services, which I always recommend if it is offered. They will not permit virtual downloads or affiliate links (because they DO have final value fees, so they care about off-site sales). There is a way to promote your website URL using their special banners.

Offering your products at the above sites can be very cost effective. What you need to do is study each site carefully. Conduct the same sort product and site research as you would on eBay. Look at features, read the rules, and take advantage of tutorials.

YOUR BEST FRIEND - EBAY CLASSIFIED ADS

When most people think of eBay they think "auctions". There is no question that the eBay auction paradigm can be used very effectively in internet marketing.

But there is a lesser known way for infopreneurs to cash in on eBay that has nothing to do with auctions. It is called "eBay Classified Advertising". It is GOD'S gift to the affiliate marketer. It can be used to generate direct sales, and to build a massive double-opt-in mailing list. We covered this earlier, but it is worth repeating here.

Advertising off-line, in publications that accept classified ads, can be very profitable and should not be overlooked. All but the smallest off-line ads are quite costly, so most use the minimum-size two-line ads to generate leads. These ads are priced by the word, offer little in the way of "selling", and are generally squeezed together with dozens of competitor's ads.

EBay Classifieds, on the other hand, can be huge and bold and include hundreds of words and many pictures. An equivalent size off-line ad would be prohibitively expensive, hundreds if not thousands of dollars. The eBay cost? Zero for "local classifieds", around $10 for a 30-day exposure across the entire eBay site!

The KEY to using eBay Classifieds profitably is the fact that these ads respond to searches made by eBay shoppers who you can target 100%! Everyone searching for your type of offer is a potential buyer. Your job is to create a

KEYWORD RICH AD, starting with the title of the ad. You learned how to accomplish this in the preceding chapter.

With eBay Classifieds there are no final selling fees to eat into your profits. And probably most important there is no "feedback" provision which precludes the habitually-unsatisfied or outright fraudulent buyers from leaving negative feedback about you and your products. Unfortunately there exists a universe of idiots out there in cyberspace who get their jollys castigating innocent sellers just for the fun of it.

Most of the successful eBayers I know use this format to build their mailing lists. They offer a free report and send the visitor to a website where they sign up for the freebie and can be directed to an affiliate offer, killing two birds with a single rock! But there are many others who skip this process, which admittedly takes more steps and more time, in favor of simply sending the visitor directly to an affiliate offer. Personally I use both.

A word of caution. EBay "Rules" can be very confusing and ambiguous, and even worse, change frequently. What is true today is not necessarily true tomorrow. As pointed out above, for years fortunes were made selling digitally-downloaded reports through eBay auctions until this was outlawed.

To check on eBay's latest rules, go to pages.ebay.com/help/sell/f-ad.html. It is a good idea to click on everything and read it all. It takes a few hours but could save you serious grief.

Also do the same at: pages.ebay.com/help/policies/listing-links.html. Irrespective of the "letter of the law" it is quite apparent from all of the ads on eBay that they do not rigorously enforce their restrictions. Pull up lots of ads and see for yourself.

It is a good idea to check out other classified ads to see what eBay is permitting (or turning a blind eye towards, rules-against notwithstanding) at any given time. If you see many ads doing exactly what you want to do (e.g., sending visitors away from eBay to non-eBay email-boxes or to affiliate websites or to your own website or email autoresponder) it is a pretty safe bet you can do the same.

Under "What Is Not Allowed On eBay Classifieds" is a list of almost fifty "no-nos". Read it, and abide by it.

This is actually a pretty good list for you to follow in all of your internet marketing, because most of the items would be prohibited in any medium you might choose. I strongly disagree with eBay's present exclusion of "e-cigarettes" because that is a very profitable affiliate category and seems to me to be in the public good.

I also have no personal moral problem marketing "nude art" as long as it is non-pornographic, but apparently eBay sees all nudity as bad. Affiliate programs for any sort of weapons are also specifically excluded, as are all "adult" products.

You can post 25 local ads per day, all FREE! Each ad can be posted in only one category, and in one chosen ZIP code. Posting that many ads daily, and doing it properly, is quite a chore, but if you could somehow end up posting 750 ads a month it is quite unlikely that you would not generate a significant income!

There also exists in eBay a different level of Classified ad that is not quite free but offers some serious advantages. This is running Classified Ads directly on eBay.com. If you access pages.ebay.com/help/sell/formats.html you will see a detailed comparison under "Selecting A Selling Format".

In this option you state a price, the buyer contacts you, and you handle the transaction personally, for example, on your website.

Most ads run for 30 days, although there is a "Good Until Cancelled" option. Either way you are charged a small "insertion fee" every 30 days. The fees charged are based on the category of product selected. You are NOT charged a final value fee, primarily because eBay has no idea how many of something you have sold.

Classifieds on eBay are a serious bargain! Each 30-day period presently costs only $9.95. The first picture in the ad is free. Additional pictures cost only $0.15 each. There are a number of "upgrades" that can add an additional $6.10/30-days, or $16.05 total, still a major bargain over off-line classifieds. A big ad with ten pictures keyword-targeted to a specific niche audience costing under $18.00 is a real bargain.

The upgrades are intended to make your ads stand out in a crowd. I can't make a strong argument for using them, because it is the wording of your title and ad that drives visitors to your site, but using them can't hurt either.

With eBAY Classifieds you can sell on any eBay country site regardless of where you reside or from what country your eBay account was initially registered. Just note that fees and allowable products do vary country to country. Digital products are the most relevant example of this. They are AOK in the UK but a no-no in the USA!

The same is true for outside linking. In reality you will find some ads running with outside links featuring affiliate products. So join the crowd until such time as eBay decides to tighten their rules or better police them.

Many marketers will post classified ads linking to their own paid-for listings on eBay. They set up identical Classified

Ads ending by the hour and linked to the paid-for listing giving the product a high profile. Though you are keyword-limited to 55 spaces in your eBay "Buy It Now" titles, you are not limited in putting keywords and phrases throughout your classified ads. You want to appear once for a large number of search terms.

You can put virtually anything on this page, including a link to your website. The only restriction here is that any products you offer on your website that you are selling on eBay must be priced $1.00 higher than on eBay auctions

If eBay's "Rules Of The Moment" are not permitting payment links in your classified ads put an opt-in form in lieu of a payment button. When the buyer opts in with their name and email address, they click on a bar that says: "Click To Receive Ordering Information" that takes them directly to the payment page.

You also will be collecting names for your email list, and for anyone who does not order you can email them to get them to reconsider!

Regardless of costs and restrictions selling through eBay Classified Ads represents perhaps the single best internet marketplace. Promoting your affiliate offers, or your own products, or your website, using eBay Classifieds to drive traffic is by far one of the easiest and most cost-effective ways to earn a very significant internet income.

YOU *CAN* HAVE YOUR OWN *PRIVATE* AUCTION SITE!

If you are so inclined you can compete with other online auction sites all by yourself! This is not for newbies, but worthy of mention because it can be a very profitable business model.

I can think of four good reasons to set up your own personal auction site:

It can generate a lot of income;
It can help promote your website;
It can attract visitors to your affiliate ads;
It's a lot of fun!

You will need special auction software the same as you would need special software to create your own unique products affiliate universe. Go again to InternetAuctionSite.com. In the list down the left side click on "Auction Software".
You will be presented with a long alphabetical list of software products with thumbnail descriptions of each. Some are eBay enhancement tools, some are for live auctions, but many are designed specifically to allow you to have your very own auction site. Some can be purchased outright; some can be leased on a monthly basis. They are not at all inexpensive, but should pay for themselves over time.

Having your own private auction site is not something an internet newbie should consider, but in the context of multiple streams of internet income it is yet another way to diversity your portfolio

FINAL THOUGHTS

You now have all of the information you need to start your eBay marketing adventure. Once you get the hang of it you will find that the time required to market on eBay vis a vis the profits possible are well in line with other of the many possible multiple streams of internet income business models.

JUST GO FOR IT!!!!

CONCLUSIONS TO PONDER

You have in front of you a book, physically in your hands on an e-reader, that can change your life if you choose to read it and follow one or more of the success paths presented.

If you are unemployed or under-employed this information could be salvation. If you are in a job that you know will never bring you the goodies that only money can buy, starting to supplement your income with an on-line adventure could set you on a path you never thought possible. **But you must take action.**

The internet is extremely dynamic. It literally changes month to month. New ideas and new techniques are published in monthly magazines such as *Websites.* Google, which is responsible directly and indirectly for the bulk of our internet income, adds new tweaks at a rapid clip. They also constantly evolve their rankings algorithm.

The social media sites Facebook , MySpace, YouTube, Twitter and Pinterest are regularly adding features and enhancing the social-interaction experience. Almost anything that matters to us as internet marketers changes often. Too often.

Because of the dynamic nature of the internet, virtually anything written before 3Q- 2012 will contain outdated, harmful to follow, information. Do not be misled by all of the wonderful "FREE" publications you will be offered as bonuses or "Private Label Rights" material or incentives to purchase various internet courses.

Just look at the copyright dates. Most will be around 2003-2004! Some I've seen are as old as the late '90s. Rarely will one be as recent as 2010, and even that is probably mostly outdated.

Certain of the popular best-selling "National Best Seller" hard-cover books on earning internet income have **never** been updated. One in particular has so many link-references in it that no longer exist that it's laughable! Amazingly, it still sells, to the peril of its readers who will end up more confused than helped. The majority of this old stuff is potential fish wrappings!

There's a lot of excellent **current** training out there. I buy and learn from it continuously. If you don't stay on top of new developments your competition will bury you. At the very least you will waste a lot of time and occasionally make a damn fool of yourself. Just be careful to stay away from the worthless outdated material.

Anyone who purchases this book, if they wish, will be placed on a special email list to receive FREE reports of new developments and techniques as I learn, apply, or react to them. I will also point out anything in this book that is no longer valid if such becomes the case. I'm not aware of anyone else offering to do this. Just send your email address to: author@askburt.com. INCIDENTALLY: **We never sell or _SHARE_ your email address in any way.**

No one can argue that the internet has changed the world. It has, and in ways so profound that only someone who has celebrated many decades of life can truly appreciate the changes. No one under twenty-five can begin to appreciate, even imagine, life before computers, cell phones, ipods and ipads, Kindles and Nooks and Xboxes and flat screen TVs.

Just as these new technologies have evolved over the past decade and a half, internet marketing has evolved rapidly as well. All internet entrepreneurs need to evolve with it, and to never stop learning. New ideas and techniques literally appear almost weekly. And it all began less than two decades ago. Quite amazing.

There are certain absolutely timeless principals that can be applied to internet marketing today. If you have never read "Think And Grow Rich" by Napoleon Hill, written in the 1930s, do so, and then re-read it a few times. I strongly recommend that you study its wisdom. I read it once a year. It can change your life. In my opinion it is the most profound book on marketing and on life itself ever written.

Our jobs as internet marketers is quite straight forward: _Maximize the number of customers; Maximize the amount of the average order; and Increase the frequency of those orders_. That's the whole enchilada. Master those basic principles and you have the key to boundless wealth. Reread and memorize this paragraph, because it is fundamental to your success.

Remember: **IF YOU WANT YOUR CUP TO RUNNETH OVER BE THE PERSON POURING THE PITCHER!** You have that opportunity in internet commerce.

You possess one asset that no one else in the universe can claim...... **YOU!** You are the only "you" on the planet. You are totally unique, with your own personality, quirks, and perspectives. When dealing with your customers always be honest and **be yourself.**

Your level of motivation will be key to your success. Some people need to be between a rock and a hard place before taking action. Some see the handwriting on the wall and act early. Some will take action out of pure curiosity over what might happen if they don't!

The internet is **huge**, with millions of websites and billions of visitors. The internet marketing pie is immense. As I've said before, you don't need even a small slice of the internet pie. You just need to lick the knife! I'm not a greedy person. Heck, I'd be satisfied with just a dollar a month from every person on line in the USA!

Abe Lincoln is credited with saying, as a young man, **"I will study and get ready and someday my chance will come"**. You have the material here in this book for you to study. Especially if you are unemployed or underemployed there is no better time to start getting ready than **now**. You "chance" **HAS** come. It is credibly reported that countless individuals earn a substantial income sitting in front of a computer screen from the comfort of their homes. I do. You can too.

Traffic to your internet-offers can be free or costly to obtain. Cost in terms of dollars is optional. Cost in terms of time is not. If you are not ready to invest a lot of time in your pursuit of internet riches you should not even start, because you are sure to fail. It is real work.

Despite what a lot of internet guru's ads would have you believe this is not a "few hours a week" project. Far from it. Just deciding on your niche areas of focus takes time. The simple act of deciding which of many possible profit paths, the multiple streams of internet income to follow, is time consuming in itself. Just reading and starting to absorb the material in this book is time consuming.

Everything you will be doing takes time, more at the beginning, but time is always a consideration. Finding relevant keywords, writing titles, writing ads, and writing website copy takes time. Programming your autoresponder takes time. The good news is that once you have set everything up and going it all pretty much runs itself! Eventually your "job" is reduced to updating details, monitoring to make certain your links are functional, and checking your statistics. And counting your money!

I have found that most internet training sold today is vastly "puffed up" to make its perceived value appear greater. I could expand every cChapter in this book and make it into a $997 course many thousands of pages long. And people would buy it.

I know this is true because I have bought multi-thousand page training that could easily have been condensed to a few hundred pages. The perceived value of a huge course is greater. Its true value in helping you make lots of internet cash is not.

Any single Chapter in this book could be expanded into a long, drawn out course. I could provide endless "screen shots" with details of which button to push to make something happen. I think these types of courses, filled with superfluous fluff, are always overpriced and are an insult to anyone who buys them. A button that says "click here" doesn't need a video shot of a finger pressing the button!

If my reader cannot go to a suggested website and figure out how to navigate it without seeing screen-shots on a page telling you to "click on this, go to that", with pages of idiotic illustrated instructions, then they probably could never make a living on line.

I leave it to my readers to have the initiative to search the internet for any highly-advanced training aids they might believe to be of value. Please be assured that this book gives you all of the knowledge you need to become a very successful internet entrepreneur, but you can never acquire too much knowledge. The problem that can occur is called the "paralysis of analysis". You cannot permit yourself to spend ALL of your time learning. Again, as Yoda said to Luke: "There is no try, there is just do or not do". You simply must "do".

I've done my best to share the ideas I have learned over many years that relate to making money with a computer. No doubt there are many techniques out there in cyberland that some young genius is using today to get rich and has not yet shared with the unwashed masses. If and when such information becomes available I will undoubtedly purchase it! And if I have your email address, I'll share my experiences with you.

I have learned over a lifetime not to even think of trying to reinvent the internet-commerce wheel. Let others spend years of trial and error making some technique work. Everything I know about making money on line I have learned from others, as I hope you can learn from me.

I cannot assure you that you will make a single dime applying my ideas. Everyone has a unique skill set, and some are simply resistant to learning anything new. Many lack the requisite persistence to succeed in an endeavor such as this. Being an internet entrepreneur requires study, practice, and patience, and "persistence, persistence and persistence".

Many people never see the pattern of their own self-destructive actions. They incorrectly assume that the reason things did not work out as planned must have been **due to someone else**. This is true among the ignorant and the brilliant alike, among business leaders and politicians, and us regular folk. And surely true among many aspiring internet marketers.

If you try, or have tried internet commerce and are unhappy with your results you simply have not taken the time and effort needed to get it right. Sorry folks, it ain't nobody's fault but your own.

I promise you that if you read and follow the information in this book that it is very possible for you to begin making money within the next few days. I want you to succeed and make money. Just believe in me and that what I am sharing with you works. If you become confused or don't believe you know enough just do it and learn by doing. **Action is the critical step.**

The great motivational speaker Anthony Robbins said it best: "You see, in life, lots of people know what to do, but few people actually do what they know. Knowing is not enough! You must take action." Even a poorly set up plan of action that is actually acted upon is far better than a perfectly structured plan that just sits there unused and untried. Do whatever you can NOW.

At any time just do what you can and skip what you cannot, and later do those other things when you gain experience and knowledge. I want you to go from zero to hero! **Start selling something somewhere.** Ask yourself: "How many "Buy Now!" buttons do I have on the internet this very moment?" The answer should never be: "None".

In biblical terms, I am trying to teach you to fish. I have no control over what you do with this fishing guide, where you fish, and what fish you seek, and how good you become at setting the hook.

I offer you this traditional Gaelic blessing: "May the roads rise up *to* meet you. May the wind be always at your back. May the sun shine warm upon your face, the rains fall soft upon your fields, and until we meet again, may God hold you in the palm of His hand."

GOOD LUCK AND GOD BLESS!

ABOUT THE AUTHOR

There is one very logical question you should ask: "Who are you and why should I listen to what you have to say?" It is a very valid question.

I'm going to resist the urge to show you copies of my bank statements, as many "internet gurus" are so fond of doing. These are just too easy to fake or embellish or show out of context to have any credibility. Suffice it to say I have been rather successful at internet commerce far longer than most, since 1995 in fact. During that time I have made it a point to learn as much as I can from all of the biggest names in internet marketing, and to apply that knowledge. I share all I can in this book.

I didn't invent the e-commerce wheel, nor did I try to re-invent it along the way. I simply made it my job to learn as much as I could as often as possible from those rare pioneers who blazed the trail to internet riches.

I was born in a slum called Bedford-Stuyvesant (known affectionately as "Bed-Sty") in Brooklyn, New York. (Go Dodgers!) The "hood" was an interesting mixture of immigrant Catholic Italians and Irish, Protestants, Blacks, and Hassidic Jews, about in equal proportions. Both of my parents worked two menial jobs just to put food on the table. I had no siblings, and no educated role models. My birth year was 1938. Yep, I'm an old poop in his mid-seventies! Surprised? My plan: Live to 110! Maybe 111.

I was a typical "street kid", frequent truant, hustler, shop-lifter, and a survivor in a neighborhood where survival was both an art-form and a not-always reality. My best and only real skills were staying alive and shooting pool, the latter providing sustenance cash. Back in those days today's recreational drugs were almost unheard of. Had I been born in the modern era I might well have ended up a junkie, in prison, or dead.

My first job, at age ten, was delivering staggering shoulder-hung loads of dry-cleaned clothes for a local cleaner. My first "real" job was packing and shipping bottles of arthritis pills for a company called Dolcin, under the ever-watchful eye of the meanest lady that ever lived, my wretched first boss the evil Sheila! She was the direct descendant of a long line of slave drivers!

What happened between then and a decade or so ago I won't bore you with. I had the usual nine-to-fives, learned a lot from the school of hard knocks, suffered through two divorces, and served in the Army as a grunt during Vietnam. I flew search and rescue for the Civil Air Patrol. I almost died in a SCUBA accident! I more or less raised three kids. I never quite made the "big time". During a "religious period" I even became an ordained minister! But after a succession of failed business attempts, in 1994 I found myself in Chapter 7 bankruptcy and absolutely penniless.

Fortunately I had by then married my third wife, an exceptional and beautiful very young lady who certainly didn't marry me for my money! She always believed in me, often more than I believed in myself. I'm thrilled to say we are soon to celebrate our 30th Anniversary! She is one of a kind. Post-bankruptcy, from reaching up to touch bottom, today we live in absolute paradise on a twenty-acre ranch bordering millions of acres of State lands in the High Sonoran Desert in sunny southern Arizona. We have a beautiful 5,572 square foot stone home, have travelled the world, and have every creature comfort we could ever want.

THE LOVELY MELANIE, WITH OUR VIPs COCOA AND CAPPY

What could conceivably have happened between a 1994 bankruptcy and today? From Chapter 7 and reaching up to touch bottom to total creature comfort? *THE INTERNET HAPPENED!*
Back in the mid-90s, quite by accident, a buddy of mine mentioned that he heard about a local seminar being held on Long Island. It had something to do with computers and making money on the internet. Neither of us knew diddly-squat about either one! At that time very few individuals did. It cost a thousand dollars to attend the seminar, but you could bring a friend for free. So we both scraped up five-hundred bucks and attended.

I have no recollection of who ran that two-day seminar. The focus was on buying up "dot com Domain Names" and somehow or other reselling them at a profit. Our first homework assignment was to go home and register "(OurOwnName).com". Next we were instructed to think up a lot of possibly useful words and phrases and to buy the corresponding dot com domain names. These could be bought at that time for $35 each for a year. Almost any word or phrase you could think of was available.

My friend Paul thought it was a scam and a waste of money and never bought any domains at all. For whatever reason I found it fascinating, and over the next year I bought a few every time I had an extra hundred bucks. I never tried to sell any of them. I eventually accumulated a few dozen dot coms.

One day out of the blue I got a phone call from someone who had tracked me down as the owner of one of my dot com domain names. He asked me if I would take five thousand dollars for it. I almost fainted! After a milli-second of contemplation I agreed. Score a really big one for me, $35 to $5,000.00, right? Not quite!

A few weeks later I learned to my horror and chagrin that the buyer re-sold my domain name the day after he bought it from me, for $125,000! Lesson learned. Seller beware. Make no emotional decisions **ever**. Sleep on everything. Knowledge is power. A very painful and costly learning experience to say the least.

Suffice it to say that over the next few years my focus was on learning the true value of my domain names and selling them at the then-going market prices. It is a documented fact that some domain names (unfortunately none of mine) have sold for millions of dollars each! To this day sales in the hundred-thousand-dollar-plus range are not uncommon. Domain Name auctions occur almost monthly worldwide.

These early domain experiences got me very interested in the internet overall. If dot com domain names actually had value, why was this true? Apparently there was some way to make money with .com websites. Some internet visionaries began to emerge, and some were willing to share the money-making knowledge they had learned through long and tedious trial and error.

Internet "wealth seminars" proliferated. In the late '90s I made it a point to attend every seminar I could, all around the country. I always made certain to meet the "guru" running the classes and try to pick their brains clean. Some were late teenagers, half the age of my kids! Some were clearly geniuses. Some were obviously out to make a fast buck. But all had useful lessons to be absorbed, and I was a willing sponge.
Early motivational seminars from which I learned a great deal were run by some famous individuals (Tom Hopkins, Zig Ziegler and Art Linkletter among them). Others were hosted by some younger geniuses who were lesser known by the general public. A few of the best, who were getting top grades from the internet community, were Jeff Paul (of '70s mail-order fame), Jay Abraham, Dr. Jeffrey Lant, Charles Carboneau, Darren Falter, Ken Varga, Robert Allen, and a very young man named Cory Rudl.

Cory Rudl was in my opinion the Steve Jobs of internet marketing. Cory was a young visionary who was so far ahead of his time that much of what he taught seemed far beyond the possible. Some thought he was a scam artist. He was, in fact, the real deal. I made it a point to attend all of his many seminars, and got to know him very well. Shortly after I attended his wedding reception conference he was killed in a tragic race car training accident. I believe he was 28. He left an indelible mark on internet training, and on me.

The following are a few of the photos I have accumulated over the years. These are among the individuals to whom I owe a debt of gratitude for guiding my internet and business career :

THE AUTHOR WITH INSPIRING LECTURER THE LATE GREAT ART LINKLETTER

THE AUTHOR WITH WORLD FAMOUS WRITER AND INTERNET
GURU ROBERT G. ALLEN (ROBERTGALLEN.COM)

THE AUTHOR WITH FAMOUS INDUSTRIALIST, AUTHOR AND
LECTURER KEN VARGA (KENVARGA.COM)

THE AUTHOR WITH HIS WRITING MENTOR DAN POYNTER
(PARAPUBLISHING.COM)

THE AUTHOR WITH THE INCOMPERABLE WRITER AND
INTERNET GURU DR. JEFFREY LANT (WORLDPROFIT.COM)

THE AUTHOR WITH THE GIFTED INTERNET GURU CHARLES
CARBONEAU (CASHCONNECTION.COM)

THE AUTHOR WITH THE INTERNET GURU JONATHAN MIZEL IN
THE "EARLY DAYS" (MARKETINGLETTER.COM)

THE AUTHOR WITH THE LATE CORY RUDL AT ONE OF CORY'S FIRST SEMINARS IN THE 1990s

I learned all of the internet basics from Cory. Much of his original material is still valid today. But the internet is very dynamic, and changes happen almost weekly. For example, the entire idea of marketing on social sites such as Facebook and Twitter was unknown only a few years ago, because neither social site even existed! And Google and other search engines are continuously tweaking their ranking algorithms, often with surprise dramatic and occasionally detrimental effects on internet marketers.

Over the ensuing years I was privileged to meet, and in many cases get to know well, a number of other internet marketing geniuses. Names that come to mind are John Reese, Marlon Sanders, Armand Morin, Alex Mandossian, and Jim Edwards, but there were many others. I not only learned what they taught but have profitably applied each and every concept of theirs at one time or the other.
I have purchased internet training material from literally dozens of individuals. My belief is that if I can learn one single new idea that I can convert into internet cash then the training was well worth whatever its cost. I calculate that I have spent over $97,436 on such material. And it was all well worth it.

I have courses from Yanik Silver, Gabor Olah, John Thornhill, Kim Enders, Brad Callen, Avril Harper, Matt Garrett, Socrates Socratos, and literally dozens more. I study them all, test the techniques they share, and incorporate many of them in my overall internet marketing strategy. **I never stop learning.**

Within the past three years another young marketing genius has appeared on the internet marketing scene. His name is Anthony Morrison. I met Anthony at a seminar he was running at a hotel conference center in Tucson. He was promoting an interesting new Domain Name marketing program which brought me back to my Long Island domain-seminar roots of a decade earlier! Of course Anthony had greatly refined the Domain Flipping concept to mesh with modern day realities.

I made it a point to meet Anthony in person. Because of my early experience   with domain names Anthony invited me to do an infomercial with him at CBS studios in Orlando. It was really fun to do, and of course seeing oneself on late-night TV is a pretty amazing ego trip!

Anthony has gone on to become yet another self-made internet multi-millionaire still in his twenties!

He is a living testimony to what can be achieved in internet marketing in a relatively short time starting from ground zero with little or no operating capital.

If a young man in his early twenties with very limited capital can achieve this sort of success, don't you think there is just the slightest possibility that you could make a decent living learning internet commerce techniques?

THE AUTHOR WITH INTERNET GENIUS ANTHONY MORRISON (ANTHONYMORRISON.COM) AT CBS STUDIOS IN ORLANDO

This young man has progressed far beyond the domain-selling business. He has written three great training books, and conducts internet training seminars that are second to none. I thought I "knew it all" from my fifteen years in the business, but I have learned a great deal more from Anthony and apply it profitably on a daily basis.

I have no pressing need to continue my daily internet work. I believe it was Samuel Clemens (Mark Twain) who first said: "Make your vocation your vacation", and I really do enjoy doing the tasks that are needed to earn money on the internet. I plan to do it forever. With an occasional trip to Paris thrown in!

If I can help others, especially the unemployed and under-employed to improve their lives, so much the better. If I can interest seniors such as myself in supplementing their retirement incomes that would be wonderful. Can I make life easier for stay-at-home moms and dads? I sure hope so. If I can show college students how they can reduce their loan debt I'd feel quite good about that as well.

Personally, regardless of how much money I earn on the internet it will never be enough. My dreams of creating an enduring charitable foundation to fund a worthy cause will require as much as I can ever earn. I need quite a few internet millions to make a real dent in this project. It's a five-year plan. And it will happen. The aforementioned Anthony Morrison is very philanthropic, and I'd like to copy his example.

To summarize, I have over the past decade-plus participated in every phase of internet commerce I could find. I know that **any** of it can be profitable, but I have also learned which methods are most cost effective for me, and which I found could be implemented the fastest. **I can save you years of time and and of thousands of dollars by sharing with you what I have learned through my years of study, and trial and error, and sweat and tears.**

I am certain that this book can provide you with the knowledge you need to begin your quest for internet wealth. There is absolutely no reason for you not to give this wonderful journey a try. **JUST DO IT!**

There are so many different paths to internet wealth that I cannot imagine anyone not being able to find some aspect of the endeavor within their abilities and to their liking, and within their budget. And you might just get very rich in the process!

Good luck, and GOD bless.

Rev. Dr. James Burton "Burt" Anderson, SOB*, BChE, MBA, GRI, LLO, LIB, RFP
P.O. Box 2100
Green Valley, Arizona 85622
DRJBA@askburt.com

*Sweet Old Burt!

GLOSSARY OF INTERNET, AFFILIATE & PUBLISHING TERMS

As you become involved in internet commerce you will encounter a vast number of unfamiliar terms that are unique to the internet.

The following is some of the more commonly used internet terminology with which you should become familiar. If you come across a term not defined here, Wikipedia.com is always my first choice for a definition.

3-WAY MATCHING: A way of blending ads into a web page taking into account the ads background color, font color, and font size.

404 ERROR: A message that appears on a computer screen when you arrive at a web page that does not exist.

ABOVE THE FOLD: The area of a website that appears immdediately when someone arrives at your website and does no scrolling down.

ACCEPTANCE RATE: The percentage of email accepted by a mail server. This is not necessarily the amount of email actually arriving at desired inboxes.

ACPA (ANTI-CYBERSQUATTING CONSUMER PROTECTION ACT): A Federal law that prevents domainers from registering copyrighted or trademarked names or the names of private individuals for the purpose of profit. Fines can be as high as $100,000.

ACTIVE CHANNEL: A channel hosted on a Web server that features frequently updated information

ACTIVE SERVER PAGES: Special pages that allow Web developers to create dynamic by using database-driven content. Content is generally produced on th server-side.

AD RANK: The order in which Google AdSense ads appear on your site, as determined by Google.

ADSENSE: One side of Google's AdWords cost per click ad platform. Google pays you for these ads on your website.

ADSENSE CODE: The HTML instructions for your web page that places a Google AdSense ad on that webpage.

AD UNIT: A group of AdSense ads presented as a set. A maximum of three ad units are permitted per web page.

ADVERTISER: Also known as the "Merchant", pays affiliates for sending traffic to the merchant's website to either provide information or buy something.

ADWORDS: The advertiser side of Google's ad program.

AFFILIATE: Also called "Associate". Any website owner who earns a commission (i.e., a finder's fee) for sending traffic to a merchant's website. An individual who markets another's book for a percentage of the proceeds. Certain platforms, such as Smashwords, have an available affiliate program within their platform. You can always register with clickbank.com and offer your book at a percentage split upon which you decide; you become the merchant, those who promote your product are your affiliates.

AFFILIATE AGREEMENT: All of the terms that define the relationship between an affiliate and a merchant.

AFFILIATE LINK: Unique identity links that identify the affiliate to the merchant.

AFFILIATE MANAGER: The person responsible for running the vendor's affiliate program. Many vendor's will assign you a personal affiliate manager.

AFFILIATE PROGRAM: Also known as a referral program, revenue-sharing program, partnering program, and associate program. A vendor rewards his affiliates based on number of visits, leads, or sales.

AFFILIATE PROGRAM DIRECTORY: A listing of affiliate programs categorized according to niches.

AFFILIATE SOFTWARE: The software that runs and manages an affiliate program. It includes analytics, commission calculation, and making payments.

APACHE: A popular open source public-domain Web server that provides users with CGI, SSL and virtual domains. Apache's open source code allows users to adapt the server to suit their unique needs, which provides them with strong performance, security and reliability. This is the most widely used Web server on the Internet.

APPLET: A small Java-based program that runs in a sandbox and is embedded into a website to allow users to create virtual objects that can move or interact with the site.

ARCHIVE: Large files that contain valuable data.

ASCII (AMERICAN STANDARD CODE FOR INFORMATION INTERCHANGE: The worldwide standard for the code numbers used by computers to represent all letters, numbers and symbols.

AUTHENTICATION: An ISP's technical standards by which email gateway administrators establish sender identity.

AUTHOR PAGE: The various publishing platforms provide you with adequate space to tell about yourself, and to list other books you have published.

AUTO-APPROVE: Affiliate application process whereby anyone applying to be an affiliate member is accepted.

AUTO VETTER: AutoVetter is Smashwords' proprietary technology that automatically scans your uploaded ebook and reports back to you about potential formatting problems.

AUTO RESPONDER: A computer program that detects the receipt of an email and automatically replies to the sender with a pre-programmed response.

AVAILABILITY: See Uptime.

BACK ORDER: A domainer's order to register a URL if the current registrant allows it to expire.

BACKUPS: Data from you that your Web hosts copy (typically once a day) in case of a loss of data situation. Backups allow hosts to easily restore lost data. Be certain your host offers backup.

BANDWIDTH: The amount of information transferred both to and from a website or server during a prescribed period of time. This is usually measured in "bytes". Hosting companies generally offer packages that come with different bandwidth transfer limits per month.

BANNER AD: An ad promoting a product by means of a rectangular box (the Banner) containing an image, text, gif, .jpg, or video.

BISAC: "Book Industry Standards and Communications" is the standard book category coding system. You will find drop-down menus in the publishing platforms that offer you these choices.

BIT RATE: The speed that bits, the smallest units of digital information, are transferred over a communication link.

BITS PER SECOND (BPS): It is a measurement of how fast data flows from one place to another. A 56K modem can move about 56,000 bits per second.

BLACKLIST: A list of email sender addresses believed to be sending SPAM.

BLOCK PARAGRAPH: When paragraphs are not indented, but are stretched from one side of the page to the other, that's a block paragraph. It is generally accepted that "right justified" is more readable for the viewer.

BLOG HOSTING: These are special scripts that let users automatically post new information to a website.

BLOGOSPHERE: The sum of all information available on blogs.

BLUE SCREEN OF DEATH: When a computer crashes your monitor displays a blank blue screen.

BROADBAND: Refers to internet connections with much greater bandwidth than possible with a dial-up modem.

BROWSER: (or "Web Browser"): A computer program used to view and interact with the content of Web pages on the internet.

C+/C++: Programming languages used to created server-side programs that run after compilation. C++ includes objects.

CASCADING STYLE SHEETS – CSS: Rules that determine how an HTML document is displayed by a browser and adds functionality to and controls all design elements of simple HTML pages.

CHALLENGE RESPONSE: An automated message that identifies a sender of an email as a trusted source.

CHARGE BACK: A forfeited commission due to a cancelled sale.

CLICK FRAUD: The practice of sending traffic to a merchant using automated "huitbots" where the merchant pays a commission to a scammer and not to the legal affiliate.

CLICK THROUGH: The action of a visitor to your website clicking on a link that takes them to the merchant you represent.

CLICK THROUGH RATE (CTR): Ratio of the visitors who click a link and visit the merchant's site.

CLIENT: A software program designed to contact and obtain data from a server. For example, a Web Browser is a kind of client.

CO-BRANDING: This occurs where you as an affiliate can add your logo and branding on the pages to which you send visitors.

CO-LOCATION: When a user owns his/her own Web server, but houses it in the hosting provider's facilities for easy management, a high-speed connection, security, backup power and technical support, said user is "co-locating".

COMMISSION: This is the income you earn by sending a visitor to your website to your merchants website.

COMMON GATEQWAY INTERFACE (CGI): A program that helps servers and scripts communicate, enabling interaction between HTML documents and applications.

CONTEXUAL ADVERTISING: Ads that relate to the content on a web page.

CONTEXUAL LINK: A link within the text in an article or on a website which is a highlighted word or words within the text.

CONTROL PANEL (C-Panel): A Web-based application that allows you to manage various aspects of your hosting account. This includes uploading data and files, adding email accounts, changing contact information, installing shopping carts and/or databases and viewing statistics.

CONVERSION: When your visitor clicks over to your merchant and performs some positive action that is a conversion.

CONVERSION RATE: Percentage of clicks by visitors to you website that result in you earning a commission.

COOKIE: A piece of information sent by a Web Server to a Web Browser that forces the Browser to save the information and alert the Server whenever the Browser makes additional requests from the Server! It is used by vendors to keep track of a computer user's surfing history.

COPYRIGHT: (Not "copywrite".) A copyright is the exclusive legal right, normally held by the author of a book, to copy, adapt or distribute their creation. Often a publisher will control the copyright. Wikipedia has good technical descriptions found under "Copyright" and "Authors' Rights".

CPA (COST PER ACTION): A method by which you earn a commission as an affiliate when your visitor clicks over to your merchant and takes some positive action.

CPC (COST PER CLICK): Also known as PPC (Pay Per Click). Cost when paying on a per-click basis for an individual click to your website.

CPM (COST PER THOUSAND): (M = Roman numeral for 1,000). This is the cost for every thousand page views.

CPO (COST PER ORDER): Same as PCA except a sale must result.

CRON: The ability to run programs based on a server's clock

CTR (CLICK THROUGH RATE): The percentage of your visitors who click through to the merchant's website.

DATABASE: Data stored on a Web server in a structured format.

DATA FEEDS: Product-sales information provided by a merchant to an affiliate to aid in promotion of the merchant's products.

DATA TRANSFER: See bandwidth.

DEDICATED HOSTING: When you rent or lease your own Web server that is housed at a hosting provider's facilities for easy management, a high-speed connection, security, backup power and technical support, you are buying dedicated hosting.

DEDICATED IP: See static IP.

DIAL-UP: A method of connecting to the internet using telephone lines. It is very slow compared with other "high-speed-internet" and "wireless" connections.

DIRECT NAVIGATION: This is also known as "type-in traffic". This occurs when a visitor reaches your website through their address bar.

DISCOVERY: This is an important term used in ebook publishing. It describes how "findable" your book is by a

prospective buyer. The key is **proper categorization.**
You want people to find your book whether or not they are
specifically looking for it! This is why it is so important to
publish across as many different publishing platforms as
possible.

DISK SPACE: The amount of space available for you to
house your website files on your host's server.

DOMAIN NAME: An address assigned to a website for
identification purposes that can be translated by a domain
name server into a server's IP address that includes a top-
level domain.

DOMAIN NAME SYSTEM (DNS): Keeps a database of
domain names and their corresponding IP addresses, so
that when a user searches for a domain name, the request
can be

routed to the server where the desired website resides.

DOMAIN PARKING: The ability to hold a domain name on
a hosting server without the service provider requiring that
users have the corresponding website up and running.

DOMAIN REGISTRAR: A company responsible for
managing your domain names and helping you secure the
rights to a specific domain name you wish to purchase.

DOWNLOAD/UPLOAD: This refers to electronically
getting a file from an internet location "down" to your
computer, or sending a file from your computer "up" to an
internet site. You "upload" your files to your publishing
platforms.

DOWNTIME: That period of time whae a server or browser
is unavailable.

DOUBLE OPT-IN: This is a verification process used in email marketing. The individual receiving your first email must click on a link confirming that they actually wanted the email in the first place.

DRM: This stands for Digital Rights Management, and is offered as an option by some publishing platforms. On the surface it sounds like a good idea. It is "copy protection" technology designed to prevent piracy of your work. It makes it harder for someone who has bought your book to print or duplicate it. The problem with DRM is two-fold. First of all, a dedicated book pirate can easily bypass DRM. But more important it restricts your reader from enjoying your book on different devices. Although I have never "split tested" to see whether DRM helps or hurts my bottom line, conventional wisdom is to never employ it.

EBOOK: This is a generic term for any book offered electronically, intended to be read on portable devices or downloaded from a website.

EMAIL FORWARDER: A program that will automatically forward a received email message to a specified remote email address.

ENCRYPTION: Encoding data with a cryptographic cipher so that only authorized entities can view it

EPC (EARNINGS PER CLICK): A mathematical expression of total earnings divided by each click on the merchant's link.

EPUB: This is an open industry standard ebook format It is the format used almost universally, with the major exception of Amazon Kindle which does not support it.

EPUBCHECK: This is an EPUB validation tool designed to automatically determine if an EPUB file is compliant with the EPUB standard. Many ebook platforms require its application to your book's manuscript to insure that your book will appear on customers' devices correctly. You can learn more about it at: code.google.com/p/epubcheck/.

ESCROW: A third party service that acts to protect both buyer and seller in an internet transaction.

EVERCOOKIE: A persistent cookie created with JaveScript that remains on a site even after other cookies have been deleted.

EXCLUSIVITY: A merchant's requirement that an affiliate promote no competing products on their website.

EXTENSIBLE MARKUP LANGUAGE – XML: A meta-programming language used to specify other document types being used on the Web.

EXTENSIONS: The "dot something" that follows a domain name.

FACEBOOK APPLICATIONS: These are programs within Facebook that let users share content with other users.

FACEBOOK CONTENT: Items posted on a Wall, such as status updates and recent actions. Becoming a Fan would be an action.

FACEBOOK EDGERANK: Facebook's algorithm that determines what content gets shown in users' News Feeds.

FACEBOOK FAN: Users who choose to "Like" your business page.

FACEBOOK FRIEND: As a noun, a personal connection. As a verb, to add a Facebook member as a friend.

FACEBOOK FRIEND LIST: An organized group of friends.

FACEBOOK GROUP: This is an aggregation of users having a common interest. You can create and/or join a Group.

FACEBOOK LIKE/LIKES: AS a verb, to "like" your business page means someone became a fan of that page. As a verb, to like others' comments on their Wall or News Feed. As a noun, "Likes" are the number of users who have liked your business page.

FACEBOOK NETWORK: An associated group of users based at a school or workplace.

FACEBOOK NEWSFEED: A collection of your friends' Wall posts published on your homepage.

FACEBOOK PAGE: The official Facebook presence from which your business shares information and interact s with Fans.

FACEBOOK PROFILE: Your personally stated information about yourself or your business.
FACEBOOK WALL: This is the core of a Facebook Page or Profile that collects new content.

FALSE POSITIVES: The almost one in five of the valid permission-based emails that are blocked erroneously by SPAM filters.

FAQ: Stands for "Frequently Asked Questions." All publishing platforms offer this collection of questions that have been asked by publishers in the past. Studying the entire set of FAQs will often answer every question you might have about a particular publishing platform.

FEEDER SITE: A website set up only to redirect traffic to another site.

FILE TRANSFER PROTOCOL (FTP): A commonly used method for exchanging files over the Internet by uploading or downloading files to a server. (An example would be "cuteFTP".)

FILENAME EXTENSION: A tag that appears at the end of each file name. It consists of a dot and then three or four letters that signify the type of file and format.

FIRE WALL: A software/hardware security program that splits elements of a network into various parts.

FIRST LINE INDENT: This is a style of printing your manuscript in a word processing program such as Microsoft Word. It refers to indenting the opening line of every paragraph a few spaces to differentiate it from the next paragraph. Personally I never use it.

FORMAT (noun): This is a reference to a particular electronic program. There are many different ebook formats specific to particular reading devices.

FORMAT (verb): It is used in the context of how you prepare your file in a particular way before uploading it to a publishing platform.

FORMMAIL: An application that lets users create interactive forms and include them on their websites to let visitors submit information

FRONTPAGE: A server-side, HTML editor for website creation from Microsoft

FRONTPAGE EXTENSIONS: Scripts and programs installed on a server that allow sites, or features of sites, created with Microsoft FrontPage to operate smoothly

FTP CLIENT: A software that lets two computers transfer files over the Inte

FTP (FILE TRANSFER PROTOCOL): The method of moving information files between two internet sites.

GIF: Stands for Graphic Interchange Format. It is a format used for image files, especially those with large areas of the same color.

HONEY POT: A planted email address designed to identify and trap spammers.

HARD BOUNCE: A failed email delivery due to a non-existent address.

HIT: A single request from a web browser for a single item from a server. A web page with four graphics would require five hits, one for the page and one for each graphic.

HOME PAGE: The first page of your website that a visitor sees.

HOST: A computer on a computer network that is the repository for services available to other computers on that network.

HTML (HYPERTEXT MARKUP LANGUAGE): This is the programming language commonly used to build websites, It is read and processed by web browsers (as opposed to PHP which is read by servers).

HYPERLINK: This is a clickable line of text that takes a reader elsewhere. It can be an internal hyperlink taking the reader somewhere within the book itself, as with the "clickable" table of contents. An external hyperlink takes the reader to a site outside of the book, such as your website. To create a hyperlink highlight the text, right mouse click, and select hyperlink. From the Word panel that appears on the left side chose internal or external.

HYPERTEXT MARKUP LANGUAGE (HTML): The cross-platform language in which the majority of Web pages today are written. Codes are interpreted by Browsers to be properly formatted for visitors. It is relatively easy and helpful to learn, but not entirely necessary.

HYPERTEXT TRANSFER PROTOCOL (HTTP): This is the primary protocol for transferring and receiving data on the Web. It involves a browser connecting to a server, sending a request that specifies its capabilities and then receiving the appropriate data from the server in return. (In general you do not need to type http:// in to your browser before typing in the domain name.)

IMPRESSION: Also known as a "page impression". It is recorded every time a web page is viewed.

INBOUND LINKS: Links from a remote website to your website.

INDIE AUTHOR/INDIE PUBLISHER: "Indie" is an abbreviation for "Independent", and is synonymous with "Self-Published. These are the many writers, publishers, and writer-publishers today who have come to recognize that they need neither an agent nor a traditional publishing house to successfully market their books.

INTERNET: This is the huge collection of interconnected networks that are connected using the TCP/IP protocols. It connects tens of thousands of independent networks.

INTERNET MESSAGE ACCESS PROTOCOL (IMAP): The means by which an email provider offers their interactive services.

INTERNET PROTOCOL (IP): Sets of rules and regulations agreed upon internationally for all internet functions.

INITIAL CAPS: (as opposed to ALL CAPS): "Caps" is short for "capitals". Initial caps is where the first letter of every word is capitalized. Generally articles of speech such as "the" "this" or "and", and prepositions such as "over" or "on" are only capitalized if they are the first word.

IP ADDRESS: A numerical address that domain names piggy-back. The nameserver resolves the domain name to the IP address.

ISBN: Is the acronym for International Standard Book Number.
It does NOT convey copyright. It is a digital identifier that helps second-parties (publishers, retailers and distributors) to identify your particular book to track it or communicate with others about it. It is 100% unique to each specific version of your book.

JAVA: A programming language that produces dynamic pages for websites.

JOINT VENTURE (JV): A business venture designed to take advantage of a synergy of two products or services, the sum of the venture being greater than the sum of its parts.

KEYWORDS: A single word or a word-phrase (known as a long-tail keyword) of any length which is the word or words used by a visitor to a search engine to find the information for which they are looking.

LANDING PAGE: The first page seen by a visitor to a website. (See "portal").

LINK CLOAKING: A way to hide the real destination of a hyperlink.

LINK FARM: A website set up solely to create links to other sites in an effort to improve search engine ranking. These are not looked on favorably by search engines.

LOG FILES: These are text documents that document activity on a website or server.

MAILBOX: An individualize account where email messages are received.

MAILING LIST: A list of email addresses that facilitates sending a single message to a group of email addresses simultaneously.

MALWARE: A generic term to describe programs that are placed on your computer without your knowledge, designed to extract all manner of personal information.

MANAGED HOSTING: A system whereby you own or lease a server that is located with a service provider. All of its management needs are taken care of by on-site personnel beyond your need to input or control anything.

MEATGRINDER: This term is proprietary to Smashwords. It refers to their software that takes your .doc file once it is properly formatted and converts it to all of the other formats required by the various ebook readers.

METADATA: This is every piece of information that pertains to your particular book. It facilitates your customer finding your book. It includes everything from your title and cover, the ISBN, your book description, your biography, the category classifications, and your price.

META TAG: A specific piece of HTML coding that contains information not normally displayed to the visitor. They are typically used to help search engines categorize a web page.

MOBI: This is the format used by Amazon Kindle, as opposed to EPUB. It is also called a .prc file. (This has nothing to do with the .mobi top-level URL extension.)

MODEM (*MODULATOR / DEM*ODULATOR): A device that connects a phone line to a computer.

MULTI-LEVEL MARKETING (MLM): Also called "network marketing". It involves buying products wholesale, selling them at retail, and sponsoring other people to do the same.

MySQL: A relational database encountered in the building of websites.

NAMESERVER: These are the servers that issue an IP address for a given domain name.

NCX: This is short for "**N**avigation **C**ontrol File for **X**ML". It is the Table of Contents summary that accompanies a book presented in EPUB format.
]
NETIQUETTE: Internet etiquette.

NETIZEN: Someone who uses internet resources.

NEWBIE (NOOB): A new or inexperienced internet commerce or self-publishing person.

NUCLEAR METHOD/OPTION: This is a term coined by Smashwords for a system by which an author can strip out Microsoft Word's various unintended glitches. It creates a "virgin" copy of your text from which to begin proper formatting.

OPERATING SYSTEM (OS): A program that can manage computer or server hardware so that it provides the desired operations.

OUTBOUND LINKS: These are links on your webpage that lead to web pages on another domain.

PARASITEWARE: Programs that are placed on your computer without your knowledge that attach themselves to programs you commonly use (such as your browser) and force you to use their program in lieu of your chosen program.

PDF: This is short "**P**ortable **D**ocument **F**ormat". It is a .pdf format created a decade ago by Adobe Systems. It is a fixed-layout format that freezes the layout of a book and its word positions. It is the standard for books sold on websites and downloaded by purchasers to their computers. It is not compatible with ebook readers.

PERFORMANCE BASED AMRKETING: A generic term for affiliate marketing.

PERFORMANCE INCENTIVE: A "bribe" from a merchant to an affiliate designed to encourage better results.

PHP: Technically "hypertext preprocessor". This is the programming in a website that is read by the web server, as opposed to HTML which is read by the web browser.

PIN: An item put onto a Pinterest pinboard.

PINTEREST PINBOARD: The electronic bulletin board where Pinterest users post pictures and any theme-based material.

PLUG-IN: A small item of software that adds some feature to the software on a website.

POINT OF PRESENCE (POP): "POP" has dual meanings. It is a physical geo-location to where a network can be connected. Or:

POST OFFICE PROTOCOL (POP): The email retrieval standard by which email messages are downloaded and manipulated on a computer.

PORTAL: This is the main point of entry to a website, synonymous with "Landing Page".

POSTING: A single message "posted" (entered) into a netword communication.

PREMIUM CATALOG: This is unique terminology used by Smashwords. It refers to the set of publishing platforms outside of Smashword's own store. To be included in the "catalog" you must upload very specialized file formatting in accordance with their massive "Style Guide". (Think Fiverr!)

PROTOCOL: Rules governing the sharing of information between two parties.

REDIRECT: This is where one URL sends visitors directly to a different URL.

REFLOWABLE TEXT: Electronically delivered books, ebooks, are formatted very differently from printed books. While print book text is rigidly fixed, reflowable text can shape-shift across any size reading device screen. This can be anything from a huge computer screen to the smallest iPhone. Readers can alter the font size and spacing to suit their personal needs.

REGISTRAR: A company offering domain registration services.

REGISTRY: The central URL authority for domain name extensions.

RESIDUAL EARNINGS: Affiliate programs where the merchant pays the affiliate commissions for all present and future customer purchases.

RETAILER: This is the company that sells your ebook directly on its websites, such as Amazon or the Smashwords store.

ROAS (RETURN ON ADVERTISING SPENDING): The revenue generated per dollar of advertising spent. An ROAS of "4" means you earned four dollars revenue for each dollar spent on advertising.

ROI (RETURN ON INVESTMENT): What you earn equated to everything you spent to earn it.

ROOT SERVER: Servers containing software and data necessary for locating name servers containing authoritative data for top level domains.

ROUTER: A hardware device that communicates   with your computer to the network sending you the electronic internet information.

RTF: This is shot for Rich Text Format. It is a format that permits any word processor to open your book, and allows manipulation of the fonts before printing (something that a .pdf file does not permit).

SALES LETTER: The text on a website designed to entice a visitor to make a purchase.

SEARCH ENGINE: A system for looking up information on the web. (Google is the best-known search engine.)

SEARCH ENGINE OPTIMIZATION (SEO): This is the practice of designing websites so that they rank as high as possible in search results made on search engines.

SECURE HTTP (SHTTP): An HTTP protocol that uses encryption to protect the traffic between the Server and Browser.

SECURE SOCKETS LAYER (SSL): A website encryption (evidenced by a "Certificate") that can be purchased that enables absolutely data-secure transactions between browsers and servers.

SENDER SCORE: A 0 – 100 rating of how easy it is to get email to a particular in-box.

SERVERS: These are specially- networked computers that handle client requests including Web pages, data, email, file transfers and more.

SERVER SIDE INCLUDES (SSI): Special files that instruct servers to add dynamic information (e.g., time countdown) to a webpage before it is sent to a viewer.

SHARED HOSTING: A system in which multiple clients and websites share a single server. Each account has specific limits on how much space they get and how much data they can transfer. This is the most basic and affordable type of hosting. The downside is if one client manages to crash the servers you go down with them!

SHOPPING CART: Software that lets website visitors select, add and remove products and pay for them online. This software can automatically calculate extra price considerations, such as tax and shipping. It then sends all of the information to the merchant once the transaction is complete.

SIDELOAD: This refers to copying a file directly from your desktop or laptop computer hard drive, or a flash drive, directly to an electronic reading device.

SIMPLE MAIL TRANSFER PROTOCOL (STMP): A way to transfer email messages from server to server.

SITE BUILDER: An application offered by most hosting service providers. It allows you to create a website from scratch based on predesigned templates without requiring knowledge of HTML. The finished sites then run on the host's servers and can be accessed and used through any Web browser.

SITE MAP: A file on a website page that has links to everywhere else on the website.

SMASHWORDS SATELLITES: This is a series of narrowly focused ebook sites operated by Smashwords. They are intended to facilitate buyer search by narrowing their search parameters.

SOFT BOUNCE: A failed email delivery due to a temporary matter such as a full in-box or busy server.

SPAM: Unsolicited email, generally containing advertising.

SPYWARE: Software secretly installed on your computer that is used to provide a third party with your personal information.

SQUEEZE PAGE: The first page of a website a visitor sees if the intent is to gather an email address before the visitor reads the Sales Letter.

STATIC IP: A unique and unchanging IP address given to a website by the hosting provider.

STREAMING: The playing of audio or video files without executing a full download.

STRUCTURED QUERY LANGUAGE (SQL): A programming lannnguage cooommonly employed to update and perform queries on databases.

SUBDOMAINS: These are third-level domains, addresses that replace the typical "www". This sends visitors to special

URL (i.e. subdomain.website.com) that requests data from a different directory within the original website.

SUPER AFFILIATE: The best performing affiliates. It is reported that 1% of all affiliates are responsible for 90% of all affiliate commissions.

SUPPORT: Technical help provided by Web hosting companies, usually via phone or email, to correct any problems that customers may encounter.

SURFING: The act of looking for information on the web.

TABLE OF CONTENTS: Often referred to as the "TOC" it provides the reader with a summary of your chapter headings. In ebooks this TOC must be formatted in such a way that a reader can click on a chapter name in the TOC and be taken directly to the start of that chapter.

TARGETED MARKETING: Offering the right product to the right buyer at the right moment.

TCP/IP: Stands for **T**ransmission **C**ontrol **P**rotocol/Internet Protocol. This is a suite of software protocols universally used by every kind of computing system.

TELNET: Standard internet protocol for accessing remote systems.

TERMINAL: Generic for a hardware device (e.g., your **P**ersonal **C**omputer) that allows you to send commands to a remote computer.

TEXT LINK: A link with no graphical image.

TOP-LEVEL DOMAIN (TLD): The domain name element to the far right of the address (i.e. .com, .net or .org).

TRACKING CODE: Refers to the hidden tracking code to track sales conversions.

TROJAN HORSE: A form of malware or virus designed to obtain your personal information.

TRAFFIC: The data being transferred over a network, typically between the Browser and Server

TWITTER TWEET: A short message sent from one Twitter account to another.

TWITTER RETWEET: A tweet that is forwarded to another Twitter member.

UNIFORM RESOURCE LOCATOR (URL): This is your "domain name". It is the standard for giving the address of a resource on the World Wide Web that makes up your Web page's full unique address using alphanumeric characters.

UNIQUE CLICK: A click from a visitor counted only on the first visit by means of recording the visitor's IP address.

UNIX: The most popular operating system used for servers on the World Wide Web.

UNMANAGED HOSTING: This is a system whereby you own or lease your own server and are fully responsible for the management of it. This includes troubleshooting, maintenance, applications and security, and is not recommended for anyone who is not an industry professional.

UPTIME: The amount of time in a 24-hour period in which a system is active and able to service requests. Most hosts claim 99%+.

VIRALITY: This is a term with its roots in biology (i.e., viruses). It describes the spread of any data across the internet. This can be through word of mouth, or word of **mouse**! All of the social networking platforms, Facebook, Twitter, MySpace, Pinterest, YouTube or whichever can, " as a virus can spread across the population", spread the word (both good and bad) about your book across the internet. Forums also do this as well. Many substitute the words "Auto-Effective Marketing" for "Viral Marketing" because of the negative implication of a virus!

VIRUS: A malicious program that infects your computer for the purpose of mining your data or corrupting your files.

WEB HOSTING: This is the service that provides a physical location, space and storage, connectivity and services for websites that allow your files to be accessed and viewed by internet users. Sites are created and then uploaded to a Web hosting service provider's server. Some services provided include email addresses, free site builders and databases, among many other things.

WEB MAIL: A service that facilitates sending, receiving and storing email messages.

WHITELIST: Opposite of "blacklist". A list of sender addresses that a recipient manually approves for delivery into their email in-box bypassing SPAM filters for those addresses.

WIKI: This is a kind of website within which the content can be edited and altered from the web browser in which it is being viewed.

WILDCARD DNS SETTING: When your domain name server setting points the following to your website: www.yourdomain.com; yourdomain.com; www.yoursubdomain.yourdomain.com, and yoursubdomain.yourdomain.com.

WORLD WIDE WEB (WWW): Often incorrectly used as a synonym for "the internet". It is the universe of all web servers that serve web pages to web browsers.

WORM: A self-replicating virus that alters or destroys specific programs.

XML (EXTENSIBLE MARKUP LANGUAGE): A general purpose code that differs from HTML in that it allows the user to define the mark-up elements. It is used in applications such as site maps and RSS feeds.

###

www.ingramcontent.com/pod-product-compliance
Lightning Source LLC
LaVergne TN
LVHW022300060326
832902LV00020B/3195